Enactive Psychiatry

Psychiatry is enormously complex. One of its main difficulties is to articulate the relationship between the wide assortment of factors that may cause or contribute to psychiatric disorders. Such factors range from traumatic experiences to dysfunctional neurotransmitters, existential worries, economic deprivation, social exclusion and genetic bad luck. The relevant factors and how they interact can differ not only between diagnoses but also between individuals with the same diagnosis. How should we understand and navigate such complexity? *Enactive Psychiatry* presents an integrative account of the many phenomena at play in the development and persistence of psychiatric disorders by drawing on insights from enactivism, a theory of embodied cognition. From the enactive perspective on the mind and its relation to both the body and the world, we can achieve a new understanding of the nature of psychiatric disorders and the causality involved in their development and treatment, thereby resolving psychiatry's integration problem.

SANNEKE DE HAAN is a philosopher and postdoctoral researcher in the Philosophy of Psychiatry within the Department of Culture Studies at Tilburg University, the Netherlands.

T0371255

Enactive Psychiatry

SANNEKE DE HAAN

Tilburg University

CAMBRIDGE
UNIVERSITY PRESS

CAMBRIDGE
UNIVERSITY PRESS

University Printing House, Cambridge CB2 8BS, United Kingdom

One Liberty Plaza, 20th Floor, New York, NY 10006, USA

477 Williamstown Road, Port Melbourne, VIC 3207, Australia

314-321, 3rd Floor, Plot 3, Splendor Forum, Jasola District Centre, New Delhi - 110025, India

103 Penang Road, #05-06/07, Visioncrest Commercial, Singapore 238467

Cambridge University Press is part of the University of Cambridge.

It furthers the University's mission by disseminating knowledge in the pursuit of education, learning and research at the highest international levels of excellence.

www.cambridge.org
Information on this title: www.cambridge.org/9781009246033
DOI: 10.1017/9781108685214

First published 2020
First paperback edition 2022

A catalogue record for this publication is available from the British Library

Library of Congress Cataloging in Publication data
Names: Haan, Sanneke de, author.
Title: Enactive psychiatry / Sanneke de Haan.
Description: Cambridge ; New York, NY : Cambridge University Press, [2020] |
Includes bibliographical references and index.
Identifiers: LCCN 2019043495 (print) | LCCN 2019043496 (ebook) | ISBN
9781108426060 (hardback) | ISBN 9781108685214 (ebook)
Subjects: LCSH: Psychiatry – Philosophy. | Mental illness – Philosophy. | Mental
illness – Physiological aspects. | Mind and body.
Classification: LCC RC437.5 .H335 2020 (print) | LCC RC437.5 (ebook) | DDC
616.89001/9–dc23
LC record available at https://lccn.loc.gov/2019043495
LC ebook record available at https://lccn.loc.gov/2019043496

ISBN 978-1-108-42606-0 Hardback
ISBN 978-1-009-24603-3 Paperback

Contents

Figures

Preface

It doesn't take more than three months of living to discover that we are all connected to each other's cruelty and to each other's kindness.

Deborah Levy, *The Cost of Living*

When I first started working at a psychiatric hospital as a philosophical researcher, someone advised me to keep a diary of all the things that struck me, as a newcomer and relative outsider, before I started to take them for granted. It was good advice, but unfortunately, I didn't follow it. I do remember some quite puzzling things, though. It is one of these early puzzlements that has motivated this book.

At team meetings, when we talked with and/or about patients, we talked about how they were presently doing and feeling, how they experienced the different forms of therapy they engaged in, and we talked about their lives outside of the ward: about their family situations; their jobs or schooling and future perspectives; their housing and financial situations; their relations to their partners, family members and friends. We did not talk about brains, though. We discussed various forms of medication, their advantages and side effects and how patients felt about and reacted to them. But neurotransmitters were not part of the conversation.

At scientific meetings, however, it was the other way around: we talked mostly about brains and hardly about anything else. Most research was neuroscientific research, directed at finding the underlying mechanisms of different disorders. Similarly, if we engaged in more theoretical discussions, many of my colleagues seemed to subscribe in one form or another to the idea that psychiatric disorders are diseases of the brain.

But how were they related: patients' brains, their experiences, and all the other things we talked about? Wildly diverse things seemed to affect patients' well-being – traumatic experiences, dysfunctional neurotransmitters, existential worries, economical deprivation, social relationships, genetics – and these, moreover, seemed to influence one another: traumatic experiences, for instance, altering the brain and affecting the quality of relationships, and that in turn inducing existential concerns. For each patient, the relevant factors and how they interact may differ too. How are we to understand and navigate this mind-boggling complexity? That is the topic of this book.

In what follows I present a model that integrates the many phenomena that play a role in the development and persistence of psychiatric disorders, drawing on insights from enactivism, a form of embodied cognition. Psychiatry's integration problem can be solved if we adopt an enactive view on what the mind is and how it relates to the body and the world. From this enactive perspective we can elaborate a new understanding of the nature of psychiatric disorders and the causality involved in their development and treatment. As a philosophical work this volume does not propose any novel forms of treatment or provide analyses of specific psychiatric disorders; rather, it offers an integrative theoretical framework that helps us understand what happens in various forms of treatment (e.g. the effects of medication vs the effects of psychotherapy) and that helps relate different types of research findings (e.g. neuroscientific data and phenomenological analyses).

This book is a philosophical work, but I did not write it mainly for philosophers. First and foremost, I hope to reach all of those who are interested in better understanding psychiatric disorders: those who work in mental health care (psychologists, social workers, psychiatrists, nurses), those who do scientific research into psychiatric disorders, and those who find themselves affected by psychiatric disorders as a patient or a patient's friend or family member. To enhance the book's readability, I have tried to stay clear of all-too-technical discussions and banned most intra-philosophical debates to the footnotes. Philosophers with an interest in psychiatry, the mind–body problem, and/or embodied cognition may, however, still find enough of it to their liking.

In the first chapter I introduce psychiatry's integration problem: the difficulty of relating the heterogeneous phenomena that may play a role in the development and persistence of psychiatric disorders. In practice, many mental health professionals work holistically in a pragmatic and eclectic way. Such pragmatic approaches often function well enough. Yet an overarching framework provides orientation, treatment rationale, a shared language for communication with all those involved and the means to explain treatment decisions to health insurers and to society at large. It also helps relate findings from different areas and types of research. To do that, such a model should give an overview of the relevant aspects involved and an account of how they are related. I propose four main aspects or dimensions of psychiatric disorders that a model should ideally take into account: the experiential, physiological, socio-cultural, and existential dimensions.

In the second chapter, I briefly discuss the currently available models for psychiatry. They can be divided into (1) one-sided and reductionist models, (2) complementary or dualist models and (3) integrative models. Single-aspect models can offer valuable insights, but they do not help to solve the problem of integration, as they do not take into account the whole range of factors that are in play. Complementary approaches are more encompassing but fail to show how the aspects relate. Reductionist models, such as the nowadays popular neuroreductionist, view that psychiatric disorders are brain diseases, do offer an integrative perspective but oversimplify the complexity of psychiatric disorders, making them both improbable and ethically disputable. The integrative models, such as the biopsychosocial model and the network model, go a long way. The biopsychosocial model, however, insufficiently shows how the dimensions relate, and while the network model offers a helpful mathematical template, it presupposes rather than provides an integrative theory. We still lack a framework that integrates all four dimensions in a non-reductionist manner. That is where enactivism comes in.

In Chapter 3, I outline the enactive perspective on cognition – the most rigorous of embodied and embedded approaches. Cognition is defined in terms of 'sense-making': the evaluative interaction of an organism with its environment. I explain that sense-making is essential to life, implies values, and is affective. I also urge the importance of distinguishing basic from existential sense-making and discuss its implications for our understanding of the relation between cognition, perception, and action. I explicate this enactive ontology of the mind and clarify how it differs from a more traditional approach. This will then serve as the overall background in terms of which we can start to explain the precise way in which an enactive ontology can bring together the experiential and the (neuro)physiological dimensions (Chapter 4), the socio-cultural dimension (Chapters 4 and 6), and the existential dimension (Chapters 5 and 6).

A big part of the integration problem concerns the difficulty of relating the physiological and the experiential dimensions of psychiatric disorders: body and mind. In Chapter 4, I first sketch the ways in which the mind–body problem is at stake in psychiatry and how a dualist opposition is still deeply engrained in how we conceive of both causes and treatment of psychiatric disorders. While we want to acknowledge the differences between matters physiological and psychological, we do not want to adopt the unsatisfying accounts of their relation as offered by dualism and reductionism. By taking continuity rather than opposition as its starting point, the enactive life–mind continuity thesis has the potential to offer a helpful alternative perspective on the mind–body problem. The life–mind continuity thesis argues that physiological and sense-making processes necessarily go together in the process of living. Given the fundamental dependency of living beings on interactions with their environment, they require some (basic) sense-making capacities in order to survive. The viability of the life–mind continuity thesis depends on adopting a solid account of emergence. I discuss several conceptions and conclude that emergence is best understood in terms of fusion.

From an enactive perspective, then, the relation between physiological and experiential processes necessarily includes living beings' relations to their environment. It thus reconfigures a two-place relation (mind and body) into a three-place one (mind, body, and world) and stresses their mereological co-dependency. In other words, the physiological, experiential, and environmental/socio-cultural dimensions are all part of one person–world system. This in turn has consequences for how we conceive of the causality involved between these three dimensions. I argue that this is best understood as organisational causality. Within this organisational causality we can distinguish more global from more local processes and effects, which in turn allows us to differentiate between various causes and forms of treatment of psychiatric disorders.

I end the chapter with an evaluation of the enactive framework as elaborated so far. I conclude that even though it has much to offer in terms of an integrative view on the physiological, the experiential, and the environmental/sociocultural dimensions of psychiatric disorders, it does not yet encompass the existential dimension, which is crucial for a useful framework for psychiatry.

In Chapter 5, I introduce the existential dimension and show how it is at play in psychiatry. The existential dimension refers to our capacity to take a stance on ourselves and on our interactions with the world and others. This reflexive capacity introduces a different relation to the world, in which not only survival but also the aim to lead a good life counts. This existential dimension is an important aspect of psychiatry: patients' relation to themselves and their situation can play a constitutive and/or a modulatory role in psychiatric disorders. Besides, existential considerations come to the fore in psychiatric practice through patients' relations to their diagnoses and treatments. This does leave us with the dilemma of how to fit the existential dimension, and the values that come along with it, into a naturalist approach to psychiatry.

The enactive approach is a naturalist approach, but so far, it has neglected the existential dimension. In Chapter 6, I discuss how the enactive approach can be enriched by adopting this existential dimension. This requires reconsidering (1) sense-making as existential sense-making, (2) values as existential values and (3) environments as sociocultural worlds. I explain existential sense-making, how it differs from basic sense-making and whether this amounts to a 'cognitive gap'. Turning to values, I distinguish between valences (i.e. basic values) and values (i.e. existential values). I discuss three main theories on the relation between values and naturalism – a subjectivist, an objectivist, and an evolutionary perspective – and show that each has its drawbacks. Following the enactive ontology as developed in Chapter 3, I propose a relational view on values as relational realities, which avoids the pitfalls of objectivist, subjectivist, and evolutionary theories and allows values to be incorporated within a naturalist approach. With the capacity for stance-taking, the environment we live in becomes a world imbued with existential meaning and values. The development of this capacity is itself dependent upon and supported by being part of a sociocultural community with specific socio-cultural practices. The existential dimension has thus reconfigured the organism–environment system into a person–world system that integrates all four dimensions we started out with.

With this enriched enactive perspective in place, we can now turn to the implications of this view for how we understand the nature (Chapter 7), causes, and treatment (Chapter 8) of psychiatric disorders. I argue that psychiatric disorders are structurally disordered patterns of sense-making. Generally, the way in which the person makes sense of her world is biased in a specific direction: the world appears overly threatening, or meaningless, or overly meaningful, or chaotic. The person's sense-making is not appropriate or insufficiently attuned to her situation. She will find it difficult to adjust her sense-making to the situation at hand, and this difficulty in adjusting and attuning typically results in overly rigid patterns of interactions. Psychiatric disorders thus pertain to persons in interaction with their world. I discuss what makes them *psychiatric* rather than somatic disorders and what makes them *disorders* rather than cases of normal sense-making. I then illustrate disordered patterns of sense-making by looking at patients' changed experience of the world. The activity of sense-making discloses the world as a field of relevant affordances, and consequently, disordered sense-making discloses an altered field of relevant affordances. I end the chapter by discussing some conceptual consequences of the enactive view on psychiatric disorders. This shows that an enactive approach dissolves several conceptual dichotomies that stem from the (implicit) adoption of the dichotomous mind–world topology that enactivism challenges.

In the final chapter, I discuss what an enactive approach implies with regard to the causes and treatment of psychiatric disorders. Much research in psychiatry is devoted to finding the 'underlying' causes or mechanisms of specific disorders. From an enactive complex systems perspective, however, this is a problematic metaphor, as it encourages the adoption of a vertical hierarchy in which symptoms are taken as signs at the surface for what is going wrong underneath – which is typically taken to refer to (neuro)physiological processes. In contrast, following the integrative enactive view, none of the four dimensions is more fundamental than any of the other, since they refer to different excerpts of one and the same system. Nothing underlies disordered patterns of sense-making: the pattern itself is all there is to it. The enactive adoption of a complex dynamical systems view further implies that causes are only causes in a specific context, thus nuancing the notion of originary causes. The initiating factors of psychiatric problems may, moreover, not be the same as their maintaining factors. Finally, the complexity of the system means that for different patients, their problems will probably have different developmental trajectories. To navigate this complexity, personalised network models could be used, using the four dimensions as the major groupings of relevant factors. These network models can then be personalised, with regard to both the specific factors to be included and the nature of their influences.

With regard to treatment, taking an encompassing perspective on the entire person–world system may at first sight seem too complex to be workable. However, the complexity of the system also implies that there are many routes to change. An enactive approach does not a priori exclude any type of treatment. This does not mean that anything goes, however. Personalised network models show how different treatments have different effects and how one and the same treatment results in different outcomes for different patients. The enactive focus on the person in interaction with her world implies the relevance of the role of patients' environments. Part of treatment may consist in finding an appropriate *niche* for this person to flourish. Besides, from an enactive view, abilities themselves have an interactional character, and different settings can thus affect our abilities. Psychotherapy can be regarded as prasticing sense-making in a helpful setting, making it a practice of participatory sense-making.

By the end of the book, I hope to have shown that an enactive view on the mind and its relation to both body and world provides a valuable new understanding of psychiatry's old problems. While this view may at first seem more complex, in the end, it offers a clarity and unification that are otherwise hard to come by.

Acknowledgements

This book is an adaptation of my PhD thesis in philosophy at Heidelberg University ('An enactive approach to psychiatry'), which was supervised by Thomas Fuchs and Gerrit Glas. I thank both of them for our many helpful discussions along the way. Thomas gave me the chance to work at the psychiatric hospital and be part of the stimulating Marie Curie Research Training Network 'DISCOS' (disorders and coherence of the embodied self). He introduced me to phenomenological psychopathology and showed how philosophy can have real-life relevance. Our conversations have shaped my thinking – and it was a remarkable new experience for me to have to agree with someone so often. Gerrit similarly supported me to pursue the questions that are important to me. He helped me always to keep in mind the relation to clinical practice of any philosophical discussions and to see things from a systemic perspective.

Hanne De Jaegher first introduced me to enactivism, together with Ezequiel di Paolo, and it felt like a philosophical homecoming. Hanne has the liveliest of minds, and I'm glad that we get to share the joy of thinking, both as colleagues and as friends. I would like to thank her for her encouragement throughout this project – spurring me just to say what I want to say.

Working at the psychiatric hospitals of Heidelberg University and the University of Amsterdam has taught me a lot. I am grateful to my former colleagues for letting a philosopher into their midst and to the patients who shared their experiences with me.

Over the years, I have talked about the ideas in this book with a fair number of people – too many to mention everyone. I would particularly like to thank Jelle Bruineberg, Jan Degenaar, Roy Dings, Zeno van Duppen, Sonja Frohoff, Lena Kästner, Jonathan Led Larsen, Judy Luigjes, and Han van Wietmarschen for helpful discussions and feedback.

A special thanks goes out to my friend and companion in thinking Richard Gipps, who masters the fine art of offering the right mixture of challenge and encouragement. I much enjoyed our discussions. They also made this a better book. I am grateful too for his proofreading of the entire manuscript, saving me from many mistakes.

Finally, I would like to thank my family and friends for being who they are and making my life nicer, which, from a systemic perspective, has undoubtedly been good for this book too. And above all, I want to thank my partner, Wouter, who patiently endured my preoccupation with this book, supported me in so many ways, and reminded me that (almost) anything is possible. I am so lucky to have found you! A lot has happened since I first started writing this book – the biggest, most existential change being the birth of our wonderful daughter Ida. I am incredibly happy and grateful that you are now part of our lives. The two of you mean the world to me.

1   The Need for a Model

1.1   INTRODUCTION

In her article 'Why Psychiatry Is the Hardest Specialty', Dew (2009)
sketches the everyday difficulties of psychiatric practice. She writes,
'Being a psychiatrist means dealing with ambiguity all the time . . . I go
to work and listen to someone describe a vague uneasiness felt for
a lifetime. Then after about 45 minutes I'm asked to assign it a name'
(p. 16). Of course, as Dew remarks, assigning a name to something
does not make it true. But what she chooses to call it (depression,
demon possession, or – a possibility that the author does not consider –
non-pathological unhappiness) is not arbitrary: 'How I choose to con-
ceptualize this person's complaint is not merely a matter of my own
intellectual satisfaction; in addition to the implications for what
treatment is applied, what I say will probably become an integral
part of this person's life story' (p. 16). To make things even more
complicated, we could add that this conceptualisation may even itself
affect the course of the problems.

Dew explains the problem as a lack of a comprehensive view on
(1) what is wrong with the patient and (2) what she as a psychiatrist is
doing. Although she starts from the idea that psychiatrists are trying
to 'make sense of someone else's brain', this conception obviously
does not prove to be of much help in her practice:

> *I have to have some sort of model for what I'm doing.* So sometimes
> I think, 'She needs her serotonin levels tweaked, that's why she
> feels this way.' The truth is I don't really know why she feels this
> way. If I asked the right questions, I'd probably find something that
> happened in her childhood that could be considered traumatic. If
> not, I could probably find something in her current life that is

a 'stressor'. I could develop a sense that this problem is more 'psychological' than 'biological' (as if thoughts and feelings weren't biological events and there were really two organs inside her cranium). The one thing I can't think, that I really can't tolerate at all, is that I don't know what's wrong and I don't know what I'm doing that is helping.

(p. 16, italics mine)

The idea of making sense of someone else's brain not only falls short of providing a model for what she, as a psychiatrist, is doing in practice but it also fails to encompass the various sorts of 'causes' or influences in play in psychiatric disorders. These range from traumatic experiences, relational conflicts, and dysfunctional neurotransmitters to genetic bad luck. It is already hard to figure out how each of these influences develops independently. But the hardest thing, according to Dew, is 'to imagine all of the causes happening together, responding to each other, making each other worse, compensating for each other, benefiting the person, harming the person, comforting the person, killing the person' (p. 17). She concludes, 'That's why psychiatry is the hardest specialty' (p. 17). What she lacks is a comprehensive view on her patients that would help her connect all the possible causes of their problems and the possible interactions between these causes.

In this book I want to address this problem and present a model that integrates the many phenomena that potentially play a role in the development and persistence of psychiatric disorders.

I.2   PSYCHIATRY'S PROBLEM OF INTEGRATION

Medicine is a discipline in which natural sciences and the life-world meet. In order to help people with their complaints, doctors will search for dysfunctions and treat these guided by applied knowledge from the natural sciences. They translate problems into medical diagnoses, and in so doing, they have to switch between the patient as a person and the patient as an organism.[1] The tension between the patient as a person in his life-world and the patient as a body for scientific and medical investigation characterises the whole field of medicine. In psychiatry, however, matters are even more complicated. In somatic medicine, diseases can typically be regarded as alien intrusions, as external disruptions or at least as a problem of the body-as-an-organism only. Surely patients are involved as persons too; they need to cope with having this disease and maybe change their lifestyles. In psychiatry, however, the personal dimension goes much further, as psychiatric disorders pertain to the patient as a person. For it is not the

---

[1] Three terminological remarks. Firstly, I prefer to use the term *patient*, because it emphasises the passive element of being affected by something. *Patient* comes from the Latin *patiens*, which means 'one who suffers'. The term *client* has the advantage of stressing the rights of the person seeking psychiatric help. The downside of this term, however, is its suggestion of a business model and the client as an autonomous agent, free to choose between the options on offer according to her own will and insights. This picture of autonomous agency is already controversial in general, and it is certainly a distortion of those who turn to mental health care for help: their problems will often include an impairment in precisely the capacity to freely think, act, and feel as one deems right. The use of the term *patient* is meant to do justice to the vulnerable position someone with psychiatric problems finds. This of course does not deny the importance of taking the autonomy, experiences, and wishes of the patient seriously. It's an inherent difficulty in psychiatry to balance proper care and respect for patients' autonomy, avoiding both neglect and paternalism. I think it is unhelpful to stash these difficulties away and pretend this complicated patient–caregiver relationship is a simple client–provider relationship.

Secondly, I use the term *psychiatric disorder* rather than *mental disorder* or illness, because the term *mental* may suggest a Cartesian dualism that I want to stay clear of. An objection that has been formulated against the use of *psychiatric disorder* is that it may suggest 'that only psychiatrists are trained in the diagnosis and management of these conditions' (Stein 2010). That is a valid objection, and I certainly do not want to suggest that psychiatrists are the only experts, but still I find the Cartesian objection more weighty.

Relatedly, I speak of psychiatry as if this were a homogeneous field. In real life, those professionals who are concerned with treating patients with psychiatric problems are typically part of different services or organisational structures – such as social work, private or public psychotherapy practices, specialised clinics, psychiatric hospital wards, home care – and come from different disciplines. With my use of the term *psychiatry* as shorthand for this diverse field, I do not mean to imply that psychiatrists would be the alpha and omega of mental health care. In fact, the integrative approach to psychiatric disorders that I will present here precisely implies an acknowledgement of the importance of the other disciplines involved in mental health care, such as nurses, social workers, and psychologists, and rather calls for an integrative organisation of these diverse services.

liver, or the heart, or the lungs, or some other organ that is the problem; the problem, rather, concerns one's way of perceiving, thinking, feeling, behaving: experiences that make us who we are.[2] As a consequence, it is much harder for patients suffering from psychiatric disorders to distance themselves from their disorders.

In order to do justice to its complex field of investigation and treatment, psychiatry has always drawn on a combination of insights from the medical sciences and the humanities in general and from neurobiology, psychology, and philosophy in particular (see e.g. Jaspers 1913). Since the notion 'psychiatry' first emerged in the eighteenth century (Marneros 2008), theories about the exact nature of its objects of concern have continuously shifted their emphasis between those various disciplines: from phrenology, to psychoanalytical and anthropological conceptions, to the focus on the role of society and social structures in social and anti-psychiatry, to the paradigm of (neuro)biological psychiatry that has gained dominance during recent decades. Each of these paradigms advocates a very different understanding of what psychiatric disorders are. Should we understand them as brain diseases? From that perspective, patients' experiences are the result of one or more underlying problems in the brain. Research needs to be directed at finding these underlying mechanisms and, it is hoped that, we can subsequently find their biomarkers and develop interventions that target these mechanisms. Or, are psychiatric disorders, rather, the result of unresolved inner conflicts, as the more psychoanalytically minded would suggest? In that case, medication could possibly provide support, but it will not cure the problem. Or should we understand psychiatric problems as the expression in an individual of a social problem, as social psychiatry would argue? Or do psychiatric problems point to existential struggles, and should we focus on what stands in the way of patients' ability to engage with the world in a meaningful way?

---

[2] Some claim that psychiatric disorders are simply the problem of an organ too, namely the brain. Further on, I will discuss such neuroreductionist models and explain what is problematic about them.

These perspectives are so different that one gets the impression that there may be no way to reconcile them, with the result that one must instead choose between them. But the patient is both a biological organism and a person striving for meaning, and their social world seems to matter as well. How, then, should we understand the nature of psychiatric disorders? Should we indeed choose one of these perspectives, or could there be a way to reconcile them? This is no mere theoretical issue, for how we conceive of the nature of psychiatric disorders has important practical consequences. What is the problem, how can we assess it, and what could have caused it? – how one answers these questions will determine which treatments are preferred and which research gets funded. What should we focus on? Genes? The brain? Early attachment? Inner conflicts? Socioeconomic deprivation?

Besides, how one conceives of the relation between patients' experiences, their physiological processes, and their environment also matters for how one connects findings from (neuro)scientific research to psychiatric practice. Nowadays, psychiatry can profit from insights from genetics and epigenetics, from molecular biology and from neuroscience. Particularly the advancement of neuroscientific techniques like EEG, PET, and fMRI has greatly enlarged the pool of methods psychiatry has at its disposal. In fact, current research is mainly focused on tracking down deviations in the functioning of the brains of patients suffering from various psychopathologies. This has led to the collection of a huge array of data on the neurophysiological factors that are involved in psychiatric disorders: the brains of patients with a major depression show deviations in the levels of specific neurotransmitters (Nutt 2008). Schizophrenic patients show a decrease in grey matter and enlargement of the ventricles (van Os and Kapur 2009). Patients suffering from borderline personality disorder show abnormalities in their amygdala activity (O'Neill and Frodl 2012) and so on. With the increasing popularity of brain imaging techniques, more and more of these correlations between diagnosed illnesses and deviant brain processes are documented.

The challenge is to find a way to make these findings useful for psychiatric practice. Although the correlations that have emerged from this research are many, they have not led to the envisioned breakthroughs in psychiatric interventions and biomarkers for diagnoses and drug responsiveness. Little is known about the causal relations and possible mechanisms involved. The more we get to know about the functioning of our brains, the more complicated this turns out to be. In particular, the plasticity of the brain makes it an astonishing organ – and one that is notoriously difficult to study. For the application of research in neuroscience it is crucial to understand how brain processes are linked to experiences and to interactions with the environment.

It is by no means obvious how to relate such different aspects as physiological processes, experiences, existential concerns, and sociocultural influences and the different sorts of knowledge that they yield. This is what an integrative framework should help with.

I.3   THE USE OF MODELS

In both its practice and its research, psychiatry thus needs to find a way to integrate the different aspects of patients' problems. In practice, many of those working in psychiatry already work holistically in a pragmatic and eclectic way. Without using any explicit, overarching theoretical framework,[3] they aim to consider all the factors that cause and maintain their patients' problems. Such pragmatic approaches often function well enough. So why develop a framework at all? As Dew's example makes clear, one's view on the nature of psychiatric disorders influences one's decisions about treatment. If psychiatric disorders, for instance, are regarded as diseases of the brain, then solving patients' problems at their root involves changing their brains. If, on the contrary, psychiatric disorders are regarded as existential crises, treatment should be directed at addressing patients' existential concerns, not their brains. Likewise, one's view on which aspect(s) of

---

[3]   I use the terms *framework, model,* and *account* in a loose, interchangeable way.

psychiatric disorders are most central will affect decisions on how funding for both treatment and research gets allocated. Besides, one's views on the nature of psychiatric disorders will impact one's views on the people suffering from them. Is depression a disease just like cancer? To what extent do we deem patients to be responsible for their problems? For psychiatric patients, their views on their disorder affect their very self-understanding. And the views of their family and friends and their therapists, nurses, and other professionals on psychiatric disorders concern them personally.

Still, one might ask why we should develop an *integrative* framework, and why it should be *explicit* rather than functioning implicitly in the background. The reason why the framework should be integrative is simply that if it does not account for how the diverse factors potentially at play in psychiatric disorders are related – it is of no help for solving the integration problem. A non-integrative framework can be useful in other ways, but not for the difficulty of connecting brain processes, patients' experiences, and the effects of social circumstances. As we will see in Chapter 2, there are different routes to integration, with the two main directions of reductionism and some form of holism.

An explicit integrative framework has several advantages. Given the impact of one's views on treatment, funding decisions, and (self-)understanding of patients, it seems a matter of decency to be able to explicate them in order to make them contestable. But there are more pragmatic reasons as well. In fact, the difficulties that Dew (2009) describes pertain precisely to the limits of practical pragmatism in the absence of a good theoretical grounding. An explicit integrative framework can help communication. In particular, it can provide (1) orientation, (2) treatment rationale, (3) a shared language for communication with all those involved, and (4) the means to explain treatment decisions to health insurers and society at large.

1.3.1   Orientation

A theoretical framework can be useful for a better understanding of what works and especially *how* and *why* it works that way. It helps to know what one is doing and why one is doing it. An integrative framework helps us keep an eye on all the aspects of treatment, to switch between different ways of looking at the patient and his illness and to keep an overview. Is the patient unable to do something, or is he not trying hard enough? Is it primarily a physiological dysfunction, or do the patient's problems stem from social difficulties? Or is it a bit of both? How do these two interrelate? And even if we can point to an originating cause, how much use is this to improving the patient's current situation? Besides, such assessments are not just a matter of a proper diagnosis at the outset: during treatment, the emphasis may need to shift again.

A good framework also helps to relate scientific findings on the heterogeneous aspects of psychiatric disorders – for psychiatric research, too, is splintered. Biological psychiatry, for instance, investigates which brain networks show deviations in patients with schizophrenia (Alexander-Bloch et al. 2013) and phenomenological psychiatry investigates questions like the changes in the experience of time for depressed patients (Fuchs 2001; Wyllie 2005; Ghaemi 2007), while social psychiatry, for instance, investigates the family dynamics that drive patients to anorexia (Minuchin et al. 1978/2009). Even if these outcomes are intended to contribute to an integrative approach, not much integration is achieved as long as there is no guiding idea for how to connect these elements.

1.3.2 Treatment Rationale

This follows from Section 1.3.1: if one knows what one is doing and why one is doing it, one has a treatment rationale. An integrative framework can shed light on how intervening on one aspect (e.g. sleep) affects other aspects (e.g. mood). The use of a framework does not mean that one definitive treatment pops up just by looking at the framework; rather, it helps to keep an overview of all influences that could play a role and could be intervened on and to change course if the intervention is not having the intended effects.

1.3.3 Communication

A good, integrative framework aids communication. Given that there are various, very different perspectives on the nature of psychiatric disorders – as primarily physiological, or sociocultural, or existential problems – these different perspectives also imply different types of language and different frameworks for explanation. One easily ends up talking at cross purposes if one interlocutor adopts a physiological and the other an existential perspective. An integrative framework should offer a common ground and a perspective that bridges these differences. In this way, different types of expertise can be connected – both amongst various health care professionals and between health care professionals, and patients and family.

1.3.4 Justification

Mental health care professionals need to be able to justify their treatment decisions to the insurance companies that pay for it. If one wants to defend a holistic approach against economising tendencies, one will have to argue for it. For that, a solid theoretical grounding is indispensable. And it's not just insurance companies that require explanation and justification. After all, it is in the end a political decision of how many funds will be allocated to mental health care and to research. What do we need that money for and how do we use it to improve the situation of patients suffering from psychiatric disorders? A good framework can provide the premises for answering these questions.

Simply put, the primary function of a theoretical framework is thus that it helps one to know what one is doing and why one is doing it. Now any model faces the difficulty of finding the right balance between structuring, ordering, and simplifying on the one hand, and encompassing all the relevant aspects and relations on the other hand. There is both the risk of the model being too complicated, therefore offering no help in structuring the complexities of reality, and the risk of oversimplifying reality; leaving out relevant aspects or connections. What are the relevant aspects of psychiatric disorders that an integrative framework should take into account? What is it that needs to be integrated?

I.4   DISCERNING THE DIMENSIONS INVOLVED IN PSYCHIATRY

In what follows, I suggest that we can discern four main dimensions of psychiatric disorders as indispensable for understanding the nature of psychiatric disorders. These are the experiential, the physiological, the sociocultural, and the existential dimensions. Each of these can in turn be further specified, but these are the main elements. The first three dimensions more or less reflect the elements of the biopsychosocial model. I take it that these are generally accepted as relevant aspects of – or, depending on one's view, influences on – psychiatric disorders. I want to add one more aspect to this list: the existential dimension.

The *experiential* dimension refers to patients' experiences.[4] These experiences are both the starting point and the final measure of any treatment. A good understanding of patients' experiences is therefore a crucial part of psychiatric practice.

The physiological dimension includes genetic, anatomical, biochemical, and neurological aspects of psychiatric disorders. Despite the diversity of these aspects, they group together in the sense that

---

[4]   I speak of the *experiential* dimension rather than of the *psychological* dimension for reasons of clarity. The notion 'psychological' encompasses a wide range of phenomena and categories, ranging from unconscious processes, to behaviour, to the concept of personality. Because of this potpourri, *psychological processes* can refer to both first-person experiences as well as third-person descriptions, or categorisations of these experiences. Avoiding the term *psychological* forces one to be more precise about what exactly one is referring to. In particular, I want to distinguish between the experiences of the person and an observer's perspective on these experiences. The experiential dimension refers only to the first. From the enactive perspective that I will be developing here, these diverse phenomena and categories that now fall under the heading of 'psychological' can be accounted for in a different way. For instance, unconscious processes can be understood as patterns of interaction that the person is not aware of. *Behaviour* refers to a person's interaction-patterns as described from an outside perspective. And *personality* can be understood in terms of engrained interaction patterns, following a history of coupling which shapes a person's current preferred kind of interactions.

they all involve bodily processes, most of them taking place outside of our awareness.

The *sociocultural* dimension refers to the fact that we do not live in a vacuum: that 'no man is an island' (Donne 1624); that we are always in interaction with our environment. We are part of specific sociocultural communities and of our social network of family, friends, and acquaintances. Our norms, habits, and (self-)interpretations are all shaped by the practices of the social groups we are part of. The individual's psychiatric problems cannot be understood in isolation from their social context, both currently and in the past. Patients' current problems can be mitigated or reinforced by their relations, and their socioeconomical situation can also play a role (e.g. jobs, finances, housing, discrimination). Our past social interactions are relevant too: how we grew up, which coping styles we have learned to adopt, our practices of emotion-regulation, our emotional literacy, the view we have on our problems, and how we tend to talk about and react to them. In all these ways, patients' current situation and their problems cannot be seen in isolation from their material, sociocultural context.[5] At the very least then the social-cultural world needs to be taken into account as an important feedback loop regarding patients' problems.

Besides, on a macro-level, the sociocultural dimension is at stake in psychiatry as well, through the determination of what we consider to be normal and abnormal. This estimation takes place within and is to some extent shaped by a sociocultural community. No action, thought, perception, or feeling is in and of itself pathological: it always depends on the context of which they are part of. Suspicion may be warranted, an aggressive reaction can be appropriate in a specific situation, and so too can feeling sad or being pre-occupied with something. The assessment of whether or not actions, perceptions, emotions, and thoughts are pathological is a matter of their *appropriateness* within the specific situation of this person. When

---

[5]   I call this dimension the sociocultural dimension to keep the term manageable, but it also includes the material, economical, and political aspects of patients' life-worlds.

does mourning for a deceased loved one end and a depression start? Which ideas count as accepted religious convictions, and which do we consider to be delusional? To some extent, such estimation of appropriateness depends upon the norms of a sociocultural community. And, as both cultural differentiation and the Western history of psychiatric disorders show, such norms for normality can shift according to place and time.

The *existential* dimension refers to the way in which people relate to and make sense of themselves and their situation. It is a special form of the experiential dimension and so important for psychiatry that it constitutes a dimension of its own (de Haan 2017). Consider, for example, panic disorder. A fundamental part of this disorder is that patients experience regular panic attacks. But on top of that, patients *fear* these panic attacks. It is this anticipatory fear that motivates them to avoid specific situations. The avoidance in turn prevents these patients from having experiences that would correct their fearful anticipations (Beck and Clark 1997). The patients' *stance towards* their experienced and expected panic attacks thus forms a crucial part of the disorder as well. Such stance-taking on one's situation is what I mean by the existential dimension. We do not just experience things, but we can also *relate to* our experiences. We can take a stance on the situation at hand and on ourselves; on what we do, think, and feel. We do not coincide with our here and now, but can relate to ourselves and our situation. From a structural perspective, we can say that the existential dimension refers to a *reflexive relation*, in the sense that it refers to itself.

This relation is typically an *evaluative* relation. Just as our experience of the world is not of a neutral collection of objects but is rather engaged and motivated by our concerns, so too our experience of ourselves and our interactions is motivated and evaluative. We can be ashamed of present or past wrongs, we can be proud of ourselves, we can lie and feel guilty about lying, and we can dread things in the future, or look forward to events in pleasant anticipation. Moreover, although stance-taking presupposes reflective abilities it includes more than just deliberative reflection: stance-taking can also be *unre-flective and implicit* in our actions. That is, we need not have a well-formulated, thought-through, explicit standpoint on things: our stance on something may be implicit in the way we behave. Sometimes we are not even aware of these stances. I might for example act on certain norms of femininity that I am not aware of, and that I might even reject if I would become aware of them.

This means that the 'existential' dimension, as I use the term, does not exclusively or even primarily refer to the big questions of life, such as who we are, what we should do, and what we consider to be a good life. Thanks to our reflective abilities we can ask such questions and formulate answers to them, but our existential relatedness is at play much more generally and pervasively in our everyday lives: in what we do and also how we do it. My use of the term *existential* rather follows the literal meaning of the Latin *ex sistere* or *ex stare*: to being or standing outside of something.

The existential dimension deserves special attention in psychiatry. Psychiatric disorders concern one's capacities for adequate perceiving, thinking, feeling, and acting: experiences that are at the heart of who you are. In other words, psychiatric disorders affect the person qua person. And as we are stance-taking, reflective beings, our stance on ourselves and our situation co-determines the way we feel, perceive, think, and act. One could even argue that psychiatric disorders emerge with this stance-taking ability of persons (Fuchs 2011a). The idea is that because we do not coincide with what we do, because we can take a stance on our situation and ourselves, we can suffer from estrangement and anxiety. This in turn may develop into full-blown psychiatric disorders such as schizophrenia or depression.

Existential relatedness is at stake in psychiatric disorders in various ways. First of all, the way in which patients relate to themselves and their situation may be an inherent element of the disorder itself, such as the disabling fear of panic attacks in anxiety disorders. The fear of the fear co-constitutes the problem. In such cases, the existential stance plays a *primary* role in the disorder. Secondly, psychiatric disorders can also *include* patients' stance-taking. For instance, part of being depressed consists of having no hope for future change and a distorted perception of the past. Thirdly, the existential relation is present in processes that are in a sense secondary to the disorder, but can nevertheless have an enormous impact on the course of that disorder and on the patients' well-being. Especially feelings of shame and guilt can have important *modulatory* effects. Patients with obsessive-compulsive disorder, for instance, typically are able to distance themselves from their obsessive and compulsive behaviours and recognise them as disproportional or odd, but that often only amplifies their feelings of shame and anxiety, making matters worse. In general, many patients with psychiatric disorders are ashamed of their experiences and their shame can lead to the avoidance of social contact – adding to their problems the adverse effects of social isolation. Feelings of shame can also prevent patients from seeking help, in particular at an early stage during which better results might have been achieved with smaller interventions.

In psychiatric practice, the existential stance of patients comes to the fore in various ways. For instance, patients relate to their diagnosis, which may raise questions like: What does this say about me? How will others react? How will it affect my future? The decision whether or not to take medication may also involve existential considerations. It can be an unsettling idea to take medication that is aimed at changing experiences that in part make up who you are. And if these pills do change your feelings in a way that you would object to, will you then still be in the position to notice these changes? The existential dimension also shows up in the possibility of suicide – which is the main cause of death in psychiatry. Moreover, several forms of treatment are specifically directed at changing patients' attitudes or evaluative stance. I will further elaborate on the existential dimension and its role in psychiatry in Chapter 5.

I.5   CONCLUSION

Many diverse factors can play a role in the development and persistence of psychiatric disorders. Given their diverse nature, it is particularly hard to envision how they relate; how neuronal mechanisms,
for instance, are connected to existential worries. How we relate these
factors is however highly relevant. It touches upon fundamental
issues such as: What are psychiatric disorders? What is the primary
cause of illness? How does medication influence psychiatric disorders? How does therapy influence psychiatric disorders? Our (implicit)
picture of the connections between experiences, brain processes, and
social relations shapes our views on causality and optimal treatment.
And even though in practice mental health care professionals and
patients may navigate quite well without the use of an explicit framework, such a framework does help one get a better grip on what one is
doing and why one is doing it. In this chapter, I have proposed four
main dimensions that are in one way or another at stake in psychiatric
disorders: the experiential, physiological, sociocultural, and existential dimension. A helpful account of psychiatric disorders should spell
out how these relate.

2 Currently Available Models in Psychiatry

2.1 INTRODUCTION

There are already quite a few models available for psychiatry. With so many on offer it is reasonable to ask if we really need yet another. Here I will briefly discuss several common and influential models and highlight their strengths and weaknesses. My aim here is not to provide comprehensive introductions to all of them; my only goal is to evaluate the available models with regard to their suitability to function as a *general, integrative framework* for psychiatric disorders. Following the main functions of such a framework as outlined in Chapter 1, I will use two main criteria: (1) are all four dimensions of psychiatric disorders taken into account? and (2) is a clear account given of how these dimensions relate? In short, I will look at the models' scope and integrative powers.

As we will see, many current models focus on only one or two aspects of psychiatric disorders. Although these models offer numerous valuable insights, I will argue that as *general* models for psychiatry they are too one-sided. Furthermore, I will argue that such models that focus on one aspect and are moreover *reductionist* are particularly ill suited for psychiatry. Some models are more encompassing, but do so by taking a dualist route. This solution too is unsatisfying, given that one of the main functions of a model for psychiatry is to provide a workable idea of how its various aspects are connected. We will then proceed to examine the integrative approaches that have already been developed and see what still needs to be done.

2.2   SINGLE-ASPECT MODELS AND REDUCTIONIST MODELS

Most theories of psychiatric disorders have accentuated one of their aspects. Sometimes this is out of a wish to provide a counterbalance to the dominant paradigm of that time, and sometimes it is out of the conviction that this aspect is more central than others to psychiatry. A one-aspect model can become reductionist if all other aspects are argued to somehow stem from or be grounded in this one crucial aspect. One-aspect models include such diverse models as neurophysiological, phenomenological, Daseinsanalytical, psychoanalytic, and social approaches to psychiatry. What they have in common is that they focus mainly on one of the dimensions of psychiatric disorders, be it physiological (biological and neuroreductionist models), experiential (phenomenological and psychoanalytical approaches), social (social psychiatry), or existential (Daseinsanalytical and existential approaches). This is of course a crude categorisation: phenomenological and psychoanalytical approaches, for instance, also take into account the social dimension in the form of personal relations and patients' relations to the world in general, and all approaches pay attention to patients' experiences. But their scopes are limited: the phenomenological and psychoanalytical approaches do not typically have a story to tell about how patients' experiences relate to their physiological processes, and conversely, biological psychiatry does not typically factor in existential considerations.

One-aspect models can offer valuable insights, but they do not help to solve the problem of integration, as they do not take into account the whole range of factors that are in play. For this reason they cannot fulfil the important function of connecting and ordering all those aspects that are met with here. Now, these single-aspect models do not necessarily aspire to provide an exhaustive account of the nature of psychiatric disorders. They highlight an important dimension, without thereby denying that there may be other important aspects involved as well. Insofar as these models do not aspire to be exhaustive, it would not be fair to hold it against them that they aren't. They just cannot serve as the kind of framework that we are looking for here, as we are precisely seeking for an integration of the heterogeneous aspects of psychiatric disorders.

The only way in which one-aspect models can be integrative is by being reductionist, that is, by attempting to reduce all factors to one primary or underlying dimension. In that case, there *is* a claim to a specific order; namely that other aspects are subordinate to this one dimension. Of the before-mentioned one-sided models only biological psychiatry offers an integrative, reductionist account. At one time bets were placed purely on genetics, but nowadays the most common and popular variant is a neurophysiological reductionism which maintains that psychiatric disorders are brain diseases. Patients' experiences are symptoms, expressions of underlying problems in the brain – be it neurotransmitter imbalances, malfunctioning brain parts, disturbances in connectivity between different parts or networks of the brain, or some complex combination of these. The same goes for patients' existential stances. Any interaction with the world, including patients' sociocultural embedding, is now only seen as relevant to the extent that it influences the brain. Even though the precise mechanisms and causal pathways in the brain are not yet clear, the idea is that this will come: the brain is just so massively complex that it takes much more time and effort to apprehend it.

The advantages of this neuroreductionist paradigm are evident. First of all, it is obvious that the brain is intimately connected with our experiences: a blow on the head will leave us unconscious; brain injuries can affect our perception, thinking, feeling or acting; and psychotropic drugs can change how we feel. This intimate connection between experiences and the brain makes it a natural move to grant the brain a prominent position in our understanding of psychiatric disorders. Research conducted from this neuroreductionist paradigm has indeed provided insights into the neurophysiological processes involved in psychiatric disorders. In principle, these insights can be used for the development of new forms of treatment. Another advantage is that this approach is well grounded in scientific research and as such employs reliable methodologies. Moreover, like any reductionist model, it has the advantage of offering a (putatively) coherent picture of how the various aspects of psychiatric disorders relate: namely, that all other factors can be reduced to the neurophysiological aspect. Even though what happens in the brain is enormously complex, as an integrative framework it still offers a straightforward hierarchy of layers and levels. And, finally, the neuroreductionist model has the advantage that it renders psychiatry more similar to other medical specialties: just as cardiologists specialise in the organ of the heart, psychiatrist specialise in the organ of the brain – which is considerably more concrete and identifiable than the mind.

A clear model is indeed preferable, as long as it does not oversimplify matters. In all reductionist models there is the risk of *unwarranted* reductions; unwarranted in the sense that important factors and processes are not sufficiently acknowledged and taken into account. The neuroreductionist model is attractive – but is it also correct?

2.2.1   *Evaluation of Neuroreductionism*

The first thing to note is that it is not quite clear what is meant by the statement that psychiatric disorders are brain diseases. Perhaps the idea is that psychiatric disorders are *caused* by independently distinguishable brain disorders? Or should we take the statement to imply that psychiatric disorders are *epiphenomena* of brain disorders, and to imply that the idea of 'downward causation' from psychological to neurological disturbance should be ruled out? Or should we regard experiences as being *identical* with certain brain states? Or maybe it is a pragmatic claim about what constitutes a viable *treatment*? Or is it rather a claim about *constitution*: a claim that it is factually mistaken to look outside of the skull – to the rest of the body or to the proximal environment – when trying to locate psychiatric disorders? These are obviously very different claims. We can, however, safely assume that proponents of the brain-disorder view on psychiatric disorders in one way or another attribute causal primacy to the brain. What happens in the brain is taken to somehow be more important than other factors.

Examining the Evidence

What is the evidence for this assumption? Proponents of neuroreductionism could point to the effects of brain damage, to findings from neuroimaging techniques, and to the effects of neuromodulation treatments like deep brain stimulation. Let's look at these examples in turn.

Functional Loss as a Result of Damage to Specific Brain Regions

We know for a fact that brain damage – for instance, due to an accident or a brain tumour – can lead to the loss of certain abilities. If damage to brain region A affects function X, then might we not say that function X is 'located' in brain region A? This may seem self-evident, but matters are not so straightforward. First of all it should be noted that the brain is plastic to such an extent that other regions can sometimes take over the provision of functions that are initially lost. This makes judgements on the basis of individual cases highly problematic. Besides, in order to allocate specific functions to specific regions, one would ideally need a double dissociation between functions and brain regions: brain region A affects function X but not Y, while brain region B affects function Y but not X. The functional losses of patients with brain damage, however, usually only allow for a single dissociation: in their case, damage to brain region A affects function X but not function Y. But even if one is able to find such double dissociations, by itself this still does not warrant adopting a modular model of the brain.[1] The main difficulty is that both individual brains as well as

---

[1] For a careful discussion, see van Orden and colleagues (2001). They discuss the problematic aspects of double dissociation, such as its theory dependency and the unreliability of the statistics involved in comparing patient groups. They explicitly reject the assumption that double dissociations are evidence for a modular model of the brain: 'Both single causes and modules are a priori assumptions, neither follows necessarily from the appearance of a double dissociation' (p. 115).

individual damages are too diverse to be easily comparable. Nowadays neural network models of the brain have become more popular, which means that the localisation of functions in specific brain regions is less obvious. A more fundamental problem with the evidence from functional loss is that even if we can reliably implicate the involvement of a certain brain region in a certain function, this still only implies that this brain region plays a *necessary* role for this function – but not that it is *sufficient*.

Data from fMRI Studies

In the past decades increasingly sophisticated techniques have been developed for non-invasively measuring activity of the brains of living humans, such as PET (positron-emission tomography), MEG (magneto encephalography), EEG (electroencephalography), and fMRI (functional magnetic resonance imaging). Especially fMRI has become a very popular neuroscientific tool. At a first glance, the coloured blobs that indicate brain activity may seem the perfect illustration of the credibility of a neuroreductionist approach. There are several strings attached though. First of all, fMRI uses indirect parameters: it does not measure neuronal activity directly, but measures the blood flow and blood oxygen level in the brain. It is important to note that these parameters cannot discriminate between *inhibition* and *activation* of neurons: an increase in the BOLD (blood oxygen level dependence) signal can be caused by either the firing or the inhibition of firing of neurons. Secondly, fMRI requires complex statistical programming in order to filter out the relevant information from the 'noise'. The vast amount of data can easily lead to 'false positives', as is nicely demonstrated by the famous case of the dead salmon that showed activity along the midline of its brain while being exposed to an emotion recognition test (Bennett 2009; Bennett and Miller 2010). Thirdly, different scanners provide different results: to achieve similar results, one should preferably use the very same scanner, or at least a scanner of the same brand and tesla-force, otherwise results are likely to vary.

The results as presented in the fMRI pictures are thus no direct representation of what is happening in the brain. And this is even less so if techniques such as 'masking' and 'subtracting' are used to make sense of the data. Masking entails removing 'uninteresting' data and analysing only the data from those parts of the brain that one expects to be interesting. All activation that shows up outside the skull (!) is, for instance, routinely masked. That there can be such activity recorded is because the results of the scanning need to be mapped onto a template brain in order to be comparable to other participants. However, each individual brain is different, in the same way that all faces are different: they all contain noses, mouths, and eyes, but their specific shape and their relative positions will differ. So sometimes the individual's brain will not quite fit within the brain template and activation will show up outside of this template. Other masks reflect the investigators' hypotheses and, again, statistical skills (Parrish 2006). 'Subtracting' means that the activation of the brain in 'default mode' is subtracted from the activation pattern that shows up during exposure to the stimuli. The underlying assumption is that the highest activation will reflect the main site or network involved in the specific experience under investigation.

Another important caveat is that fMRI takes place in a highly unnatural situation. This is of course true for most experimental settings, but in case of fMRI its ecological validity is very limited. Test-persons lie in the narrow fMRI tube, usually with their heads fixed in place, watching stimuli on a screen. The machine makes a lot of noise. Only very limited interaction with the environment is possible: one can press a button, watch a video clip, occasionally talk to the researcher(s) in another room. This impacts the scope of the research paradigm and the validity of the findings. The final and most important caution, however, is that correlation does not imply causality. Thus the mere pointing to (some of) the neural processes that take place as someone is having a specific experience does not in itself amount to a discovery of these experiences' 'underlying mechanism'. We have at best found a neural signature or neural narrative, but no conclusive evidence.

Effects of Neuromodulation Treatment

One of the most compelling of cases for a neuroreductionist understanding of psychiatric disorders is provided by the effect of neuromodulation treatments like transcranial magnetic stimulation (TMS), transcranial direct current stimulation (tDCS) and deep brain stimulation (DBS), After all: you stimulate the brain and the psychiatric symptoms disappear. Or that at least is the hope. TMS and tDCS are non-invasive: they involve the application of a magnetic force or electrical current to the outside of the skull. Despite much research, TMS and tDCS are not widely used in clinical practice because clear evidence of their usefulness is so far lacking (Mitchell and Loo 2006; George and Aston-Jones 2009). Only TMS treatment is regularly used for patients with depressive disorders. However its effects are limited: only 30 per cent of the patients who received TMS treatment during six weeks showed improvements in their condition (George et al. 2010).

DBS is an invasive form of neuromodulation and a relatively new, experimental treatment for psychiatric disorders. It is one of the most direct ways to manipulate a specific part or network of the brain, through implanted electrodes, typically on both hemispheres. It is, in effect, like a pacemaker for the brain. The effectiveness of DBS is still a matter of research (Kopell et al. 2004; Mayberg et al. 2005; Wichmann and DeLong 2006; Servello et al. 2007; Greenberg et al. 2010; Luigjes et al. 2013), but it is clear that *when* it works, DBS has the potential to almost instantly change patients' experiences – and profoundly so (de Haan et al. 2013b, 2015b). These effects of DBS seem to motivate a neuroreductionist view on psychiatric disorders. After all, if problems (partly) disappear through directly intervening on the brain, must it not have been a problem of the brain to begin with?

In fact, we cannot draw that conclusion. If some intervention helps, we cannot conclude that this intervention has thus targeted the primary cause of the problem. A fire can be extinguished by a bucket of water, but a lack of water is not what caused the fire to begin with. The number of patients with alcohol addiction goes down when the prices of alcohol go up, but this does not mean that a low price of alcohol causes addiction.

Furthermore, the effects of DBS are not so straightforward as they may seem. Firstly we must ask why does DBS work for some patients but not for others? Here, other factors than the patients' brains come into play – the quality of their social support for instance – casting doubt even here on the primacy of the brain. Secondly, it would be misleading to trace back the effects of the overall treatment to DBS alone. First of all, the DBS intervention itself takes place in a certain context: before they arrive on the table of the neurosurgeon, patients have already been through a whole trajectory, then they are carefully selected and tested to see if they are eligible for treatment. With such a special treatment, the 'expectancy effect' may be particularly high. If they 'pass' and are operated upon, they will need to return to the hospital weekly to adjust the settings of the device (which of the four electrodes is used, at what voltage and bandwidth?) to find the optimal settings for each particular patient. This intensive care may take several months. Apart from these weekly visits, patients often engage in cognitive behavioural therapy (CBT) or some other form of psychotherapy as well and this too seems to play a vital role (Mantione et al. 2014). The DBS treatment thus already involves more than stimulation of the brain alone.

Besides, the eventual effect of treatment will include secondary effects as well. Looking at the effects of treatment it seems a more likely scenario that DBS lowers patients' experience of anxiety which in turn allows them to engage in CBT which in turn helps to diminish the compulsive behaviours (de Haan et al. 2015b). With less time spent on the compulsions, patients may find they have time to look for a job again. This in turn provides a helpful structure in terms of day-night rhythm, social contacts, and increased self-esteem.

Finally, placebo effects may play a role too: a randomised controlled study on DBS for major depression patients (Dougherty et al.

2014) found that after a sixteen-week period there was no significant difference in response rate between the groups receiving proper versus sham stimulation. The effects of DBS treatment thus do not offer conclusive evidence for the causal primacy of the brain in psychiatric disorders either.

All in all, the above examples should not tempt us into making the so-called localisation fallacy (Wimsatt 1974, 2000; Fuchs 2008; Bechtel and Richardson 2010): i.e. into assuming that we can locate specific experiences or functions of the whole in one of its parts. The neuroreductionist quest for finding biomarkers for psychiatric disorders and developing new forms of (pharmaceutical) treatments has so far not been successful either – despite the huge amount of money spent on neuroscientific research since the 'decade of the brain' was announced in 1990. Proponents of the neuroreductionist view acknowledge this lack of progress, but they still remain convinced that their assumption of the brain's centrality is correct (Kapur et al. 2012; Krystal and State 2014).

The absence of useful applications of neuroscientific research in psychiatric practice has been blamed on the failing of diagnostic manuals: if only we had better ways to group patients we would get 'cleaner' and thus more useful data. The two main diagnostic manuals, *DSM-5* and *ICD-10*, group patients according to syndromes, i.e. groups of symptoms. Since the presence of a disorder typically depends on the patient possessing a selection of these symptoms, say five out of eight, two patients with the same diagnosis may in fact have quite different symptoms. The complaint is that the ensuing diagnostic labels contain groups of patients which are too heterogeneous, making it difficult to find underlying mechanisms and causal pathways. Besides, the idea is that similar mechanisms may play a role *across* different disorders, but such potential commonalities are hard to discover as long as research groups are organised according to the *DSM-5* and *ICD-10* labels. In other words: diagnostic labels do not map well onto neuroscientific research.

To solve this problem and bypass current diagnostic labels to further neuroscientific insights the American National Institute of Mental Health (NIMH) has instituted the Research Domain Criteria (RDoC) programme. The RDoC is meant to improve the study of mental disorders and inform prospective diagnostic manuals by focusing on psychological constructs such as 'threat', 'attention', 'perception', 'language', 'arousal', and 'reward responsiveness', instead of psychiatric disorders as defined by our current diagnostic labels. These psychological constructs are grouped into several domains, and studied on several levels, or units of analysis, ranging from genes, molecules, and cells to brain circuits, behaviour, and self-reports. This results in a matrix of research results. The hope is that this new approach will further the discovery of underlying mechanisms and their biomarkers.

Although the RDoC explicitly aims to 'integrate the fundamental genetic, neurobiological, behavioral, environmental, and experiential components that comprise these mental disorders' (NIMH 2008), it, at the same time, assumes a neuroreductionist view on what mental disorders are. For the hinging point of all these levels is assumed to be *brain circuits*. As Insel (2013) the former director of the NIMH who instigated the RDoC programme writes: 'mental disorders are biological disorders involving brain circuits that implicate specific domains of cognition, emotion, or behavior'.

Again we find the unexamined preference, characteristic of neuroreductionist approaches, for isolating just one component – a particular neurological dysfunction – from within a complex and recursive web of causal influences. Furthermore, we find here no account of *how* what happens in the brain relates to our experiences and to our interactions with the world. Neuroreductionist may object that this is not fair: that the RDoC programme is precisely set up to answer this question, to connect insights from different scientific disciplines. There is, however, a deeper problem here: putting these heterogeneous insights into one matrix does not yet provide the answer to the real issue, namely how to relate them. That requires an explanatory framework that does more than merely point to the brain as the place where the magic happens.

2.2.2   Arguments against Neuroreductionism

In light of this lack of empirical evidence that psychiatric disorders are first and foremost disorders of the brain, the assumption of the brain's causal primacy appears to be a matter of faith, rather than a matter of fact. There are however good reasons to doubt the neuroreductionists' unquestioned faith. For the fact that the brain is *implicated* in all psychiatric disorders does not mean that the brain therefore has a *special causal status*. Whatever changes in the brain may be a *reflection* rather than a cause: after all, everything we do changes our brains – but that does not yet make our brains the cause of everything. If I cut my finger, it hurts. At that moment, all kinds of neuronal processes will take place in my brain, and if I would have been brain-dead I would not have felt pain, but that does not make those neuronal processes the *cause* of my pain. Expert golf players show a different neuronal activation pattern when preparing for their swing than novice players (Bezzola et al. 2011). Does that make this neuronal activity the cause of their expertise? No, they have become expert golf players through years of practising, working on their technique, having good coaches, and some amount of talent. All this practising has affected the brain; the brain *reflects* this practice, just like their muscles do. Our brains are highly plastic: their present anatomy and functional connectivity depends on our previous experiences and interactions with our surroundings – again like our muscles reflect our history of activating them.

Even if certain neuronal processes do play a causal role, we cannot isolate these processes in the brain from the rest of the body or from our interactions with the world. For instance, if someone's amygdala is more easily activated than average, this may make them more vulnerable to develop post-traumatic stress disorder (Koenigs and Grafman 2009). The over-sensitivity of the amygdala may however in turn be the result of previous traumatic experiences (Rauch et al. 2000). Such 'neural vulnerabilities' are likely themselves reflections of previous experiences. What then would count as a primary cause here? The neural vulnerability, the present traumatic experience, or the experiences that led to this neural vulnerability? To allocate primacy to one of them seems nonsensical. And even if such neural vulnerabilities are just a matter of bad luck, they are in themselves not enough to explain the occurrence of psychiatric disorders.

From a neuroreductionist perspective, other factors that might contribute to the development and persistence of psychiatric disorders seem less relevant than what happens in the brain. But neuroreductionists surely cannot deny the effects that certain experiences or life-events may have on our mental health – for better or for worse? One line of reasoning that is often used to still grant these other, non-neuronal, factors some causal efficacy is that they only work *to the extent* that they influence the brain. Psychotherapy, for instance, is assumed to work only in so far as it changes the brain.[2] The real causal work is still done by the neural changes. So if patients get a job, or a relationship, or a better house, or if they succeed in changing their coping strategies through psychotherapy, these changes affect the brain, and in the end it is these changes in the brain that cause them to feel better and behave differently. The causal force remains located in the brain, but we can still accommodate the fact that such changes in patients' situations or psychology can have a large impact. In this way, one can apparently commit to neurophysiological reductionism without giving up on the importance of psychological or social influences – as long as one maintains that the brain is the real mechanism of change here.

This may sound plausible enough, but it is deeply flawed. Let's look in some more detail at the reasoning that is here in play. Suppose that patient (P) first is depressed (P(d)) in situation A. Situation

---

[2]   As Kandel (1999b) writes: 'It is intriguing to think that *insofar as* psychoanalysis is successful in bringing about persistent changes in attitudes, habits, and conscious and unconscious behavior, it does so by producing alterations in gene expression that produce structural changes in the brain' (p. 519, my italics).

A changes into situation B: say the patient finds a job. The patient now feels much better (P(h)). The reasoning here is that it is actually the brain that causes this change:

P(d) is caused by brain state (BS(d)).
Situation B turns brain state (BS(d)) into brain state (BS(h)).
Brain state (BS(h)) causes P(d) to become P(h).

But what we *know* is that

P(d) was in situation A;
P(d) was in brain state BS(d);
P(d) moves into situation B;
P(d) becomes P(h);
P(h) is in brain state BS(h).

Can we conclude from this list that BS(d) becoming BS(h) is the cause of P(d) becoming P(h)? This is a problematic move. First, from a commonsensical perspective the relevant difference is a change in situation, namely finding a job, and therefore this should be treated as the primary cause of the patient feeling better. For it is after the situation changes that the state the person is in changes – including her brain. Suppose the situation had remained the same, and all that had changed was that the patient had started drug therapy: in that case the neuroreductionist would not have hesitated to point to the drugs as the primary cause of the change. Finding a job and taking medication perform the same role – yet for the neuroreductionist finding a job does not have the same status, and is supposed to be effective only indirectly.

The arbitrariness of assigning the brain a special causal role here also comes to the fore if we compare it to other physiological processes. If we compared the physiological state of P(d) in situation A with the physiological state of P(h) in situation B, we would find that many physiological processes – such as hormonal, cardiac, bowel, and neural processes – have changed. After all, simply being less stressed would already imply such differences. And yet it is supposed to be only these *neural* processes that are the underlying cause of the change from P(d) to P(h). Why single out only neural processes? Why not say that it was 'actually' the changes in the digestive system that caused the patient to become healthy? One answer might be that if the brain had not changed, the person would not have changed either. But if she would not have gotten the job, she also would not have changed. The fact that the brain changes does not imply that it was therefore the *cause* of the patient feeling better. The changes in the brain could also *reflect* the changes of the patient feeling better – while she feels better *because* of her job. The brain is a part of the person, and being depressed *includes* certain brain processes just like being happy includes other brain processes.

A neuroreductionist model jumps from the fact of the brain's implication in psychiatric disorders to the unquestioned assumption of its causal primacy. As such, it a priority and thus unwarrantedly simplifies psychiatric disorders.

2.2.3   *Ethical Objections*

The adoption of a neuroreductionist model not only impacts practical matters, such as what type of research is most likely to get funding and which treatments appear as most promising – but it also raises some ethical concerns. Putting patients' experiences, existential stances, and their interactions with their world in second place comes at a cost. The focus on their brains potentially affects patients' experience of agency, of expertise, and their self-understanding in general.

In the most extreme forms of neuroreductionism the subject herself is regarded as an illusion that our brains fabricate for us. We might think we are agents in any substantial sense, that what we think and decide and feel makes a difference to what we do, but in reality our considerations are all confabulations that come after the fact (Metzinger 2003; Wegner 2003; Gazzaniga 2012). Human beings, they claim, are not free agents but instead are governed by non-conscious, sub-personal, neurophysiological processes. We are not in control, our brains are. The steps in this reasoning seem to be as follows:

1 person and her experiences *becomes* body (causally determined) and mind (free);
2 body (causally determined) and mind (free) *becomes* brain (causally determined) and mind (free);
3 brain (causally determined) and mind (free) *becomes* brain (causally determined) and illusion after the fact (causally determined).

In this way, patients' experiences drop out of consideration as irrelevant. The fundamental role of one's body and of interactions with one's (social) surroundings are left out, leaving a brain-centred model which conceives the brain as a monadic, self-sufficient entity.

Not all neuroreductionists are such hardliners of course, but the focus on the brain does imply a shift in the role that is played by patients' experiences and agency. If psychiatric disorders are brain diseases, the locus of control is in the brain too. For many patients, this in fact fits with their experience that they cannot help it to be in this situation: if they could control what they are suffering from (e.g. depressed mood, social anxiety, compulsive behaviour), they would have long since put an end to it. Placing the responsibility in the brain moreover has the advantage that it frees patients from blame. It is not a lack of character on their part, it's simply bad luck with how one's brain is wired. Initially, one of the main motivations for a neuroreductionist understanding of psychiatric disorders was precisely to get rid of the blame-discourse. 'Addiction is a brain disease, and it matters', Leshner (1997, p. 45) wrote. Addiction is probably the most blame-sensitive of psychiatric disorders, and it was hoped that a neuroreductionist view would diminish the blame and therefore the stigma surrounding it. More generally, it has been suggested that by regarding psychiatric disorders as brain diseases, psychiatric patients are enabled to distance themselves from their afflictions in the same way as is possible for 'somatic' diseases. And it is suggested furthermore that this would have the welcome effect of destigmatisation: for one surely cannot be blamed for what one cannot influence (Pescosolido et al. 2010). The hope was that suffering from a psychiatric disorder would thus attain the same 'status' as suffering from a somatic problem: that people suffering from depression would no more be told to 'man up' than people suffering from cancer.

Laudable as this aim is, there is no such thing as a free lunch. Less responsible also means less able. The supposed effect of destigmatisation comes at the cost of diminishing patients' agency and responsibility. Moreover, the destigmatising effects of neuroreductionism turn out to be disappointing. It has even been argued that regarding psychiatric disorders as diseases of the brain rather has a *negative* effect on the assumption of psychiatric patients being dangerous, as well as on benevolent attitudes towards patients (Corrigan and Watson 2004). Besides, blame is only one aspect of the stigma of psychiatric patients, and not even the most decisive one. Another study (Pescosolido et al. 2010) found that having a neurobiological conception of psychiatric disorders did increase the likelihood of support for treatment, but did not reduce stigma. Quite the contrary: the occurrence of stigmatising reactions seemed to increase; again, especially with regard to the assumed dangerousness of psychiatric patients. In the light of such studies, it makes more sense to fight stigmas not by *estranging* people from psychiatric disorders (as mysterious brain disorders that are out of their control), but rather by *familiarising* them with these disorders (as disorders that are quite common and could happen to anyone).

Besides, the transfer of the 'real influence' from the subject to its brain also entails a transfer of who is the expert on experiences (Fuchs 2011a). This encourages a far-reaching dependency on experts: those who can 'read' your brain know what is really on your mind. Many of those charmed by a neuroreductionist model of psychiatric disorder will also look forward to a future in which we could rely on 'objective' measures for diagnosing psychiatric disorders rather than having to rely on the subjective accounts of patients themselves. Patients' own experiences, however, remain the starting and endpoint of psychiatric treatment – and they remain their own experts.

From an ethical perspective, neuroreductionism thus raises concerns regarding the implied status of patients as helpless victims of their brain, thereby downplaying patients' agency, responsibility, and possibilities for taking charge and changing things. Cutting the person out of psychiatry and focusing on the brain only is an unnecessary amputation of psychiatry and a disservice to patients.

2.2.4   Summing Up

The main problem with a neuroreductionist model of psychiatric disorders as brain diseases is that it assumes an unexamined preference for the brain's causal role, thereby oversimplifying the complexity of psychiatric disorders and the factors involved in their development and persistence. It involves a localisation fallacy, and encourages a downscaled role for patients – regarding their experiences and agency, their bodies and their environments. This is not to say that the brain is unimportant. The critique of the *model* does not mean doing away with all its neurophysiological *insights*. Quite the contrary, any model of psychiatric disorders would be incomplete if it were to leave out the neurophysiological dimension: that would be just as one-sided. The challenge is do justice to the complexity of psychiatric disorders and assign physiological processes, including neuronal processes and their proper place. The wish to avoid reductionism is, thus, the wish to not leave out or overlook such elements as are essential to the understanding and treatment of psychiatric patients.

That the brain plays a vital role in our capacity to experience – and thus in psychiatric disorders as well – goes without saying, but it is not the whole story. After all, the brain is an organ that depends on the rest of the organism for its functioning, which in turn depends on its interactions with its environment (Chiel and Beer 1997; Fuchs 2018). Given the brain's plasticity, any understanding of what is happening in the brain requires us to take the person's history of interactions into account. Brain processes by themselves cannot suffice to explain experiences, let alone psychiatric disorders, even though they are surely involved.

2.3   COMPLEMENTARY/DUALIST MODELS

Apart from one-sided and reductionist models there are also complementary or dualist models of psychiatric disorders. A recent dualist model is values-based psychiatry (Fulford et al. 2005; Fulford 2008a, 2008b). The idea is that we should do justice both to the scientific side of psychiatry, studying and treating malfunctioning physiological processes, and to psychiatry as a practice in the life-world where patients show up as persons with their specific concerns. The dualism here is between the facts – the domain of science – and values – the domain of the life-world. This dualism does not quite neatly map onto the four dimensions I have singled out as the ones that need to be integrated in order to give a proper account of the nature of psychiatric disorders. It does, however, try to tackle the same problem of integration, only through a different lens.

Values-based psychiatry stands up for the recognition of the values that are involved in psychiatry: not as something to be avoided but rather as a positive entrance to the life-world of patients. It presents itself as complementary to evidence-based psychiatry (Fulford et al. 2005). That is, values-based psychiatry defines its domain on the basis of a fact-value distinction in which the complements stay dichotomous (Fulford et al. 2005). It proposes a division between psychiatric *research* that takes place under the auspices of strict science and the psychiatric *practice* on the other hand that takes place in the life-world and is guided by values. Research has the facts, practice has the values. The facts are within the neurophysiological paradigm, the values within the values-based paradigm.

The advantage of this model lies in its recognition of the fundamental role of values in psychiatry. It is not reductionist and offers a broad model of evidence-based medicine alongside values-based practice. By positioning these two dimensions as complementary, the values-based approach presents an and/and rather than an either/ or approach. This makes it appealing.

However, although it takes an important stance and provides a much needed alternative to the neurophysiological model, values-based psychiatry does not yet go far enough. Values are included, but only as a *complement* to the objective scientific facts. Besides, these values should not be thought of in any *substantive* sense: values-based psychiatry in fact adopts an 'anti-realist' conception of values (Fulford 2008b, p. 183). That means that this approach adheres only to 'the logical separation of description and evaluation' (p. 183): there are the facts, and there is the individual evaluation of these facts which makes these facts 'value-laden'. The values of values-based psychiatry refer only to such individual evaluations, to such subjective ascriptions of values to the objective facts.

Such a separation is not only highly problematic from a philosophical perspective, but the proposed fact-value distinction also does not do justice to what actually happens in science. For in scientific research too, values are at stake. The traditional scientific paradigm is not without values but rather testifies to some *specific* values, such as objectivity and neutrality. Evidence-based medicine too cannot be 'value-free' (Gupta 2014). This comes to the fore when one considers a very basic issue: how to determine whether a specific disorder is present or not. A pure description of facts is principally incapable of such a determination. For a description of facts may point to differences between states, but the facts do not offer a standard to decide which differences amount to a disorder. And even when we have facts about the probability distribution, this only allows us to say something about the likeliness of a state occurring – and not about whether this state should be regarded as a disorder. Defining disorders necessarily entails a normative element (Sadler and Agich 1996). In fact, Fulford and colleagues (2005) are aware of this difficulty. They write that finding out more about the causes of human experience and behaviour 'will do nothing to resolve questions about exactly which kinds of experiences and behaviours are *negatively evaluated* [italics added] and, hence, *pathological'* (p. 82). Still they contend that scientific research itself should not be 'biased' and that the strict 'disentangling of value from fact' (p. 83) should serve as a safeguard of science's value-free delivery of facts. But this is a simplistic conception that has been challenged for decades (cf. Kincaid et al. 2007). Moreover, in psychiatric practice this fact-value distinction will not be easy to uphold either, as many phenomena cannot be easily divided along these lines. Medication for instance, seems to sit firmly in the realm of the evidence-based neurophysiological psychiatry. But what is fact and what is value? Fact is that the effectiveness of medication does not solely depend on its chemical properties. The common occurrence of so-called placebo effects points to the impact of other factors: the relationship between patient and doctor, the expectations of the patient, the colour of the pill. Here the 'subjective evaluation' shapes the 'objective facts' – which is inexplicable from the dualistic division as proposed by values-based psychiatry.

In general, as a framework for psychiatry, complementary models are insufficient, for they offer no account of how the various aspects relate. A dualistic 'solution' does not really answer this problem but rather circumvents it. The recourse to dualism does not do justice to the fact that the psychiatric patient is one person and that the distinction between physiological facts on the one hand and existential values on the other cannot be neatly drawn. This also implies that the dualistic picture of values-based psychiatry does not give the existential dimension and the related values its proper place. I will come back to the role of the existential stance and values in Chapters 5 and 6.

2.4   INTEGRATIVE MODELS

So far the one-sided, reductionist, and dualist models have been found to not live up to the promise that a theoretical framework should fulfil. Integrative approaches precisely aim to mend this. The main integrative options are the classical biopsychosocial model, and the more recent network model, and embodied approaches.

2.4.1   The Biopsychosocial Model

The call for a more encompassing, integrative approach to psychiatry is not new. In fact, Engel (1977) introduced the biopsychosocial model (BPS) to offer just that. In his classic article, Engel criticised the dominant biomedical model in psychiatry, and instead stressed that psychological and social factors are just as relevant as physiological ones for understanding and treating disorders. Interestingly, he argued that psychiatry should not try to squeeze itself into a limited medical model, but that it should rather serve as an example to other medical specialties that would also profit from a more encompassing approach. The BPS is thus intended as a model for medicine in general. Engel (1977) illustrates this by pointing to the similarities of diabetes and schizophrenia: even though one is a 'somatic' and the other a 'mental' disorder, both disorders require us to take into account both psychological and social factors. And in his article 'The Clinical Application of the Biopsychosocial Model', Engel (1980) discusses the treatment of a patient with an acute myocardial infarction, to highlight in which respects a BPS approach would have differed from the traditional biomedical one.

As its name indicates, the main additions of the BPS model compared to the biomedical model are that it also takes psychological and social aspects of disorders into account. Concretely, this means that physicians should also take into consideration their patients' personality and psychological reactions to what is happening. Moreover, the social environment of patients should be included as well: their relations with their loved ones, as well as the larger setting of their professional life and cultural community, are all relevant. Engel (1980) stresses that this attention to psychological and social factors is not merely a matter of being a nice, compassionate doctor, but is rather an essential part of medicine. How the patient reacts to his condition, and how his loved ones react, are *medically* relevant. The personality style of the patient is relevant because physicians rely on a proper understanding of the experiences and behaviour of their patients. It is, for instance, useful to know if the patient is reluctant to acknowledge any need for help, for that implies that the physician needs to be more proactive and inquisitive. As for the impact of social factors, Engel (1980) cites, as an example, the fact that the patient's illness could have a destabilising effect on the people around him, which in turn may have a destabilising effect on the patient. He therefore concludes that 'attention to Mrs. Glover's well-being [is] a necessary element in Mr. Glover's care' (Engel 1980, p. 543).

With regard to the relation between these three aspects, Engel draws on general system theory (GST) as developed by von Bertalanffy (1950). GST was developed as an alternative to the traditional 'mechanistic view' of science which holds that 'in order to state exact laws for any field, and to render it an exact science, it had to be reduced to physics and chemistry' (p. 140). Even though the methodology of analysis and reduction has been successful in these fields, for a wide range of phenomena it seems less useful. Especially when it comes to describing living organisms, basic biological phenomena, and sociological phenomena, which are 'essentially problems of organisation, orderliness, and regulation, resulting from the interaction of an enormous number of highly complicated physico-chemical events' (p. 140). Instead of trying to explain what is happening at the level of the system as a whole by reducing it to what is happening at the level of its elements, von Bertalanffy proposes that we investigate whether there are exact laws that govern that system-level. A 'system' is defined as 'a complex of interacting elements $p1$, $p2$ ... pn. Interaction means that the elements stand in a certain relation, R, so that their behaviour in R is different from their behaviour in another relation, R' (p. 143). GST, then, is 'a logico-mathematical field, the subject matter of which is the formulation and deduction of those principles which are valid for "systems" in general. There are principles which apply to systems in general, whatever the nature of the component elements or the relations or "forces" between them' (p. 139). The ultimate goal is that GST may provide a 'Unity of Science', because it applies to all systems, in all fields of science.

For Engel (1980), systems theory provides the means to connect the biological, psychological, and social as different levels of a 'hierarchically arranged continuum' (p. 536). Each of these levels forms a dynamic whole, a system of itself, but each of them is at the same time part of the higher order, more complex systems as well. Importantly, Engel stresses that each of these levels or systems requires its own methods, its own research questions and explanations that are 'unique for that level' (p. 536). In contrast to von Bertalanffy's unifying aspirations, Engel states that 'in no way can the methods and rules appropriate for the study and understanding of the cell as cell be applied to the study of the person as person or the family as family' (p. 536). The biological, psychological, and social systems each have their boundaries 'across which material and information flow' (p. 537).

The BPS model provided an important step forward, and both Engel's critique of the biomedical model as well as his arguments for a more integrative approach to medicine remain just as valid and relevant as they were forty years ago. There is room for improvement though. In three respects: first of all, the BPS model relies on GST to explain and model the relation between the three aspects. Although Engel (1980) is right that a systemic approach is intuitively appealing, it should offer more than that. But the BPS remains vague when it comes to explicating the precise nature of the interactions between these separate systems. Engel stresses the qualitative differences between the biological, psychological, and social systems, but this of course makes the question about the nature of their interactions all the more pressing. The mention of 'material and information flow' (p. 537) across the system's boundaries is not very informative. As a consequence, the BPS model has been criticised for insufficiently integrating the three perspectives (Drayson 2009; Ghaemi 2009; van Oudenhove and Cuypers 2014), and for thereby fostering an eclectic style in psychiatric practice in which everything is equally important, and anything goes (Ghaemi 2009). Without a clear view on how to order the biological, psychological, and social aspects, there are also no clear guidelines for how to proceed when it comes to diagnosis and treatment. In fact, Engel (1980) does say where to start, namely at the level of the person, that is, the patient (p. 537). But still, the difficulty of ordering all relevant factors, which are moreover of different kinds, remains. This is a difficulty that faces all approaches that aim to be integrative while doing justice to complexity.

Moreover, the ways in which to think of and to model systems, has in the meantime evolved considerably. In particular, complex systems theory, dynamical systems theory, and network theory have been further developed to model complex, interacting, and non-linear processes – the kind of processes at stake in psychiatric disorders. So for the pursuit of a similar aim, we now have different means at our disposal.[3]

Lastly, the BPS model does not explicitly acknowledge the existential dimension. To be sure, the way in which patients evaluatively relate to their disorder and their situation in general is implicit in the psychological aspect: Engel (1980) for instance mentions the relevance of whether or not the patient has *accepted* the reality of his illness (p. 540). The disadvantage of leaving the existential stance implicit, is that it is thereby not recognised as a *specific loop* of the overall system. For all disorders, but especially for psychiatric disorders, it is useful to distinguish the patients' experiences from their *stance on* or attitude towards these experiences. This is useful for assessing the experiences of patients: is someone prone to deny or relativise symptoms, or is she somewhat hypochondriacal and inclined to quickly regard her experiences as potential symptoms? And treatment too can be targeted at changing patients' experiences, or rather at changing their stance on their experiences. Given the special importance of the existential stance for understanding and treating psychiatric disorders, it is helpful to recognise it as a separate dimension.

---

[3] I will not go into the exact differences in the mathematics of these various models. For an overview of the relevance of these new systems' approaches for biology and cognitive science, see Moreno et al. (2011).

2.4.2 Network Models

Recently, another model has been proposed as an organising framework for the 'integration of different levels of explanation' in psychiatry (Borsboom 2017, p. 11). The idea is that mental disorders follow a network structure in which the components of the network (so-called nodes) correspond with psychiatric symptoms as listed in the *DSM*. To put *DSM* symptoms in a network model means that the model allows for direct causal connections between symptoms, as well as for feedback loops. This may seem self-evident, but it stands in stark contrast to the commonly held 'latent variable' models in which the disease is supposed to be the one cause of each of the separate symptoms.

The advantage of a network model is that it offers a way to model complexity – and psychiatric disorders with all these heterogeneous factors involved are certainly complex. Assuming the possibility of causal interactions between symptoms makes sense too. Besides, the network model can shed light on the high rate of double diagnoses in psychiatry: many of the symptoms of different disorders already overlap, and if one, moreover, assumes causal connections between symptoms (e.g. sleeping problems lead to difficulties concentrating) then one can easily see how problems could be spreading from one symptom to the next; activating a new cluster of symptoms, that is, a disorder. Another advantage of network models is that they are easy to individualise and to adopt in practice: different patients can have different symptoms which can, moreover, be differently connected. For example, for the one patient getting enough sleep may be vital, whereas another patient might be especially sensitive to social isolation.

Despite these advantages, network models do not offer the integrative account they promise. They *presuppose* an integrative theory (or any theory) rather than provide one. Network models are only a mathematical tool, an empty template, in which the nodes and their connections can refer to anything. Network models cannot tell us what to include in the network, since the network model cannot by itself tell us what is and is not relevant. This is why Borsboom and colleagues rely completely on the lists of symptoms of the *DSM* to determine the content of their networks. The symptoms form the network and all the rest are 'external factors'. But this is highly unsatisfactory: it means that it does not include (potential) causes that are not *DSM* symptoms, and since *DSM* symptoms refer only to patients' experiences and behaviour, this means leaving out a lot of potential causes; ranging from brain changes to unconscious emotions to environmental influences. This is quite a drawback for a model that is supposed to provide an integrative framework. It also means that the network model as proposed by Borsboom and colleagues does not include positive, strengthening factors – even though that would make a lot of sense from a clinical perspective. There is nothing in the network model itself that poses this limitation – but one needs to have an idea of what is and isn't relevant, for the model won't tell you.

Furthermore, network models by themselves also cannot tell us what is normal and what is abnormal. They define mental disorder as 'the (alternative) stable state of a strongly connected network, i.e., the state of disorder that is separated from the healthy state by hysteresis' (p. 9). Pathological networks are thus those with a strong connectivity between their nodes in combination with the feature of 'hysteresis': the dependence of the state of a system on its history, which means that even if one removes the triggering cause of a disorder, the symptoms continue to activate each other. But of course, neither the connectivity strengths between nodes, nor the occurrence of hysteresis in a network means that this network is in any way abnormal. Again, this definition only works if one already presupposes the abnormality of the nodes as being 'symptoms' in the first place. But whether or not something should be seen as a symptom is something the network model cannot tell us. The general problem of the network model is that no model will tell you how to apply it, one needs a theory for that – but the network model lacks such a theory.

This lack of a theory or an ontology shows up in another problem too: the network model tells us nothing about the nature of the relations between the nodes. In particular, it cannot help to distinguish between causal and constitutive relations – which is unhelpful of a model that is supposed to be a tool for mapping causal trajectories. Again, one needs an understanding of what it is that one is modelling in order to make that distinction. Network models thus presuppose an integrative theory of the various factors in psychiatric disorders and cannot offer such a theory itself.

2.4.3 Embodied and Enactive Approaches to Psychiatry

The relevance of enactive theories for psychiatry and psychopathology has been recognised for some years now. Enactive ideas have been called upon to develop a unifying theory on autism (Klin et al. 2003; De Jaegher 2013), for a better understanding of depression (Slaby et al. 2013; Maiese 2018), schizophrenia (Kyselo 2016; Maiese 2016; Krueger 2018; Fuchs, forthcoming; Gipps, forthcoming-b), anxiety disorder (Glas, forthcoming), and dissociative identity disorder (Maiese 2016). Enactive accounts of emotions (Colombetti and Thompson 2008; Colombetti 2010) are relevant for psychiatry, as is Ratcliffe's (2008, 2009) embodied account of existential feelings.[4] More general outlines of how embodied, embedded cognition and enactivism may relate to the field of psychiatry have been provided too (Fuchs 2007, 2009, 2018; Drayson 2009; Fuchs and Schlimme 2009; Hutto 2010; McGann et al. 2013; Myin et al. 2015; Maiese 2016).

What these different publications have in common is, first of all, their rejection of reductionist biomedical or brain-centred approaches to psychology and psychiatry. Instead, they stress the

---

[4] Not to be confused with what I am calling the existential stance. Ratcliffe's (2008) 'existential feelings' refer to background orientations, to ways of being attuned to the world – comparable to Heidegger's (1927/1978) notion of mood. The existential stance, by contrast, refers to the implicit or explicit evaluative stance that people take on themselves, their experiences, and their surroundings. The existential stance has a reflexive (i.e. self-relating) structure, whereas Ratcliffe's existential feelings are general, pervasive, implicit orientations to the world.

relevance of taking into account a broader picture, including the role of the body (Gallagher and Væver 2004; Fuchs 2005; de Haan and Fuchs 2010), and of interactions with the (social) environment (Klin et al. 2003; Gallagher 2004; Hobson 2009; McGann et al. 2013; Myin et al. 2015). Our focus, they suggest, should not be on the brain only, but rather on the whole 'brain-body-environment' as one dynamical system (Fuchs 2009, 2018; McGann et al. 2013). Moreover, several authors argue specifically for acknowledging the relevance of patients' experiences, pointing to the links with classical phenomenological psychopathology (Fuchs 2009, 2010a), and the research paradigm of neurophenomenology (cf. Varela 1996; Colombetti 2013). Adopting an embodied or enactive framework encourages a pluralistic approach to treatment (Fuchs 2009; Colombetti 2013), which should notably include body and movement-oriented therapies (Fuchs 2009; Röhricht et al. 2014). With regard to the implications for how to conceive the development of psychiatric disorders, it is suggested that an embodied, systemic approach calls for a more complex notion of causality, such as circular causality (Fuchs 2009, 2018).

Embodied and enactive approaches to psychiatry are very promising, especially with respect to their encompassing scope, and potentially also with respect to their integrative powers. However, as Colombetti (2013) recently noted: 'enactivist ideas so far have not been applied to develop worked-out theories and methods in psychopathology' (p. 1088). Drayson (2009) too, pointed out that if psychiatry were to adopt an embodied cognition approach, 'a new model of psychopathology would be required' (p. 338). Still lacking is a *general enactive framework for psychiatry* that can provide an integrative perspective on the nature, causes, and treatment of psychiatric disorders – one that helps dissolve several longstanding conceptual debates such as whether psychiatric disorders are real or whether they are social constructs, whether we should conceive of them as gradual or as discrete phenomena, or whether psychiatric diagnoses are objective or value-laden. My aim here is to develop such an integrative framework, which can serve as the basis for further enactive modelling in psychiatry.

2.5 SUMMARY

Summing up, currently available models leave out one or more dimensions and/or do not sufficiently show how the dimensions relate. The network model is somewhat different in that it offers a helpful template, but this model presupposes rather than provides an integrative theory. What we still lack is a framework that integrates all four dimensions in a non-reductionist manner. Ideally, a model should acknowledge the complexity of these factors and their mutual influences and help to get a grip on these interactions. It should take the development of the person and her problems into account. It should be encompassing without being dualist, and it should be integrative without being reductionist. Ideally, then, a model should provide a holistic perspective without being vague.

3   Introduction to Enactivism

3.1   INTRODUCTION

The problem of integrating the heterogeneous factors involved in psychiatric disorders is a central one. This difficulty of how to connect all the possible aspects of psychiatric disorders and their mutual interactions bears on important issues, such as how to understand the causality involved in psychiatric disorders and how to understand the effects of different treatments, including medication and psychotherapy. An integrative account of psychiatric disorders addresses these issues. Reductionist models are problematic in their oversimplification of the complexity of psychiatric disorders and their failure to give an account of how other factors are supposed to influence the brain. Dualist models do not solve the integration problem, but rather pass it by. And the integrative models available fall short because they remain vague on the precise relation between the factors involved (BPS and network model), or are not actually integrative accounts (network model). The paradigm of embodied and embedded approaches to cognition is a promising newcomer, but has so far not been elaborated into a proper framework for psychiatry.

In this chapter, I will outline the enactive – the most rigorous of embodied and embedded approaches – perspective on cognition.[1] Cognition is fleshed out in terms of 'sense-making'. I will explain this

---

[1]   The other main version of an embodied and embedded approach to cognition is the extended mind theory as put forward by Clark and Chalmers (1998). They argue that the mind can extend into the world; that it is arbitrary to limit the mind to what is happening 'inside the skull'. They propose that a part of the world can (temporarily) be part of our cognitive processes if that 'part of the world functions as a process which, were it to go on in the head, we would have no hesitation in accepting as part of the cognitive process'. Extending the inner is, however, quite different from overthrowing the very inner mind–outer world division – as enactivism proposes. In other words: extended mind theory still accepts the basic dichotomy of inner minds and outer

notion and spell out its implications for our understanding of the relation between cognition, perception, and action. I will explicate this enactive ontology of the mind and clarify how it differs from a more traditional approach. This will then serve as the overall background in terms of which we can start to explain the precise way in which an enactive ontology can bring together the experiential and the (neuro)physiological dimension (Chapter 4), the sociocultural dimension (Chapters 4 and 5), and the existential dimension (Chapters 5 and 6).

3.2   MODELS OF PSYCHIATRY AND MODELS OF THE MIND

What is so special about enactivism? Why should enactivism succeed where other integrative models fail? So far we have looked at several models of psychiatric disorders, but we have not examined what conception of the mind they imply. But if we are trying to understand mental illnesses, we need to understand what we mean by 'mental'. What makes enactivism such a promising starting point for an integrative framework of psychiatric disorders is that it proposes a view on the nature of the mind that is radically different from the common view on the mind that reverberates in other models of psychiatry.

Even though dualism has long gone out of fashion, the common view on the mind still bears its heritage. Not in the sense that we would think there are two different *substances*, one material and one mental, but rather in the way we are still used to thinking in oppositions: of mind and body, internal and external, and subject

worlds; it only proposes to be more liberal when it comes to drawing the lines between them. Enactivism however challenges this very dichotomy (Di Paolo 2009a).

Some recent literature has applied an extended mind approach to psychiatric disorders (Cooper, 2017; Hoffman, 2016; Krueger, 2018; Roberts, Krueger, & Glackin, forthcoming). Although the enactive approach and the extended mind approach both reject the idea that psychiatric disorders could be explained by referring only to what is happening inside the individual, specifically its brain, and although they both acknowledge the fundamental role of patients' social and material environments, they fundamentally differ when it comes to explaining how physiological, experiential, and environmental processes relate. This has the important consequence that extended mind approaches are still trying to localize disorders and find their 'underpinnings' – distributed as these may be. As we will see, from an enactive view these localisation attempts do not make sense. See also: (de Haan, forthcoming).

and world. On the one hand we have the outer world, objective reality, and on the other hand we have our minds: inner, subjective, hidden. The world is out there, the mind is in here. How then are we in touch with reality? How do we bridge this gap between inner and outer? The idea is that we receive information from the outside world through our senses and that we use this input to construct an inner model of the world. This leads to the so-called Cartesian anxiety (Bernstein 1983/2011): are these inner representations a proper reflection of the outside world? If so, we can obtain objective truth, if not, we are lost in illusions. That is, either our mind is a 'mirror of nature' (Rorty 1979), or what we perceive is not reality at all, but merely a projection of our inner minds. A similar worry arises with regard to our contact with other people. With our minds hidden away from one another, we cannot even be sure that others have minds of their own. And if they do, the problem remains as to how we manage to 'read' these hidden, inner minds. With our minds secreted away, trying to guess what is on the other's mind is like playing a game of Battleships: dropping bombs in the sea in the hope you hit something underneath.

This traditional, dichotomous view has been described recently as a 'mediational model' (Dreyfus and Taylor 2015) and a 'sandwich model' (Hurley 2008) of the mind. The model is mediational because it supposes that we 'grasp external reality through internal representations' (Dreyfus and Taylor 2015, p. 2). It resembles a sandwich in that the model 'regards perception as input from world to mind, action as output from mind to world, and cognition as sandwiched between' (Hurley 2008, p. 2). And it is dichotomous because it implies the topology of an inner mind versus an outer world. From such a perspective, psychiatric problems appear as problems with the internal processing of sensory inputs. The senses themselves are working alright, so we don't have a problem with the input; something is instead going wrong then in the inner modelling of the outer world, in the processing of the information from the senses.

It is easy to see how this model of the mind as an inner zone meshes with the neuroreductionist model of psychiatric disorders. For if the mind is inner, and its job is to process sensory input and steer (bodily) output, it seems natural to turn to the brain as the place where the magic happens – and where the internal mechanisms that have broken down in psychiatric disorders may be found. And so we get theories of schizophrenia as involving a failure of the inner mind's model of outer reality to properly evaluate and make accurate predictions regarding future incoming sensory stimuli, which is in turn linked to deviations in the brain such as dopamine levels and diminished prefrontal connectivity (Sterzer et al. 2018). Both obsessive-compulsive disorder (OCD) and addiction are suggested to involve problems with the inner modelling of reward, which is thought to depend on various brain circuits (ventral and dorsal striatal circuits), including specific parts of the brain (e.g. the prefrontal cortex, the insula, the nucleus accumbens) and, again, the dopaminergic system (Figee et al. 2011; Fontenelle et al. 2011; Noël et al. 2013). Depression has been characterised as a negative bias of the inner model, with negative biases in attention, memory, and representations of self and others, which have been linked to a host of neural mechanisms (Disner et al. 2011). These short descriptions obviously do not do justice to how sophisticated such models can be, but what is relevant here is that they all share the same format, the same implicit framework of the mind and of mental disorders, namely: something is going wrong with patients' internal models of the world, and since this model is formed in the brain, we should expect to see these problems instantiated in deviations in their brains' anatomy or functioning.

Enactivism proposes a very different understanding of the mind and its relation to the body, to the world, and to perception and action. In fact, Varela, Thompson, and Rosch introduced the enactive approach in their book *The Embodied Mind* in 1991 precisely out of dissatisfaction with the cognitivist view of the mind that dominated the cognitive sciences at that time. Cognitivism is a variant of the traditional model of the mind described above. It regards the mind as an information processing system that manipulates mental representations of the outside world by means of specific rules. Mental representations have content by virtue of their ability to correspond with (things in) the world. At the same time, however, mental representations have a certain functional structure that makes it possible to study them independently of these contents. Consequently, cognitivists maintain that cognition can (to some extent) be studied in isolation from the world in which it is embedded. The preferred metaphor adopted by this view is that of the human mind as computer, a metaphor which includes the distinction between hardware and software. The mind now is the software running on the hardware of the brain.

Varela et al. pointed out that in pursuit of the formal structures of information processing and symbolic representation, the cognitive sciences had drifted away more and more from everyday human life. Mind had become narrowly defined as the device we use for problem-solving. They worried about this narrow view of cognition and the subsequent detachment of the cognitive sciences from our everyday experiences. In *The Embodied Mind* they introduced the term *enactive* to denote their alternative research programme:

> In the enactive programme, we explicitly call into question the assumption – prevalent throughout cognitive science – that cognition consists of the representation of a world that is independent of our perceptual and cognitive capacities by a cognitive system that exists independent of the world.
>
> *(Varela et al. 1991, p. xx)*

Instead, Varela et al. proposed a view of cognition as a form of 'embodied action':

> By using the term *embodied* we mean to highlight two points: first that cognition depends upon the kinds of experience that come from

having a body with various sensorimotor capacities, and second, that these individual sensorimotor capacities are themselves embedded in a more encompassing physiological, psychological, and cultural context. By using the term *action* we mean to emphasize ... that sensory and motor processes, perception and action, are fundamentally inseparable in lived cognition.

(pp. 172–3)

Four main characteristics of cognition come to the fore in this conception: (1) cognition is *embodied*; (2) cognition is *embedded*; (3) cognition is a form of *action*, and (4) action and perception are intrinsically intertwined. This means that we cannot understand cognition in isolation from the bodily being that is doing the cognising, nor from the environment that it is directed at. If we see cognition in this way, Varela, Thompson, and Rosch argued, we can bring together our everyday experiences and the scientific study of the mind in the cognitive sciences. And this is important, not just to foster our understanding of the mind, but also because how we think about the mind and ourselves has ethical implications. For our scientific views influence our understanding of ourselves and others and our views on agency, autonomy, and responsibility.

Even though cognitivism has lost ground in the cognitive sciences since the publication of *The Embodied Mind*, the views that have come to replace it still follow a similar inner–outer topology of mind and world.[2] The enactive programme has

---

[2] Popular recent varieties of this picture are for instance predictive-processing models which assume a back-and-forth between predictions generated by an inner model and corrections or confirmations of this model through our sensory input, depending on how much our sensory input deviates from our predictions. These models come in many forms. Some (especially those that are more action and dynamics based) have been argued to be compatible with an enactive outlook on mind and world (Bruineberg and Rietveld 2014; Kirchhoff 2015a, 2018; Bruineberg et al. 2018). However, the structure of an inner model that gets updated through our interactions with the world also fits with a traditional mediational or representationalist model of the mind (Hohwy 2016), and this is how predictive-processing models are typically understood and used in neuroscience.

evolved too. In the last twenty-five years many different forms and applications of enactivism have been developed (cf. Torrance 2005; Stewart et al. 2010; Di Paolo and Thompson 2014). Some focus on perception (O'Regan and Noë 2001; Noë 2004; Myin and Degenaar 2014), others on social cognition (De Jaegher and Di Paolo 2007); on formalising and modelling important concepts of autonomy, agency, autopoiesis (Barandiaran et al. 2009; Barandiaran and Egbert 2014; Di Paolo et al. 2017); on language (van den Herik 2017; Di Paolo et al. 2018), mathematics (Zahidi and Myin 2016), musicality (Krueger 2011; Matyja and Schiavio 2013; Schiavio and Høffding 2015) and archaeology (Malafouris 2013; Garofoli 2015). Other enactivists have developed a strong line of critique on representationalist views of the mind (Hutto and Myin 2013, 2017). What binds these different theories, what makes them *enactive*, is that they share some core ideas of what cognition is and what it is not and how it could best be studied.[3]

---

[3]   Enactivism is neither the only nor the first articulation of an embodied, embedded or ecological understanding of the mind. In 1909, Jacob von Uexküll (1909) introduced the notion of *Umwelt* and of the functional circle (*Funktionskreis*) between what an organism can perceive (*Merkwelt*) and what it can do (*Wirkwelt*). In 1940, Victor von Weizsäcker (1940/1986) elaborated this with his theory of the *Gestaltkreis*. Uexküll and Wesiak (1986) later distinguished the functional circle (*Funktionskreis*) of the organism and its environment from the situational circle (*Situationskreis*) of human beings and their world. Ecological psychology (Gibson 1979; Reed 1996; Chemero 2003) draws on these predecessors to explain psychological processes in their proper environmental embedding. Within the phenomenological and philosophical anthropological tradition we find similar views on the relation between person and world and the role of the body therein, such as Heidegger's (1927/1978) notion of being-in-the-world, Plessner's (1928/1981) description of human's excentric position, Jonas' (1966/2001) connection of life and mind, and Merleau-Ponty's (1945/2002) investigation of the crucial role of the body as well as his (Merleau-Ponty 1942/1963) perspective on overcoming both dualism and reductionism through his notion of the structure of behaviour. Within the analytical tradition, kindred spirits are for instance Ryle's (1949) lucid critique on the traditional dualist picture of the mind and Wittgenstein's (1958) scrutiny of imprecise, confusion-inducing reasoning and his focus on the primacy of practices. Many more names could be listed, but a historical exegesis is not so relevant for the questions we are trying to answer here. Enactive theorists draw on (some) these insights and combine them with insights from current research into artificial intelligence (Pfeifer and Iida 2004); biology, neuroscience and developmental systems theory (Oyama et al. 2003); and dynamical systems theory (Kelso 1995; Beer 2000). The term *enactive* thus denotes a specific understanding of how mind, body and world relate that has been voiced before. I see 'enactivism' as the current best, most rigorous articulation of this view. What further makes enactive theories stand out is

The latter, methodological strand has always been strong,[4] but here I will focus on the enactive ontology of the mind that motivates these methodological commitments and that will help with psychiatry's integration problem.

3.3   COGNITION AS SENSE-MAKING

According to a dichotomous conception of the mind as inner and the world as outer, cognition is something that happens in the mind, on the basis of the material delivered to us from outside by our senses. We construct an inner model of the outside world and use this to design and guide our actions. With this division between the inner mind and the outer world, the mind should somehow represent the world. Our senses bring us the raw, neutral data which are processed by the mind, ordering and assigning meaning to it.

Enactivism rejects this inner–outer division of mind and world. Instead of presupposing a gap between mind and world, enactivists argue that organism and world are dynamically coupled. This has to do with the very constitution of living beings: contrary to non-living aggregations of matter, living beings rely on a constant exchange with their environment in order to maintain themselves. Living beings are self-organising unities; they actively maintain their own boundaries by interacting with their environment. That is, in order to remain alive, living beings need to eat and breath and defecate. In an environment that consists of many other living beings whose needs may be detrimental to their own, organisms need to find their way and adapt to the dynamics of

their explicit engagement with the natural sciences and their embracement of complex dynamical system theory as their preferred mathematical model.

[4]   Enactivism's main methodological foci are (1) an emphasis on the relevance of investigating first person, lived experiences; (2) the aim to connect these first person experiences with the third person perspective of natural science; (3) the acknowledgement of the complicated role of using cognition in trying to understand it; and (4) the acknowledgement of the irreducibility of the special sciences (i.e. its non-reductionist agenda) (Varela et al. 1991; Stewart et al. 2010).

their environments. They need to discern what is edible from what is not, and what is dangerous from what is safe. For their own survival then, they need to make some sense of their environment. And this *sense-making*, this activity of an organism, interacting with its environment, is cognition. The mind is not a separate faculty, nor something inner, it is not hidden in the brain where it is causing actions; the notion of 'mind' instead refers to a type of interaction with the environment.

Ryle (1949) nicely dismantled the tendency to regard the mind as something *over and above* some behaviour as a 'category-mistake'. He argued that by opposing matter and mind as two separate things, concepts to do with the mind are incorrectly applied. He gives some examples. Suppose a foreigner visits Oxford or Cambridge and after being shown the libraries, the colleges, the scientific departments and administrative offices, remarks: 'I have now seen all these buildings and the people working in them, but where is the University?' We would have to explain that the University is not something over and above what he has seen, but that what we call 'the University' is 'the way in which what he already has seen is organized' (p. 16). Similarly if a child were to watch the march of a military division and, after seeing the battalions, batteries, and squadrons march past, asked 'But when is the division coming?' this too would be a category-mistake. For the battalions, batteries, and squadrons *form* the division: once again the division is not something else, something apart from these. A final example is of a foreigner who watches a game of cricket for the first time and, after having explained to him the functions of the bowlers, the batsmen, the fielders, the umpires, and the scores, asks: 'But who is doing the team-spirit?'

We are making the same mistake, Ryle argues, when we look for some extra ingredient, the mind, to explain intelligent behaviour. I see someone interacting skilfully with their environment and ask how their mind is steering their body. With its concept of 'sense-making' enactivism offers an alternative to this reification of the mind.

Sense-making can be defined as an organism's evaluative inter-action with its environment.[5] This means that for enactivism the central unit of analysis for understanding mind or cognition is not an isolated individual agent, let alone its brain, but rather the *organism–environment system*. This is a complex, dynamical system: the relations between its parts are characterised by (mutual) reciprocity and by all sorts of feedback loops, leading to a complex tangle of processes interacting over time. Besides, sense-making is an activity, a temporally extended process, and as such requires a dynamical, developmental perspective. Below I highlight three characteristics of this environmentally and temporally situated process; it is: essential to life, implies values, and is affective. I also urge the importance of distinguishing basic from existential sense-making.

3.3.1   Living Implies Sense-Making

Living beings rely on making sense of their environment for survival. This implies that sense-making, in its basic form of distinguishing (perceiving) what is supportive of one's existence and what entails threats, is *inherent to all living beings*. It is in this sense that life and 'cognition' or 'mind' are continuous. This is the so-called life–mind continuity thesis (Thompson 2007; Di Paolo 2009a). The life–mind continuity thesis offers an alternative perspective on the relation between the body and the mind in which these are explicitly not regarded as two distinct entities, or processes.

The central assumption is that matter is not opposed to cognition, and that matter in specific organisations can give rise to qualitative differences. It is not just the (tiniest) parts that determine the characteristics of matter: it is their mutual *relations* too. This is the central idea of the notion of *emergence*: the

---

5   Thompson and Stapleton (2009) suggest a similar definition – 'sense-making is the intentional and normative engagement of the system with its environment' (p. 28) – as do Di Paolo and Thompson (2014): '"Sense-making" describes behaviour or conduct in relation to norms of interaction that the system itself brings forth on the basis of its adaptive autonomy' (p. 73).

properties of the whole depend not only on the properties of the parts, but also on their organisational structure. Different organisational structures of the same matter give rise to different kinds of processes. Following this view, cognition and matter are not two separate things; rather, matter in specific (self-organising) patterns *is* minded. I will discuss the relation between body and mind, and the role and interpretation of emergence more elaborately in the next chapter.

3.3.2 Sense-Making Entails (Basic) Values

In sense-making, there is something at stake. The fundamental dependency of organisms on their surroundings implies that the interaction between organism and world is not neutral: the organism has specific needs and concerns and what the environment offers is evaluated accordingly. Depending on the specific characteristics of the organism, its abilities and concerns, the elements in the environment have a specific value or meaning for it. In this way, our 'needful freedom' as Jonas (1966/2001) calls it, entails a very basic form of values. We could call these 'basic values' or 'valences', to differentiate them from the existential values that we will discuss in Chapter 6.

It is important to point out that these valences, or more generally the 'sense' of things, is not bestowed upon them by the organism. The term *sense-making* could be understood in a too active way, as if the meaning of things in the world was 'generated' by the organism. By stressing only the active part of organisms, and not their receptive part, it is easy to slip into a subjectivist conception of meaning being 'projected' by the organism onto a neutral world.[6] Such an overly

---

[6]   Several enactivist authors at times use terminology that could easily invite an overly activist or even subjectivist interpretation of sense-making. Thompson (2007), for instance, speaks of the 'construction' of meaning (p. 54) and states that 'significance and valence do not pre-exist "out there", but are enacted, brought forth, and constituted by living beings' (p. 158). Similarly, Varela et al. (1991) talk about the 'constitution' of the perceived world (p. 164), and Weber and Varela (2002) state that organisms 'fashion a world of meaning from within' (p. 115). Colombetti (2013) writes that 'the organism's structure, interests, and goals' play a constitutive role in 'what is constructed as salient' (p. 1098). More examples could be given. Still, it is quite clear that subjectivism does

active, almost subjectivist reading misconstrues sense-making. Sense-making is neither passive information-absorption nor active projection: it is a *relational* function. That is, the sense-making of organisms depends both on what is given in the environment, what is in fact out there, and on the organisms' abilities and concerns. The biological make-up of the organisms, their abilities – such as their ways of sensing and moving – and their long-term and current needs and concerns all determine how organisms make sense of their environment, and what sense they make of it. But they do not make these senses up: the valence of an object for a specific organism depends just as much on the factual characteristics of that object.

Von Uexküll and Kriszat (1956) give the example of an oak. The tree is there and is real, but different organisms will make sense of it in different ways. For the forester, the oak is wood. For the fox the roots of the oak provide a place to dig a hole to be safe in, whereas the ants walk on the bark of the oak, with all its heights and valleys, to search for food. The bark beetle is also searching for food, but within the oak. None of these experiences of the oak are subjective 'projections' of the respective organisms, since they are all grounded in the oak's objective existence and characteristics, and in its objective specific relation to the each of these living beings. There are the *objective* properties of the oak on the one hand, and the *objective* properties of the organism on the other hand: taken together, these two imply certain *objective* facts about their *relation*. For instance, the suitability of the oak as food for the bark beetle is such a *relational fact* or *reality*; it is a function of the properties of both

not fit with the fundamental enactive principle of the structural coupling and co-determination of organism and environment. One reason for stressing the active part of the organism rather than its receptive part may be that it is precisely this active part that traditional conceptions of both perception and cognition have omitted. Besides, the language used is often ambiguous. For example, when Thompson (2007) writes that an autonomous system (e.g. an organism) '*determines* the cognitive domain in which it operates' (p. 43, italics mine), this could be taken as something that the organism apparently does. But instead of an *act* of the organism, it could also be simply an *effect* of its specific being. Just as your length determines which shelves you can and cannot reach, so do the specific body and needs of a particular organism imply specific senses that its environment will have for it.

the oak and the beetle. The oak is thus objectively valuable for the beetle.[7] 'Objectivity' here does not imply 'a view from nowhere' (Nagel 1989), but means that the value of the oak to the beetle is neither random, nor a subjective attribution. It is real.

The specific biological being of each organism carves out some aspects of the oak as relevant. Apart from this structural influence of the organism's bodily make-up, the sense of the environment is also dependent upon the organism's current needs and concerns. If it were raining, for instance, the forester might perceive the oak as a place to shelter (cf. Heidegger 1927/1978). If an organism is hungry, food will be especially salient to it, but once sated, a safe place to rest is most attractive. The value of some aspect of the environment is thus to some extent dynamical.[8]

Apart from the potential projectionist misunderstanding of sense-making there is also a potential conceptualist misunderstanding of sense-making. When I talk about the *value* of the oak for the fox and the sugar being *meaningful* for the bacterium, I am not saying that the bacterium regards sugar *as* food, or that the fox makes sense of the oak *as* shelter. I am just saying that these things *are* meaningful to the organism. This does not entail that they are, on top of that, experienced by the organism *as being meaningful.* That is: bacteria need no concept of food to distinguish and seek out sugar, a fox is not looking for shelter 'as shelter': she does not have a concept of shelter in her head and then looks to see if anything in the environment instantiates this concept.

---

[7]   In this way, basic values or valences are what I will call 'relational realities': they are real, relational properties that cannot be reduced to either one of the relata. I will come back to this in Chapter 6.

[8]   One way to picture the difference between the structural and the need-dependent part of the value of the environment is to see the first as a landscape of potentially relevant possibilities for action (i.e. affordances) and the second as an excerpt of that: a field of presently salient affordances (de Haan et al. 2013b; Rietveld and Kiverstein 2014). This field can in turn be specified along the three axes of (1) the amount of presently available affordances – the width of the field; (2) the affordances that are already presently on the horizon – the depth of the field; and (3) the relative salience of each of these affordances – the height of each part of the field (de Haan et al. 2013b). This salience can be further unpacked: an attacking predator is salient in a different way than an alluring source of food (Dings 2017). See also Chapter 7.

Likewise, although a vervet monkey can recognise its family members within a group of monkeys, that does not mean that it has a notion of 'family' or 'kinship'. It just recognises its family members – but not necessarily *as* 'family-members' (cf. Noë 2009, p. 43). The distinguishing between monkeys already *is* the sense-making and this does not require any concept or category. The 'as' is added by us, when we are describing what sense-making is going on. The capacity to recognise some particular as of a certain kind is a more complex form of sense-making that requires a reflexive awareness, the awareness of what is distinguished, sensed, experienced – which we will later describe as existential sense-making.

3.3.3   Sense-Making Is Affective

Sense-making is not a cool, detached endeavour: the organism is *affected* by its environment. Because of our dependency on our environment, what we encounter matters to us, there is something at stake, and we are affected by it accordingly. Directly related to the evaluative, value-sensitive character of sense-making is its *affective* character. Our affects reflect the value or meaning of what is encountered. To us, for instance, a poised rattlesnake is dangerous and thus frightening, a dark-pink raspberry is delicious and thus attractive, and a cool lake on a hot day is refreshing and thus pleasing. For an eagle, the rattlesnake may be food and thus appealing when she's hungry, whereas she might not even see the raspberries as they mean nothing to her. Affects thus refer to the experienced relevance of a situation: something is appealing, repulsive, frightening, curiosity invoking ... This experience of the affective 'allure' of a situation does not typically require any conscious scrutinising: sense-making is first and foremost a direct bodily affective evaluation (Colombetti 2007, 2010; Colombetti and Thompson 2008).

3.3.4   Basic Sense-Making and Existential Sense-Making

A part from gradual differences in the complexity of the sense-making of different organisms, I propose to distinguish a qualitative shift in the very nature of sense-making that comes from being able to reflexively relate to one's own experiences: what I call the existential stance. I will argue in Chapter 6 that this capacity to take a stance (on oneself, one's experiences, one's environment) is not just a capacity added on top of basic sense-making: it rather changes the whole system to such an extent that it calls for distinguishing organism–environment from person–world interactions.[9]

Basic sense-making involves discerning the relevant aspects of the present environment; recognising food, mates, danger, etc. It is a submerged sense-making of the here and now. The meaningfulness of the environment is a reflection of its relevance for survival: what is valuable is a function of the organism's biological necessities. For those organisms capable of taking a stance, however, things change drastically. With evaluative sense-making turned upon itself comes the desire not just for survival but for dignity, for living a *good* life. The meaningfulness of our worlds and the values that guide our actions, surpass the functional, the life-maintaining: with stance-taking a different kind of values emerge, what we could call 'existential values', such as respect, honour, dignity, friendship, and love. The opening up of the existential dimension even transforms our basic biological needs. For instance: food is never just food: what you eat says something about who you are, which cultural community you are part of, and we have all kinds of rituals surrounding how to eat, what to eat, when, and with whom. The same is true of other basic biological needs such as sex and clothing. Clothes keep us warm, but we cannot avoid expressing something through what we wear – even if only that we do not care about clothes. The existential stance thus affects even the basic, life-maintaining values.

We will come back to the existential dimension and how it alters our sense-making in Chapter 6. For now, I just want to point out that the distinction between basic and existential sense-making

[9]   I do not want to claim that only humans are capable of stance-taking: it is an empirical question whether, or to what extent, other organisms are capable of such stance-taking too. As I am only interested in human beings here, I use *persons* as shorthand for humans capable of stance-taking.

leads to three different forms of sense-making: (1) basic sense-making; (2) existential sense-making as the specific reflexive sense-making of oneself, one's situation, or others; and (3) the general sense-making of persons as transformed by (2). Explicit existential sense-making (2) refers to those instances of sense-making when we explicitly reflect on something, when we pause and consider our stance towards something. When I talk about the sense-making of organisms, I refer to basic sense-making (1), but when I talk about the sense-making of persons, I refer to 'existentialised' sense-making (3).

3.4   PERCEPTION, ACTION, AND SENSE-MAKING ARE INTERTWINED

On a traditional view, cognition is partly characterised by its opposition to the body, to emotion, and to perception and action. By contrast the enactivist notion of sense-making thwarts these demarcations. Sense-making is an embodied activity, and it is affective as well. Sense-making implies a different carving out of what we are talking about when we are talking about 'the mind' or 'cognition'. The relation between sense-making and perception and action also differs from the traditional division of labour as described by the sandwich model (Hurley 2008). In their definition of cognition as embodied action, Varela et al. (1991) already point us to the inseparability of perception and action in lived cognition.

As we saw the notion of a supposed gap between mind and world opens up the difficult question of how they can relate. The main task, within this traditional dichotomous conception of mind and world, is to weigh the extent to which we are passive absorbers of what the world throws at us, or rather active constructors of what we see. How ready-made are the building blocks that perception gives us and how much construction is supplied by cognition? Enactivism, however, opts for a different mind–world topology altogether from which this problem appears ill-conceived. We are neither passive receivers of the world, nor active projectors onto it, but we are rather interactive participants in the world. We engage with the world – but not through the detour of some inner, representational processing that remote-controls our perceptions and actions. Adopting an enactive, biological perspective, perceiving is about orienting oneself, finding one's way, distinguishing the beneficial from the harmful. This activity of perceiving is fundamentally dependent upon and shaped by our movements and actions: we need to move our eyes, our heads, or our bodies in order to perceive (Gibson 1979; O'Regan and Noë 2001; Noë 2004; Myin and Degenaar 2014). It is through moving that we can observe features such as the boundaries of objects, for instance. Perceiving is something we do: we hear, see, smell, touch, and taste, by moving our heads to locate a sound, walk closer to have a better look, sniff our noses to smell a flower, run our fingers over a surface to determine its smoothness, and move food around in our mouths to taste it. Perceiving is thus not something that *precedes* acting; it is rather itself a form of acting. More precisely, perceiving is a sensorimotor process, leading to the formation of sensorimotor patterns. Sensorimotor patterns or contingencies refer to the 'regularities in how sensory stimulation depends on the activity of the perceiver' (Degenaar and O'Regan 2015). Becoming a skilled perceiver implies having an implicit grasp, or being attuned to these regularities (O'Regan and Noë 2001).

It is through moving that we perceive, but the intertwining of perception and action goes further: perception is usually *action oriented*. That is, we perceive possibilities for action rather than mere collections of objects. Gibson (1979) introduced the helpful notion of *affordance* to refer to the possibilities of action that the environment offers to a specific organism.[10] The world invites

---

[10] Affordances depend on the characteristics of both world and organism. As a relational concept, affordances fit nicely with an enactive ontology. There is, however, some debate on the degree of compatibility of Gibson's theory of perception and enactivism: Varela et al. (1991) criticised Gibson for what they perceived as downplaying the active role of the organism in perceiving, by building up his theory of perception 'almost entirely from the environment', in contrast to their own focus on the structural coupling of the animal and its environment (p. 204); Hutto and Myin (2013) offered a thorough critique on the notion of 'information' that Gibson also uses and the notion

a certain range of actions, depending on the specific organism and the specific situation at hand. That is, a teacup affords grasping it and drinking from it – for me, not for a giraffe. To a giraffe, the leaves of a tree afford tearing them off and eating them, but not for us. A fallen leaf affords earthworms the possibility of pulling it into their hole, thereby closing its opening and keeping it moist. But a leaf on a tree affords the earthworm nothing. When we perceive the world, we first and foremost perceive the possibilities for action it affords, and then particularly the ones that are in one way or another relevant to us.

The action-orientedness of perceiving thereby also attests to its motivational nature. Perceptual engagement with the environment is motivated by the concerns of the organism. Depending on the state we are in, different things catch our eyes: when we are hungry, we notice a bakery which we would overlook if we were intent on finding a vacant cab. As Merleau-Ponty (1945/2002) pointed out, we do not perceive the world as a neutral, objective space, but that we are rather attracted or repulsed by things. Instead of regarding this as a kind of affective 'colouring' of an otherwise neutral perception, enactivists maintain that perceiving itself is inherently intentional and interested.

These concerns are closely connected to the bodily constitution of the perceiver, as our bodies that carve out the space of what actions are possible and at least the contours of what actions are appealing. And perceiving is of course a bodily activity from the start, as our bodies and sense-organs determine the kind of interactions we can have with the environment. Our bodies and sense-organs afford contact with a certain bandwidth of reality: we can see colours, but not in the way fish with double cones do; we can

of content that it typically implied in talk of information. According to van Dijk et al. (2015), however, these critiques have misinterpreted Gibson's theory of perception which they claim is in fact very close to enactivism. See also Raja (2018) for a recent discussion of Gibson's notions of information and resonance. Furthermore, Gibson's theory of perception and affordances has been further developed, discussed, and revised, leading to a lively debate on the precise ontological status of affordances within the movement of ecological psychology (Turvey 1992; Reed 1996; Chemero 2003; Stoffregen 2003).

smell faeces, but we remain ignorant of the many interesting things that dogs appear to smell in it; we can hear, but not very high or very low pitches (where 'high' and 'low' are referenced to what is 'medium' to our hearing). For each of our faculties we can find an animal or plant species that can do things that are out of our range, or are of a completely different ball park all together. So even though we live in the same place as arthropods and bats, our respective *Umwelten* are very different.

On an enactive account then, perceiving is not a matter of passively being imprinted upon: it is both active and shaped by our bodies and concerns. The world is not simply given – since our bodily constitution co-determines what it is we perceive. To be sure, there is a passive element in perceiving in that we do not determine what is there to be perceived: what I see, hear and smell depends on what is in fact happening in the world. Perceiving is not so active as making things up. On an enactive account, perceiving is thus not constructing the world either.[11] Rejecting 'the myth of the Given' (Sellars 1956) does not imply the opposite: that we conjure up worlds before us. Instead of this grandiose picture of us as meaning-bestowing magicians, enactivism opts for the humbler idea that we are tied to our perspective and that our perspective does not encompass the whole richness of reality. It is still a reality that we perceive, but just a limited part of it.

Concerning the relation between perception, action, and cognition, an enactive account thus goes against the assumption that we first perceive something to which we then add cognitive processing in order to come up with an intention and subsequently perform a goal-directed action that expresses this intention. Perceiving is rather an activity of

---

[11] Like with sense-making, the eagerness to object to the passive picture of perception can sometimes invoke its opposite extreme: the recognition of the active contribution of the perceiver to the perceiving can tilt over to the idea of perceiving as *constructing* (Weber and Varela 2002; Thompson 2007; Colombetti 2013). But a simple inversion keeps one trapped in the same mind–world topology that one tries to overthrow; one has only changed the direction of the arrows. Our senses rather enable us to perceive the world – even if only a limited excerpt of it.

motivated engagement of the organism with its environment. We perceive meaningful opportunities for interactions in the world, the relevance of which invites our response, and elicits our actions. The interactions of an organism with its environment are interactions of bodily beings, moving around, sensing their surroundings. Such sensing is not just an inherently bodily and motile process, but is also inherently evaluative, discriminating beneficent from dangerous interactions. As such, perceiving is already a form of sense-making. It is not just action and perception that are intertwined, but sense-making as well.

3.5 THE ENACTIVE ONTOLOGY IS A RELATIONAL ONTOLOGY

The model of the mind that enactivism offers is thus very different from the traditional dichotomous picture on all fronts: how mind and world relate, how mind, perception, and action relate, and how mind and body relate – as we will see in the next chapter. To start with what it is not: it is clear that the enactivist ontology is not dualistic. Enactivists share a deeply rooted rejection of traditional dichotomies, such as subject *versus* object, inner *versus* outer, mind *versus* body, and perception *versus* action *versus* cognition. However, to the extent that monism is understood in terms of one or the other side of the dualist's dichotomy, enactivists reject monism as well. That is, any reductionist version of monism does not fit enactivism either. Enactivism is just as much non-reductionist as it is non-dualist.

So where does enactivism stand? Enactivism does not assume anything over and above matter – no vital force or mental substance – but it does not assume matter to be meaningless, nor to be homogeneous. Enactivism embraces the view that it is the specific organisation of matter that gives rise to a wide variety of processes. Matter in specific configurations has different properties than matter in other configurations and the properties of the entity as a whole cannot be reduced to the properties of its parts. It is thus their *organisational structure*, the relations between parts, that plays a constitutive role for the properties of the entity as a whole. If we wanted to put a name to this position, we might call it a *pluriform monism*.

The fundamental characteristic of the enactive ontology is that *relations* – and not just matter – *matter*. Relations are constitutive: both within the organism itself and between the organism and its environment. *Within* the organism, it is the organisational structure of matter which shapes the properties of the organism as a whole. This importance of the structure of matter, of the relations between elements, is known as 'emergence'. We will come back to this in Chapter 4. Apart from these intra-organismic relations, the relations *between* organism and environment are constitutive for the organism as well. We are of the world: we breathe, we eat, we drink, we defecate and urinate: we are in constant exchange with our environment. Organism and environment are coupled: they co-determine each other, both on a long-term (evolutionary) and a short-term timescale. This co-determination is both active and receptive: the organism changes its environment to some extent and adapts to it as well. But it is good to keep in mind that 'the environment' for a large part consists of other organisms that change and adapt in turn. In this way a co-determination and co-evolution takes place, where it is no longer easily determined what is action and what is reaction; rather the whole process is one of mutual adaptation.[12]

This relational ontology implies two major moves. First of all, relations presuppose relata. An enactive ontology thus requires us to 'zoom out'; to enlarge the scope of the explanandum *in space*. With regard to understanding cognition, or rather sense-making, we should look at the *whole organism* – not just at any of its parts. Moreover, in order to understand the whole organism, we should look at the organism *in its environment*. Secondly, relations are dynamic; they evolve

---

[12]   Note that the interactions between organisms and their environments are not just competitive but also complementary. Bateson (1972/2000) for instance gives the example of the co-evolution of horses and steppes: the horses eat the grass, but they also provide manure for its growth. The more you zoom out in space and time to look at the evolvement of ecosystems, the more complementary or dependence-relations show up.

over time. This requires another move of zooming out, one which enlarges the scope of the explanandum *in time*. It is not just the whole organism in its environment that we should look at: we should more specifically look at the organism *in interaction* with its environment. This interaction is a constant back-and-forth, acting and reacting, mutually adapting and changing. Because of the dynamical character of relations, it is not just the present relation that counts, but also the *history of couplings* that has shaped the present interaction. A relational ontology thus implies the need for a developmental perspective.

Following an enactive ontology then, it makes no sense to isolate and reify cognitive phenomena, both in terms of space (e.g. searching to uncover the smallest 'underlying' set of parts, typically in the brain) and time (e.g. investigate a static snapshot). Regarding relations as co-constitutive means that with the stripping away of the wider spatiotemporal context a fundamental part of the phenomena will be lost as well.

3.6 PRELIMINARY IMPLICATIONS FOR PSYCHIATRY

What does this model of the mind mean for the development of an integrative model for psychiatry? This is the topic of the coming chapters, but we can already sketch out some preliminary implications. On a traditional, dichotomous view of the mind, psychiatric problems appear as the results of failures of one or more internal mechanisms of an individual's mind. If the mind is a matter of internal information processing, then in psychiatric disorders something must go wrong in these processes. As we saw, this dichotomous picture of the mind aligns perfectly with the neuroreductionist proposal of the centrality of the brain. So what we get is a view of psychiatric disorders as problems with the capacity of an individual's brain to correctly represent the outside world and/or translate perceptual input into appropriate action.

Following an enactive perspective, the mind is not something inner, but rather refers to the activity of an organism making sense of its environment, or a person making sense of her world. Psychiatric problems then amount to something going wrong in someone's interactions with her world, in her sense-making. I will elaborate on psychiatric disorders as disorders of sense-making in Chapter 7, but at this point it should already be clear that, if we are interested in sense-making, the proper unit of analysis is the organism in interaction with its environment, or, in our case, the person in interaction with her world. Moreover, an estimation of someone's current situation also requires that the history of these interactions be taken into account. This means that it will be unlikely that we can pinpoint psychiatric disorders as occurring at a specific site, such as the brain.

With regard to our aim of integrating the four dimensions – the physiological, experiential, sociocultural, and existential – the enactive ontology of the mind offers a promising starting point. For the enactive notion of sense-making is integrative from the very start: sense-making is, after all, the activity of a bodily being interacting with her environment. Applied to persons, this means we can only understand their sense-making if we take into account their bodily nature and their fundamental embeddedness in their sociocultural world. In other words: when it comes to sense-making, the person in interaction with her world is the proper unit of analysis, and it is this dynamical system that all dimensions are part of. The four dimensions then refer to different *excerpts* of this one complex person–world system, at different levels of zooming in.

As we will see, an enactive ontology is thoroughly integrative: from an enactive perspective *none of the four dimensions can be understood in isolation from the other three.* Experiences depend on there being a bodily being in an environment, which is in our case a sociocultural world. We live in a sociocultural world rather than an environment due to our stance-taking capacities. But the development of these reflexive capacities itself depends on our being bodily, social agents who interact with others in a community that fosters this practice. Our sociocultural communities in turn both shape and are shaped by our experiences and reflexive stances. Even our physiological processes depend on the person–world system as a whole (see Chapter 6, Section 6.5). As we will see, enactivism rejects the common intuition that there is first matter and that the other processes (experiences, existential stances, sociocultural processes) are somehow added on to this matter (dualism) or are somehow derivative of it (reductionism). Following the life–mind continuity thesis, the matter of living beings is already different from the matter of objects. Matter in the specific configuration of living beings is minded – and this configuration determines the properties of the physiological processes involved too. Precisely how these four dimensions are connected from an enactive perspective will be the topic of the next chapters.

4   Body and Mind – and World

A big part of the integration problem is the difficulty of relating the physiological and the experiential dimension of psychiatric disorders: body and mind. Within psychiatry the question of how body and mind relate is not just an abstract, philosophical question but first and foremost a practical one. Are patients' altered experiences symptoms of underlying physiological disturbances? Or are psychiatric disorders rather psychological problems with physiological consequences? And how can we understand the efficacy of psychiatry's two main ways of treatment: drugs and psychotherapy? Is psychotherapy just a matter of treating the symptoms whereas drugs target the real cause? Or is it the other way around? All these questions revolve around the issue of how physiological processes affect patients' experiences and vice versa.

In this chapter, I will first sketch the ways in which the mind–body problem is at stake in psychiatry, in relation to both the causes and the treatment of psychiatric disorders. On the one hand we want to acknowledge the differences between matters physiological and psychological, but neither dualism nor reductionism provides satisfactory accounts of their relation. By taking continuity rather than opposition as its starting point, the enactive life–mind continuity thesis has the potential to offer a helpful alternative perspective on the mind–body problem. Its viability, however, depends on adopting a solid account of emergence. Emergence is an equivocal notion and not all accounts succeed in avoiding dualist tendencies, but there is at least one account of emergence that fits the enactive approach.

4.2 THE MIND–BODY PROBLEM IN PSYCHIATRY

The distinction between mind and body is omnipresent in psychiatry. The very discipline depends on it: psychiatry deals with mental illness, the rest of medicine covers the somatic illnesses. The problem of how to relate mind and body – or physiological and experiential, or, more narrowly defined, neural and psychological processes – is omnipresent too.[1] We can divide the possible causes of psychiatric disorders into physiological or psychological ones, as well as the kinds of treatment available. And it is not just external forces but also internal processes that get categorised along this dichotomy. Medication for instance falls into the category of external physiological influences, and one's hormonal and neurotransmitter levels fall into the category of internal physiological processes. Psychotherapy can be seen as an external psychological force, worrying as an internal psychological process. Qua methods, psychiatry still relies on patients' experiences and behaviour, but the search for so-called biomarkers of psychiatric disorders is now fully under way.

It is obvious that psychiatric disorders entail changed experiences. But what has caused these disordered experiences? Are depressive episodes, for instance, the result of major life-events? Can stress cause depression? Or is there an 'underlying' physiological problem that is the real cause of patients' altered experiences? Or maybe psychiatric disorders develop from a combination of physiological and psychological causes, such as a pre-existing physiological vulnerability combined with a stressful life-event. But how might these affect each other?

The same division comes to the fore in psychiatric treatment: psychiatric disorders can be targeted by means of drugs or by means of psychotherapy, or a combination of both. Even if both physiological and psychological treatment can be effective, the question

---

[1] For reasons I have outlined in Chapter 1, I prefer to speak of experiential rather than psychological processes. However, since the debate is framed in this way, I will here use *experiential* and *psychological* interchangeably.

remains *how* they are effective, and whether they are effective in the same way. What happens when anti-depressants elevate patients' mood? And what happens when psychotherapy elevates patients' mood? The intuitive idea is that medication works on physiological processes and that these in turn somehow affect psychological processes. Psychotherapy on the other hand works on psychological processes which in turn somehow have an effect on physiological processes. As we saw in Chapter 2, some would even say that psychological interventions are effective *in so far* as they influence physiological processes. The *real* change then still comes from the altered physiology.

The two issues, aetiology and treatment, are related. In general, we are inclined to think that when we can identify something as a cause, the treatment will have to be directed at that same dimension. If, for instance, a depression seems to be the result of relational tensions, it is natural to first think of treatment with relational or systemic psychotherapy. If a depression on the contrary is understood as a neurotransmitter problem, medication will be the first choice of treatment, not systemic psychotherapy. The idea is that we best use physiological means to beat a physiological problem and psychological means to beat a psychological problem. Of course matters are not so simple, and it is not necessarily the case that physiological causes are best repaired by attending to physiological processes and psychological causes by attending to psychological processes. Sometimes this is simply not possible: genetic defects cannot be 'repaired', childhood traumas cannot be undone. Other times it may not be the most effective route to change. For instance, even if a psychiatrist suspects that her patient's relationship significantly contributes to his problems, she may still find it more useful to start with individual therapy. Or it may be more fruitful to start with medication in order to induce some changes that in turn enable the patient to work on his problems in psychotherapy. Still, in general we can at least say that how we conceive of the nature of the problems at hand will affect which treatment options appear most promising.

The distinction between physiological and psychological processes makes sense: it does indeed matter whether we regard an experience as primarily physiologically or psychologically caused. A good example of this can be found in Kramer's (1997) *Listening to Prozac*. He recounts a therapy session with a student to whom Kramer had prescribed an anti-depressant the week before. Now the student tells Kramer that he is very anxious. At first, Kramer takes this to be a side effect of the medication, but then it turns out that the student has actually not taken the medication and that his anxiety stems from fearing Kramer's reaction to his disobedience. Kramer nicely describes the sudden switch in perspective that comes from considering the experience of his patient as either physiologically or psychologically evoked:

> I was struck by the sudden change in my experience of his anxiety. One moment, the anxiety was a collection of meaningless physical symptoms, of interest only because they had to be suppressed, by other biological means, in order for the treatment to continue. At the next, the anxiety was rich in overtones. Hearing that the anxiety was not a medication side effect, I had an instantaneous sense of how I appeared to the student – demanding, judgmental, punitive, powerful in the face of his weakness – and how it must feel for him to go through life surrounded by similar figures ... The two anxieties were utterly different: the one a simple outpouring of brain chemicals, calling for a scientific response, however diplomatically communicated; the other worthy of empathic exploration of the most delicate sort.
>
> *(p. xii)*

Kramer's change in reaction makes sense: there does seem to be a fundamental difference between anxiety as the result of chemical processes and anxiety as the result of tensions in an interpersonal relationship. And they indeed call for different responses too.

And yet Kramer speaks of 'meaningless physical symptoms' and suggests that it is equally inappropriate to ascribe meaning to the physical, psychologising the physical so to speak, as to deny meaning to the psychological; 'physicalising' the psychological. But if we accept these differences, there seems to be an unsurmountable gap between meaningless physical processes on the one hand, and meaningful psychological processes on the other. In other words, Kramer's shift in perspective confronts us with the apparent mutual exclusiveness of the categories of physiological and psychological.

On the one hand, such differences are undeniable – but on the other, simply accepting the dichotomy between physiology and psychology or experience is highly problematic. First of all because its basic categories are unclear: what do we mean by 'physiological' and 'psychological' influences and processes? Is 'stress' physiological or psychological? Or both? Are unconscious processes part of psychological processes? Or are 'sub-personal' processes automatically physiological? And even if we agree in our definitions, that still would not allow us to easily divide either causes or treatments into physiological and psychological forms.

The causes of psychiatric disorders are often not straightforward. There may be not just one, easily identifiable, cause of all the patient's problems. Usually various influences play a role, influences that moreover influence each other (see also Chapter 8). Clear causes are rare. Post-traumatic stress disorder (PTSD) may appear to constitute an exception: here it is clear that disorder is caused by a traumatic experience, or a series thereof. But how to categorise a trauma? Suppose someone has suffered from repeated emotional abuse during their childhood. This seems an exemplary case of a psychological cause. But is it? Emotional abuse impacts the whole person; both psychologically and physiologically. The continual experience of unsafety can lead to a lack of trust in others and difficulties in drawing boundaries in relationships. At the same time it may structurally alter someone's physiological reactions to stress, as is reflected by changes in the anatomy and functioning of the brain (i.e. the amygdala and hypothalamic–pituitary–adrenal axis; Tsigos and Chrousos 2002). And the stress affects the body too – both at the time of the abuse itself and later in life. This has been called the 'body memory' of an event: an implicit memory of traumatic events that may lead to experiences of bodily pain or tension in situations that are similar to the one in which the trauma occurred (Koch et al. 2012).

Besides, whether emotional abuse leads to a post-traumatic stress disorder or not, does not solely depend on the severity of the abuse: children differ in how much they can take; some develop ingenious ways to cope, others may be lucky enough to have a caring neighbour or teacher around, yet others manage to find a loving partner later in life who helps them recover. And 'resilience' can have a physiological dimension too, such as a genetic disposition to be more or less sensitive to stress – which could itself be the result of what previous generations have experienced, such as periods of famine affecting the genes of later generations (Heijmans et al. 2008). Whether something amounts to a cause thus depends on the context (see also Chapter 8, Section 8.2). Even traumata are thus not straightforward causes. How helpful is it then to approach this complexity with a two-pronged fork?

The same difficulty in separating physiology and psychology goes for different forms of treatment. Medication for instance, is as clearly a physiological form of treatment as one can find. But in order for medication to exert its 'physiological' effects, it should first be taken. And the patient's decision whether or not to use medication will depend on many 'psychological' factors, such as his level of trust in his psychiatrist, which in turn depends on the history of their treatment-relationship. Moreover, so-called placebo effects show that even the *effectiveness* of the medication partly depends on factors that have nothing to do with the drug itself, but are rather related to the wider context, such as the relation between doctor and patient and the expectations of the patient – which may in turn be influenced by the attitude towards medication in their sociocultural community (Ziguras et al. 2001). Again, it is questionable whether carving things up into either physiological or psychological is the most helpful way to understand what is going on.

This brings us to another major problem with this dichotomy: how can we understand the relation between these processes? Psychological processes seem somehow dependent upon physiological processes. Are psychological processes identical to physiological processes? And if so, with which specific subset of physiological processes? Neural processes? And again, which ones? Or do psychological processes somehow depend on physiological ones without being identical to them? And what about the other way around: do physiological processes also depend on psychological ones? And if there is a dependence, either mutual or unilateral, how can we understand this relation, how do these two processes work on each other?

Our answers will affect how we conceive of the nature of psychiatric disorders, which in turn affects our choice of treatment; what we consider to be the root of the problems and what we see as merely treating the symptoms. The question of influence is tied to the question of control. The implicit assumption is typically that psychological processes are under patients' own control, but physiological processes less so. Our answers will thus affect how we conceive of the agency – and the responsibility – of patients as well. Patients' own relation to their disorder is implied too, especially whether to regard the disorder as something 'external' or 'internal'.

An integrative account of psychiatric disorders has to be able to do justice to the real differences without succumbing to either dualism or reductionism. That these two appear to be the only possible answers says something about the presuppositions of the mind–body problem. These presuppositions are closely tied to an inner–outer model of the mind. An enactive account offers a way out of the impasse by redefining the relation between mind, body, and world.

4.3   THE MIND–BODY PROBLEM AND THE DICHOTOMOUS MODEL OF THE MIND

The problem of how to relate body and mind is closely tied to the traditional, dichotomous model of the mind, as described in the previous chapter. Although this dichotomous model is not dualist in the sense of accepting two different substances, one physical and one mental, it does adhere to a dualist carving of mind and world into two inner and outer realms. It typically accepts the division between the physical as the blind, meaningless, causally determined unfolding of natural processes and the mental as free, meaningful thinking. As our bodies are natural objects – observable, made of cells, part of the world, subject to the laws of physics – they belong to the realm of the physical. Our mental life, however, is different: it is inner, private, non-tangible and not subject to the laws of physics. The problem of how inner and outer relate thus finds its most intimate expression in the problem of how to connect the very different natures of our own bodies and minds.

We do seem to experience them influencing each other. Physiological processes seem to influence our experiences: drinking alcohol or taking drugs for instance can change the way we feel, act, and perceive the world. And they don't just alter our consciousness; sometimes they even make us lose it. A severe blow to the head will have the same effect. We know our brains play a special role: brain injuries can alter one's experiences, and so do neurological disorders. What happens in and to our bodies thus affects our minds. And conversely there appear to be influences in the other direction as well: we think of relaxing things and our heart rate goes down. We remember a humiliating incident and our adrenaline level goes up. More generally, we feel that we have some control over our bodies; I can move my body at will: raise my arm when I feel like it, wiggle my toes. In these cases it seems that my mind steers my body.

The trouble starts when we try to spell out how physiological processes work on experiences and vice versa. It is the old problem of dualism: where and how do these two very different processes meet? It seems we are faced solely with unsatisfying options: appointing a specific location for their encounter (such as Descartes did by singling out the pineal gland as the spot where our spirits and our body meet) is not solving the problem of how such a meeting could work. Yet it seems that nothing can. It seems that if we do want to acknowledge the influence of the mind on the body, we should probably give up on the idea that mental processes are irreducibly different from physical processes. The Swiss philosopher Bieri (1981) describes the problem through the following trilemma:

1   Mental phenomena are not physical phenomena. (Mental phenomena are subjective experiences and as such radically different from physical phenomena.)
2   Mental phenomena are causally effective in the domain of physical phenomena. (There is such a thing as mental causation.)
3   The physical domain is causally closed. (Every physical effect has a sufficient physical cause.)

These three propositions cannot all be true without leading to inconsistency: one of the propositions has to be sacrificed. If we want to hold onto both the irreducibility of the mental to the physical (1) and the reality of mental causation (2), we have to give up on the causal closure of the physical domain (3). If we want to hold onto the causal closure of the physical domain (3) and to the possibility of mental causation (2), the mental has to be reducible to the physical and now we must give up on the intuition that mental phenomena are not physical phenomena (1). Lastly, if we want to hold onto the irreducible, special nature of mental phenomena compared to physical phenomena (1) as well as to the causal closure of the physical (3), we have to give up on the possibility of mental causation (2).

We can roughly characterise the main positions in the mind–body debate by which of these intuitions they are willing to sacrifice. Physicalism sacrifices the first intuition by assuming that mental processes can be reduced to, or supervene on physical processes (we will come back to supervenience in Section 4.7). This safeguards the causal closure of the physical domain, and since mental phenomena are physical phenomena they can also be causally effective in the physical domain. Giving up on the second proposition implies epiphenomenalism: there are mental phenomena, and they are different from physical phenomena, but they are causally ineffectual. They are the by-product of physical phenomena, like smoke is the by-product of a fire. Mental phenomena depend on these physical processes for their existence, but the causal efficacy is a one-way affair. Lastly, denying the third proposition is typical for dualism. Dualism saves the intuition that mental phenomena are different from physical ones and also that they can be causally effective, and it bites the bullet of accepting that the physical domain is thus not causally closed.

Many more subtle distinctions have been made of course, but what all these attempts to solve this puzzle have in common is that they accept its presuppositions – presuppositions that derive from the traditional inner mind–outer world model. It is presupposed that there are these two opposed classes or domains or categories or perspectives or processes; the one physical, the other mental. And that each of these follows its own distinct rules. It is further assumed that the world and its objects consist of meaningless matter, and that this physical world does not need mental phenomena to exist, that the physical would basically function the same way if the mental weren't there. Mental phenomena on the other hand do somehow depend on the physical world for their existence, but they appear as something 'extra': some sort of addendum. Starting from this way of dividing matter and mind it is clear that we either grant them both their separate existence but then want for a now inconceivable bridge (dualism) or that we see how the one can be reduced to the other (typically reducing the mental to the physical, idealism being out of favour for a long a time).[2] In this way even physicalism reflects the implicit dualism of the dichotomous model of the mind by accepting the way in which it carves out mind and world: physicalism just picks one side of the divide and claims that that is all there is.

---

[2] Another telling example can be found in Robinson's (2017) entry on dualism in *The Stanford Encyclopedia of Philosophy*, where he states that 'all arguments against physicalism are also arguments for the irreducible and hence immaterial nature of the mind and, given the existence of the material world, are thus arguments for dualism'. In other words: the assumption is that if one does not want to accept a reductionist physicalist conception of the mind, one is automatically committed to a dualist conception.

Following these dichotomous assumptions, the most pressing question becomes: how can meaningless matter give rise to the meaningful mind? Or: how can it be that some physical processes 'generate' experiences? It is telling that the 'hard problem' as Chalmers (1995) famously called it, is to understand why physical processes are accompanied by experiences at all. The relatively easy questions would be to find out which 'neural or computational mechanisms' underlie specific mental functions. But the answers to such how questions would still bring us nowhere near answering the real hard why question: 'Why should physical processing give rise to a rich inner life at all? It seems objectively unreasonable that it should, and yet it does' (p. 201). After all, the assumption goes, the physical world would turn the same way without anything mental being involved.

There are, however, different ways to look at the nature of mind and world and mind and body, different ways of carving out their relations, ways that dissolve these puzzles. Enactivism is one of them.

4.4   THE LIFE–MIND CONTINUITY THESIS

Instead of assuming an *opposition* between the physiological and the experiential, between matter and mind, enactivism argues that they are rather *continuous*. If one only regards the two extremes of the spectrum, physical matter as assemblies of atoms on the one hand, and abstract thinking on the other, it may seem like we are dealing with radically different phenomena or incompatible domains. Enactivism, however, contends that matter and mind go together in a natural and essential rather than an accidental way – in living beings, that is. This is the primary step in dissolving the dualist puzzle: we are not interested in just any assembly of matter; we are interested in *living beings*, in organisms. It is not physical matter in general that we are talking about; we are rather dealing with *physiological* processes, the matter of living beings. And when it comes to living beings, their very organisational and physiological structure implies that they engage in sense-making, in other words: that they are minded, or minding beings. This is the so-called *life–mind continuity thesis* (Thompson 2007; Froese and Di Paolo 2009).[3] As Jonas (1966/2001) summarises its core idea: 'the organic even in its lowest forms prefigures mind, and . . . mind even on its highest reaches remains part of the organic' (p. 1). The presumable gap is contested, even at its extreme sides: on the one hand, there is already a basic form of sense-making implied in 'low-level' forms of life, and on the other hand, even our most abstract thinking remains embodied and embedded.

4.4.1 *Living Implies Sense-Making*

If it is relevant that we are not talking about just any assembly of matter, but rather of living beings, then what is it about living beings that makes them different from mere heaps of matter? What distinguishes matter from living matter, physics from physiology? Unsurprisingly, it is a matter of debate about how to distinguish the living from the non-living. There are several ways to approach this question: historically (either from ontogenesis or epigenesis), or systematically. The focus can be on ecological systems at large, on populations, or on individual organisms (see Thompson 2007). For our purpose, it is most relevant to try to arrive at a systematic description at the level of the individual organism.

Enactivism follows Jonas' (1966/2001) proposition that the fundamental characteristic of life is that all organisms have *metabolism*, whereas no non-living thing has it.[4] Metabolism refers to the process

---

[3] Note that the enactive life–mind continuity thesis goes further than what Clark (2001) calls the 'strong continuity' between life and mind. Clark writes: 'the thesis of strong continuity would be true if, for example, the basic concepts needed to understand the organization of life turned out to be self-organization, collective dynamics, circular causal processes, autopoiesis, etc., and if those very same concepts and constructs turned out to be central to a proper scientific understanding of mind' (p. 118, quoted from Thompson 2007, pp. 128–9). This description however remains at an *epistemological* level, whereas for enactivism the thesis is an *ontological* one. Besides, as Thompson (2007) writes, for enactivism 'the continuity of life and mind is not simply organizational, or functional or behavioral, but also phenomenological. In other words, the continuity includes the subjective and experiential aspects of mental life as well as the cognitive aspects' (p. 129).

[4] But see Villalobos and Ward (2016) for a critique on Jonas and his role in enactivism.

of exchange of matter with the environment through which the organism can maintain itself. To sustain its identity, the organism needs to transform food (matter) into its own form (matter): staying alive requires a constant flux of matter. An organism 'is never the same materially and yet persists as its same self, *by* not remaining the same matter' (Jonas 1966/2001, p. 76). Physio-chemically, the organism is constantly changing, but it still forms an organisational unity. What is special about organisms is that they maintain themselves as a *unity* in and through *interactions* with the environment.

Regarding this unity, enactivist theorists have come up with a formalisation of the basic *organisational structure* of living beings (Maturana and Varela 1987; Varela 1997; Weber and Varela 2002; Di Paolo 2005). Organisms are self-preserving through a dialectical process of transforming matter into the organisation that makes this transformation possible. As Varela (1997) puts it: 'organisms are fundamentally a process of constitution of an identity' (p. 73). The organism's process of self-preservation implies that it is an autonomous system in the sense that it specifies its own laws. In contrast to, for example, a robot that behaves according to the rules that I have programmed, a living being is not in this way externally determined: it is its own organisation that brings forth certain laws that it has to abide by.[5] The self-organisation of living beings can be operationalised as involving *autopoiesis* and *adaptivity*.

The notion of autopoiesis was first introduced by Maturana and Varela (1972/1980) to characterise the organisation of the autonomy of living beings. Living beings are autopoietic systems, in that they are:

> organized (defined as unity) as a network of processes of production (synthesis and destruction) of components such that these

---

[5] *Autonomous* thus does not mean 'unconstrained' (Di Paolo et al. 2011). The organism is not free to do as it pleases: it is autonomous in that it are its internal dynamics rather than an external set of rules that determine what behaviours are available to it. Still, as Thompson (2007) points out, we should be aware that the notions 'heteronomous' and 'autonomous' are heuristic tools and that 'what counts as the system in any given case, and hence whether it is autonomous or heteronomous, is context-dependent and interest-relative' (p. 50).

components: 1. continuously regenerate the network that is
producing them, and 2. constitute the system as a distinguishable
unity in the domain in which they exist.

(Varela 1997, p. 75)

Di Paolo (2005) rightly points out that on the present definition
autopoiesis is an all or nothing state. In this form, the definition
cannot do justice to the gradations of survival, e.g. that the autopoietic
system can be more or less fit, that interactions may be more or less
beneficial. Di Paolo therefore proposes to add the condition of 'adaptivity' to mend this problem. Adaptivity is defined as

> a system's capacity, in some circumstances, to regulate its states
> and its relation to the environment with the result that, if the states
> are sufficiently close to the boundary of viability; 1. Tendencies are
> distinguished and acted upon depending on whether the states will
> approach or recede from the boundary and, as a consequence, 2.
> Tendencies of the first kind are moved closer to or transformed into
> tendencies of the second and so future states are prevented from
> reaching the boundary with an outward velocity.
>
> (p. 438)

Di Paolo (2005) summarises both aspects as follows:

> Autopoiesis provides a self-distinct physical system that can be the
> centre of a perspective on the world, and a self-maintained,
> precarious network of processes that generates an either-or
> normative condition. Adaptivity allows the system to appreciate its
> encounters with respect to this condition, its own death, in a graded
> and relational manner while it is still alive.
>
> (p. 439)

The unity of the organism is a 'network of processes' that is distinct
from the environment but at the same time needs to interact with the
environment to stay alive. Its boundaries are 'self-maintained' (it is
the organism itself that takes care of its own continuation), but we

should be careful not to misread this self-maintenance as *self-sufficiency*. On the contrary, the autonomy of the organism includes a fundamental dependency on its interactions with its environment.[6]

The organisational unity of organisms thus already includes their relation to their environments. The organism is *structurally coupled* to its environment: the environment affects how the organism acts and how the organism acts also affects the environment. That they are structurally coupled means that they also have a history of coupling: that the organism has shaped the environment and that the environment has been shaped by the organism too. Trees, for example, shape their own preferred niche by casting shade with their crowns and capturing humidity.

As Jonas (1966/2001) points out, the relation between an organism and its environment is characterised by both freedom and need. On the one hand, the organism does not coincide with its materiality (as is the case for non-living things); it stands apart from its environment, and it can adapt itself, at least to some extent. Herein lies the organism's freedom. At the same time, however, the organism cannot escape its dependency upon the environment: it is not just that the organism *can* convert matter into its own form; it *must* do so in order to stay alive. The organism's liberty is itself its 'needful freedom' (p. 80), as Jonas calls it. It is a self-organising unity, but only by constantly interacting with its environment.

Living beings' metabolism thus makes them dependent on a constant interaction with their environments. Now this single characteristic of life already brings along many of the characteristics that we would traditionally only attribute to more sophisticated forms of life, notably our own. In particular, metabolism implies a basic form of experience, of value, and of sense-making (Jonas 1966/2001; Weber and Varela 2002; Di Paolo 2005; Thompson 2007).

---

[6]   The precise nature of the self-organisation that characterises living, minded beings is a matter of ongoing debate, as is the notion of autopoiesis itself (Hutto and Myin 2013; Villalobos and Ward 2014). For our purpose the technical specificities are less relevant: what matters is the general topology of body, mind, and world.

The organism's existence is not a given but a continuous process that requires hard work. Remaining alive is a precarious endeavour. The organism's maintaining of itself requires an estimation of its environment: what makes it live and what makes it die and some gradients in between. This means that an organism must in some way perceive and discern its environment as well as itself; to sense its own needs. A living being is a sensing being. Unassuming as this may sound, it actually implies that organisms have some sort of *experience* or *awareness* – even if only to an 'infinitesimal' degree (Jonas 1966/2001). Now the term *experience* might trigger all sorts of connotations that do not seem appropriate to apply to butterflies, ticks, fungi, or algae. To be sure, the experience of these organisms is very unlikely to be *self-aware* experience and thus to be as rich and complex as our experiences. But living beings do sense things: they are sensitive to certain aspects or events in their environment, certain aspects or events affect them in certain ways, and they react to them in certain ways too. This sensing is a very basic form of experiencing and it has a 'subjective' structure: it implies that organisms, as the sensing unities they are, embody a perspective on the world. Experiences are of a 'subjective' structure – or maybe 'subjectual' would be a better word: experiences are not subjective as opposed to objective, they are subjective as opposed to being views from nowhere. This does not mean that there is an inner homunculus or 'organismusculus' who is 'doing the sensing' or who is registering and evaluating the outcome of being affected by the environment. There is no need to assume such a doubling since the capacity to sense is implied in the very self-organising, autopoietic, and adaptive structure that characterises living beings.

Besides, from the organism's main concern of surviving, other concerns follow.[7] Its biological make-up, including its metabolic

---

[7] The definition of biological organisms in terms of autopoiesis and adaptivity does not include reproduction. Although this is of course a crucial aspect of living, some enactivists argue that it is not 'intrinsic to the minimal logic of living' (Varela 1997). I will not go into this discussion here; for an introduction, see Varela et al. (1974/1984) and Maturana (1980).

needs, bring along certain specific concerns, such as the need for food, for shelter, for sleep, for being part of a herd. These basic concerns give the interactions of the organism with its environment a specific relevance. The organism is invested in staying alive, and some interactions are definitely better suited for this goal than others. The possibilities that the environment has to offer are thus not neutral to the organism; or some possibilities are, but other things stand out as offering positive, well-being-reinforcing options for action, and others rather as entailing danger. These aspects of the environment thus have a certain *value* for the organism − albeit a basic, functional value. The organism's needs and concerns function as a kind of compass, highlighting the environment's meaning. As we saw in the previous chapter, the value and meaning of aspects of the environment are neither a projection, nor an independent, inherent characteristic of the environment, but rather the objective result of the coupling of this specific organism with this specific environment: the corollary of the characteristics of both of them.

The activity of orienting, of distinguishing between relevant and irrelevant possibilities for action, and between what is to be avoided and what is to be approached, is a basic form of *sense-making*. Sense-making is the evaluative interaction of the organism with its environment: assessing which interactions are good or bad, profitable or dangerous for its survival. The organism thus makes sense of its environment, which includes both discerning the value of what the environment has to offer, as well as experiencing its own current hierarchy of concerns. Again, this is not an 'arm-chair' activity of deliberation and introspection; again, no doubling is required here. It is instead akin to when I am hungry and in this state the apple in the fruit bowl makes my mouth water and I reach for it. I am not making any deliberate assessment, first looking inside and comparing my feeling on a chart of options, and then looking outside to compare of each object its suitability to fulfil my need; maybe we would program a computer this way, but this deliberative detour is not needed when living beings can rely on their direct experience. Organisms do not need to *know* that they are hungry, they just are, and they need not compare various parts of their environment to check if they are food; they just notice (see, smell, hear, sense) food. The interaction of an organism with its environment is a process of regulation – but not deliberately controlled: the organism adapts to its surroundings, acts and reacts, so as to attune its concerns and its possibilities for action. This process of regulation and adaptation could be regarded as an instance of *agency* – again, in a basic form.[8]

The implications of metabolism, of life, as argued for by Jonas (1966/2001) and adopted by enactivism, are far-reaching. Not only does life itself introduce the basic instances of concern, need, and freedom, but also of sense-making. Matter in specific self-organising, autopoietic and adaptive configurations is living matter, and these living beings necessarily engage in (basic) sense-making, they are 'minded'. On this enactive view, matter and mind are thus not opposed; the physiology of living beings rather implies their capacity for sense-making.

Now, we are used to thinking of what it is to 'have a mind' by taking ourselves as the standard, and not just anything we do, but especially our rather sophisticated skills like abstract reasoning and imagining. Starting from such a conception of mind it will be hard to fathom how every living being could have a mind; even invertebrates, even plants. That just seems ridiculous. But some of these hesitations dissolve if one replaces the heavy human-loaded notion of mind with the more humble and concrete notion of sense-making. Another important clarification is to explicate that there are indeed differences between our sense-making and the sense-making of bacteria. Our sense-making is shaped by our existential stance: it is existentialised sense-making, so to speak. I will come back to the necessity of differentiating basic from existential sense-making in Chapter 6.

---

[8] For an interesting discussion about the criteria for agency and agentic systems, see Di Paolo (2005, 2009a), Barandiaran and Moreno (2008), Barandiaran et al. (2009), and Froese and Di Paolo (2011).

Still, granted we understand mind as sense-making and we distinguish between basic and existential sense-making, it might still be disputed whether all living beings indeed engage in a basic form of making sense of their environments. Opponents (Adams and Aizawa 2008; Adams and Garrison 2013) may argue that it stretches the notion of sense-making too far to claim that even 'lower level' organisms like plants engage in sense-making. Proponents of the life–mind continuity thesis on the other hand point out that we should be more open-minded when it comes to recognising adaptive, i.e. intelligent, behaviour (Calvo Garzón and Keijzer 2011; Fulda 2017). Although their options for action appear rather limited compared to motile creatures, plants do act and react – only in very different ways and typically at different timescales than we do. They grow towards the light, and towards the nutrition in the soil on the other end. Some discern threats like moulds and guard themselves by, for instance, making their roots more sour and thus less attractive. There are even indications that some plants communicate through their roots, inspiring some to talk of the 'wood-wide-web'. As plant-cognition researcher Paco Calvo (2016) says: different problems call for different solutions. And why would the human and the animal solutions be deemed intelligent and the plant solutions not?

Although I am sympathetic to the life–mind continuity thesis in its full range, for our quest here it does not really matter where one draws the line; how 'low' one is willing to go. For psychiatry is about the problems of human beings and it is clear that we are sense-making, minded beings. What matters here is the radically different perspective on the relation between mind, body, and world that enactivism offers and its potential for developing an integrative account of psychiatric disorders.

4.4.2 Sense-Making Is Embodied and Embedded

The life–mind continuity thesis says sense-making is essential to living – but what does it say about sense-making? What does this thesis imply with regard to the nature of sense-making? Sense-making

emerges from the precarious organism's interaction with its environment. The capacity for sense-making thus depends on there being
a body that needs to be sustained and that requires interactions with
its environment to do so. Enactivism stresses that not only does living
imply sense-making, but sense-making, even in its most abstract forms,
remains an activity that is necessarily embodied and embedded.

Free as our thoughts and imagination are, they cannot be free in
a void. As Kant (1787/1998) wrote: 'When the light dove parts the air in
free flight and feels the air's resistance, it might come to think that it
would do much better still in space devoid of air' (A4-5, B8-9). But the
freedom of the bird's flight is of course made possible by its body, its
shape, by its feathers, by its blood circulation, by its food, and by the
air it breathes and hovers on. Like the bird needs its body and the
resistance of the air to be able to fly, our sense-making requires our
brains, our bodies, and our interactions with our world. Nowadays,
the embodiment of thinking is often very narrowly understood as the
'embrainment' (Wilson 2010) of thinking. And surely, we need our
brains – but we do not think with our brains alone. The brain is
a necessary, but insufficient precondition for thinking. That is, the
brain is indeed an indispensable organ for thinking, but it remains an
organ, and as such it is dependent upon the whole body for its
functioning.[9] This dependence goes beyond a merely accidental,
exchangeable relation. For if it were not for the body, the vulnerable

---

[9]   This is where extended mind theories (Clark and Chalmers 1998; Clark 2008) and
      enactivism part ways. Extended mind theories too stress the fundamental role of the
      environment, arguing that the mind extends into the outer world. There are two major
      differences with enactivism though. First of all, extended mind theories still rely on
      a narrow description of cognition. Only insofar as processes 'outside the skull' resemble
      those 'inside the skull' are they considered to be cognitive (Clark and Chalmers 1998).
      What happens in the brain is still considered to be the hallmark of cognition: 'If, as we
      confront some task, a part of the world functions as a process which, were it to go on in
      the head, we would have no hesitation in accepting as part of the cognitive process, then
      that part of the world is (for that time) part of the cognitive process' (p. 8). Enactivism,
      on the contrary, does not adopt the premise that what characterises cognition depends
      primarily on its localisation in the brain (Di Paolo 2009a). Secondly, even though the
      brain plays such an important role in defining what counts as cognition, extended mind
      theories do not consider either the brain or the body to be necessary for cognition. That
      is, extended mind theories see no reason why these processes could not also be

body, dependent upon its environment for survival, sense-making would not even have emerged.

But the dependence of sense-making on the body may be less controversial than the second requirement: the embedded nature of sense-making. After all, that we need the body, or at least some part of the body, to be able to think is commonly accepted. But that 'mind' requires more, that it requires 'the environment' too, is quite a far-reaching, bold claim. From an enactive perspective, sense-making *is* interacting with the environment. Living beings' dependence on interactions with their environment brings the need for making sense of it, and as such it is the needful freedom of the body combined with the resourceful (and risk-full) environment that forms the pre-condition for sense-making to occur. For us, the environment we make sense of is a social, cultural world. And our sense-making is not just directed at the specific sociocultural worlds we live in, but our (existential) sense-making capacities are to a large extent learned in and through social interactions as well – which are supported by the sociocultural communities we are part of. Our sense-making is socially constituted.

4.5   IT TAKES MORE THAN BODY AND MIND TO TANGO

So here we are, trying to relate mind and body, experience and physiology, and we find that from an enactive view, the world is inextricably included in our mindedness. And since as humans our world is a sociocultural world, this means that our mindedness must itself be socioculturally understood.

instantiated in another system, an artificial, non-living system. Enactivism opposes this functionalist assumption. For enactive theories, embodiment is not a mere exchangeable 'vat' of cognition but is rather fundamentally tied to its occurrence. Di Paolo (2009b) calls this difference 'shallow' versus 'deep' embodiment. According to this 'deep' embodiment, our specific thinking could not exist without, or in a different, body. Moreover, thinking occurs in living beings, since these are motivated to stay alive under precarious conditions, and thus need to make sense of their environment. From an enactive perspective, then, the possibility of genuine artificial intelligence would depend on a form of artificial *life*, which assumes not only some form of self-organising but also the precariousness of life and the dependence upon the environment for survival.

4.5.1 Sense-Making Is Socially Constituted

If organisms were totally self-contained and self-sufficient, there would be no need for experiences. Having experiences is the result of the particular precarious self-organisation of living beings who depend on their environments. Or, in our case, the result of our being dependent persons in interaction with our worlds. I am the one experiencing things – joy, pain, hunger, admiration – but it is the encompassing system of me interacting with my world that enables the occurrence of my experiences. In other words: it is the wider person–world system that constitutes the condition of possibility for our experiences. The relations between organism and environment and person and world are constitutive of the organism and the person respectively. Their fundamental coupling implies that 'the environment' or 'the world' is not the passive backdrop or a secondary 'add-on' to an already complete organism or person, but that both organism and person are what they are because of these interactions.

For us, our environment, our world, is first and foremost a social one. Not only because many of our interactions are in fact with people, but also because our material world and the objects we are surrounded with are mostly man-made (Heidegger 1927/1978; Merleau-Ponty 1945/2002). Even if I stay in my apartment all day and don't see anyone, sociality still permeates everything: from the fact that I live in a building, to the newspaper I read, the music I listen to, and the food that I eat: all is shaped by the specific community I am part of, with its specific sociocultural practices. Diverse as those practices are at different places, and in different times, the common fact remains that there are such practices that to a large extent shape who we are, what we do, and what our worlds look like. Sociocultural practices reflect histories of coupling. But this of course does not mean that they are static: they are continuously being shaped and re-shaped by the actions of the participants. There are trends in architecture, in food, in what is considered newsworthy or beautiful, etc. The practices are what we do, and we make the practices, and the practices make us in an inextricable back-and-forth.

And it isn't just our world that is social; our very sense-making is socially constituted. That is, we learn to make sense of the world first and foremost through our interactions with others. Even before birth, mother and child already interact, and the foetus gets familiar with the tastes of its mother's food, the sounds of their environment, the rhythm of rest and activity. Once the infant is born its interactions with its caregivers are crucial. More and more research shows how infants engage in interactions from the moment they are born and how they learn from these interactions, by imitating their caregivers, or watching their caregivers' responses (Stern 1985; Hobson 2002; Reddy 2008). When infants are confronted with a virtual cliff, a seeming hole in the floor, they look at their caregivers' expression to estimate whether it is safe for them to cross or not (Sorce et al. 1985). Infants are even sensitive to explicit learning cues: if there is a simple way to press a button with one's hand, but the experimenter uses her head instead, the infant will also use their head – unless it is clear that the experimenter could not use her hands because she is holding something. In that case, the infant will just use their hand to push the button; there was a reason the experimenter did not use her hand, so apparently it is not specifically necessary to use the head (Király et al. 2013). What is dangerous, what is relevant, what is suitable for putting in your mouth: all of this basic sense-making is learned through interactions.

More sophisticated forms of sense-making are socially constituted as well. Through social interactions like games of peek-a-boo and hide-and-seek infants and children for instance practice with perspective-taking: when can the other person see me and when can I see her (Reddy 2003; de Haan et al. 2011)? In interactions with two caregivers the child can become aware that not only she herself but also her interactions with one of the caregivers can be the object of attention of the other caregiver (Fuchs 2012). Later on, children are explicitly taught to take the perspective of others ('how would *you* feel if she would do that to one of *your* toys?') and to pause and think before rushing in to something. Through such social practices, children develop more and more elaborated skills in perspective-taking, amounting at some point to full-blown reflective capacities. We learn to think through our social interactions (Mead 1934/1962; Hobson 2002) – which are in turn embedded in specific sociocultural practices. It is especially our most abstract capacities, like calculating, that depend on our sociocultural practices (cf. Thompson 2007; Zahidi and Myin 2016).

Besides, this is not merely a social 'stage' in the development of sense-making that we at some point surpass: our sense-making rather continues to be shaped by our interactions with others and with our sociocultural communities. In many social interactions our sense-making is even joint, or *participatory*, sense-making (De Jaegher and Di Paolo 2007; Fuchs and De Jaegher 2009). Participatory sense-making refers to those cases where interactions are not just an exchange of individuals' points of view, but where the participants engage in a shared process of sense-making. This mutual sense-making can take different forms: one person can conform to the other, or there can be a more equal, back-and-forth adjustment of all participants to each other (Fuchs and De Jaegher 2009). The interaction process can also take on an autonomy of its own, when it develops in a way that none of the participants intended (De Jaegher and Di Paolo 2007, 2009). Think for instance of a couple who regularly end up having the same fight again, even though neither of them intended to start it.

So for the social beings that we are, the world we try to make sense of is a social one, and the way in which we master our sense-making skills is through social interactions.

4.5.2   *Physiological Processes Depend on Mind and World Too*

Mind depends on more than the body: sense-making is a capacity that emerges from the wider system of an organism interacting with their environment, or a person interacting with her world. For us to be able to do the kinds of sense-making that we do, we need interactions with other people, interactions which are part of and supported by specific sociocultural practices. And it is not just the mind that depends on more than the body alone; the body itself too depends on interactions with the environment. Of course, bodies typically need oxygen, something to eat, and something to drink. And air pressure, and gravity, and something to move around on or in. But the dependence is not just accidental; it is not that the external stays external: the external rather gets absorbed and shapes our bodies from the inside, so to speak. This can be seen in the many ways in which what we eat influences our bodies: shaping our mass, changing the state of our arteries, affecting our moods. Our physiological processes depend on interactions with the world to such an extent that the world is not so clearly 'outer' anymore, and sabotages any attempt at an easy divide between 'internal processes' and 'external influences'.

But the dependencies do not stop there: our physiological processes depend not only on the environment, but also on our minds. Our bodies need our minds. Without experiencing, without sense-making, organisms are either dead or they will die. Admittedly, we can nowadays keep unconscious people alive; we can keep their bodies functioning in the hope their life returns to them. But this advanced medical care comes down to doctors and machines doing the sense-making for these bodies. The model of the mind as inner fosters the inclination to think that our bodies do not need our minds; that they would function just as well without any 'extra ingredient' such as experiences, qualia, or mental life. The enactive life–mind continuity thesis however overthrows this picture. Just as our capacity for sense-making emerges from the specific configuration of a living being in constant interaction with its environment for survival, so too do physiological processes derive their properties from being part of this larger system. Our physiological processes are an emergent feature of the person–world system too. This precisely marks the difference between physical and physiological processes: matter in specific organisational patterns is alive and is minded and this configuration determines the properties of the physiological processes involved.

What we breathe and eat affects our bodies, what we experience affects our bodies, how we move affects our bodies: how we live shapes our physiology. All the way 'down' to the chemical level we can see how the context of living determines the properties of physiological processes. For instance, the effects of administering the so-called cuddle hormone oxytocin depend on what the person feels like at that moment (Bartz et al. 2011; Olff et al. 2013), much like the effects of certain drugs depend on the mood you are in when taking them. And of course placebo effects too show the importance of the social and experiential context for the precise effects of 'physiological' interventions.

These dependencies – of mind on body and world and of the body on mind and world – are not mere causal relations, but are rather constitutive. That is: mind and body, experiential and physiological processes, could not exist without interactions with the world. This is what Gallagher (2017) calls a strong sense of constitution. And they also constitutively relate in the weak sense that *how* we make sense of the world depends on both our bodies and our interactions with our world. One line of critique of the enactive (and the extended) theory of mind is that it mistakes causal relations for constitutive ones (Adams and Aizawa 2008; Aizawa 2010). Bodily and environmental processes may play a causal role in supporting cognitive processes, but that, they argue, does not yet mean that they are part of the cognitive processes themselves, as the term *constitution* suggests. However, as Kirchhoff (2015) points out, this critique assumes a specific conception of constitution as a synchronic, compositional relation between parts and whole, like the statue of David (whole) that is made of marble (parts). Diachronic relations, on the other hand, are taken to signal causal relations. From this point of view then, constitutional and causal relations rule out each other.

But these are not the only ways to think about constitution and causality (Kirchhoff 2015; Gallagher 2017; Krickel 2017). The

static view of constitution cannot apply to the dynamical processes that are implied when considering living beings and their
sense-making capacities. Nonetheless there are various part–
whole relations at play here. Even if we only consider the body
as such, we can distinguish various interdependent systems such
as the central nervous system, the blood circulation system, the
digestive system, which in turn consists of various elements
(organs such as the brain and the heart, blood vessels, bowels),
which in turn consist of specific cells. Their relations are
far from static though: they affect each other in complex
ways, with processes going on at various timescales.[10] Such
a complex, dynamical system calls for a different conception of
constitution: as *diachronic and dynamical constitution*
(Kirchhoff 2015; Gallagher 2017). It is in this dynamical sense
of constitution that our capacity for sense-making depends constitutively on our being living bodies interacting with our
environment.

The mind–body problem is about relating matter and the
mental, or experiences and physiology. But from an enactive perspective, neither mind nor body can be understood in isolation
from each other and from the world. Both experiential and physiological processes derive their existence and characteristics from
being part of the larger system of an organism interacting with its
environment, or a person interacting with her world. From an
enactive point of view, we are trying to relate the wrong things
when we try to relate physiological and psychological or experiential processes *to each other*. Trying to relate physiological and
experiential processes is like putting incomparable magnitudes
into one equation: in order to be related, they first need to be
converted into a shared magnitude.

[10]   Gallagher (2017) follows Varela (1999) in distinguishing three main timescales, which
he dubs the elementary (the milliseconds processes of neurophysiological processes),
integrative (the seconds processes of experiencing), and narrative timescales (any
processes that take longer than a few seconds and that involve memory).

4.6   MIND–BODY CAUSALITY FROM AN ENACTIVE VIEW

So far, we have looked at the mind–body problem as present in psychiatry, its roots in an inner–outer model of the mind, and the alternative enactive view of the relation between mind and body. This enactive view implies not only that body and mind necessarily belong together, but that the world needs to be included too. Now it is time to spell out what this view implies for the problem we started out with: how to understand the relation between physiological and experiential processes. How do physiological processes affect our experiences and vice versa? As we saw, from a dichotomous, inner–outer model of the mind the mind-boggling question is how a physiological process, or more specifically a neuronal process, can give rise to a mental process. The other way around is just as mysterious: how can an experience affect neuronal processes? Where and how do these processes of such different natures meet? Or is their difference in nature an illusion?

Let's look at an example to explain the enactive alternative view on the relation between physiological and experiential processes. Suppose I am reading a book in which the idea is defended that psychiatric disorders are brain diseases. I am annoyed by this: I disagree, I think that it doesn't do justice to the nature of psychiatric disorders, and I am worried that this view has potentially harmful consequences. Now suppose I were put in a scanner while I am in this state of annoyance and the scanner shows that there is heightened activity in my amygdala. What would be the relation between my feeling annoyed and the amygdala activity? Has my annoyance caused my amygdala activity to go up? Is my experience the *cause* of my neural activity? Or suppose I am annoyed, not because something has happened that annoyed me, but because I have taken a pill that stirred my amygdala. Would that mean that in this case my amygdala activity has caused my feeling of annoyance? Have these neuronal processes *caused* my experience?

From an enactive perspective these are misleading questions: both my annoyance and my amygdala activity are only understandable from the larger perspective of being a person in a world. In the first case, my experience of being annoyed is caused by the book I am reading – but this book would not annoy everybody; it would probably even make some people feel enthusiastic. The book is a cause of annoyance for me as a particular person: it is only a cause against the background of my history of reading and thinking about philosophy and psychiatry, and my caring about these matters. My experience is dependent on or is an emergent feature of this larger conglomerate of the person that I am, the context that I am in now, and the history of my interactions that have shaped me. Is this an example of an 'experiential' cause? Well, only if we add that the experience itself is not an isolated event but is rather dependent upon this whole constellation. That is to say, as long as we keep in mind that with 'experiential' we automatically include both the body and the world and the history of interactions. 'Experiential' thus does not designate the opposite of 'physical' or 'physiological'. Besides, the notion of 'cause' requires specification too: my experience of annoyance is not the cause of my amygdala activity if we understand 'cause' in a linear sense, as when one domino hits the next. The amygdala activity is rather *part of* my being annoyed. When I am annoyed this *includes* various neuronal and other physiological processes. Neuronal processes are part of and depend upon the person as a whole, in interaction with her environment. And the same goes for experiences: my experiences too depend upon my being a person, with a specific history, being engaged in a specific situation. In that sense, we can speak of a *mereological* (part–whole) relation: both experiences and (neuro) physiological processes are part of the complex system of a person coupled to her world.

How about the other case, when my annoyance is caused by a pill? That does seem to be an example of neuronal processes causing an experience. However, in this case too the physiological or neuronal cause is not as pure as it may seem. The effects of the pill depend on taking this pill: it is the *act* of pill-taking that had certain effects. Besides, this act takes place in a larger life-world context as well:

why did I take this pill? What did I expect? Was it a medical context, did someone prescribe this pill to me? If so, what were the expectations in this practice? What is my personal history with taking drugs? The effects of the pill-taking depend at least to some extent on this wider context. To dub this a 'physiological' cause would again be imprecise, as it pretends that the physiological constitutes a force all on its own.[11] And again, to say it is a 'cause' too requires clarification. The amygdala activity is not a cause in a linear way either. After all, how could that even be: a neuronal domino hitting an experiential one?

From an enactive perspective both experiential and physiological processes are what they are because of their being part of the wider person—world system. This means that in both cases the causality is not between the physiological and the experiential as such. Since they are both are part of a larger whole, we cannot map physiological and experiential processes onto each other. Physiology and experience do not add up to the whole story, nor can they be opposed. They are not separate causal systems or tracks; they are rather partly overlapping excerpts of one and the same bigger system of a person in their world. Therefore we cannot say that the amygdala activity is *causing* my annoyance; nor the other way around, that my annoyance is *causing* my amygdala to be extra active – at least not if we mean by 'causation' that there are two separate processes or systems, one physiological and one experiential, where one causes something in the other like one billiard ball hitting the next. There is no such

---

[11] Now there might be cases in which there is a purely physiological event at the basis of an experiential change. My annoyance could for instance be caused by a random twitch in my amygdala, like a random proliferation of cells can give rise to cancer. If this is the case, if all depends on a purely random physiological process, we are no longer dealing with psychiatric disorders though, but rather with neurological ones. I will get back to this in Chapter 7 when I discuss what characterises psychiatric disorders from an enactive point of view. For the discussion here it matters most that even in such a purely physiological event the kind of causality at play between the physiological and the experiential processes is of an organisational rather than a linear kind.

linear, sequential-type causal relation between the physiological process and the experiential process because we are rather looking at one and the same process, but different excerpts of it, at different levels of zooming in, typically focusing on different time-scales too.

This mereological structure of physiological and experiential processes as part of a larger system does not imply that there can be no influences from one to the other. It just requires a different under-standing of how physiological and experiential processes are related and how their influences work. The important, dualism-defeating move is to resist thinking about the causality of physiological and experiential processes in linear terms and as a two-place event. The causality involved is rather of a mereological, constitutional, or orga-nisational type.[12]

An analogy may help to understand this type of causality. Think of the causality involved in making a cake. A cake is made from various ingredients that moreover influence each other. The amount of sugar, for example, will affect not only the overall sweetness of the cake, but it also affects the yeast and thus the structure of the sponge. Adding an extra egg to the dough will affect the sponge – and thereby the cake as a whole. The added sugar or the added egg does not work 'on' the cake like one domino hitting another, but rather by being part of the cake a change in the amount of sugar or eggs *is* a change of the cake as a whole. We can understand the effect of changes in my amygdala on my mood in a similar way as changes in the amount of sugar affecting the taste of the cake. There are not two separate processes working on each other, one physiological and one mental;

---

[12]   As we saw in the previous section, the enactive recognition of living beings as complex dynamical systems calls for a reconsideration of both constitutive and causal rela-tions. With complex, intertwined processes going on at different timescales, the distinction between causal and constitutional cannot be so neatly drawn as in the traditional opposition between non-linear causality and static constitution. Is this still properly called 'causality' one might wonder? It is – as long as we keep in mind that the causality involved here is not the linear, domino-stones one, not the causality of large objects physics, but that it is rather the causality as in chemistry.

rather, by changing an element of a whole, the whole at that very moment changes.

Of course this is true in a self-evident, synchronous way: a change of a part by definition is a change of the whole. But not all changes of parts affect the whole as such. A big pile of sand is technically speaking changed when I remove one grain, but that doesn't affect the pile-ness of the whole. There are thresholds: not all local changes lead to noticeable, global effects. Adding one more grain of sugar will not make a noticeable difference in the cake as a whole, but adding an extra cup will. Similarly, not all changes in my amygdala will be noticeable on the personal, experiential level. The likelihood of local changes leading to global effects will (partly) depend on the interconnectedness of the process in question with other processes and the feedback loops involved. The effects of a local change thus depend on the larger context in which it takes place: like the effects of one ingredient will depend on the other ingredients, the effects of heightened amygdala activity similarly depend on many other simultaneous processes, such as hormonal processes for instance. Besides, in complex, dynamical systems gradual changes can sometimes lead to a qualitative turning point: tipping the system over from one stable state into another, to put it in dynamical system terms. Just as I cannot keep on adding eggs while preserving the general taste of the cake: at some point the cake will turn into something else, say, sweet scrambled eggs with jelly.

Adding sugar is a local-to-global influence, but there can also be influences the other way around. Consider the temperature of the cake as a whole: putting it in the fridge will have a different effect than putting it in the oven. Again, when we want to describe this effect, this relation between the whole and its parts, we see that it would be a mistake to invoke any linear notion of causality between them. By heating the cake, we change the cake as a whole – including its ingredients. Moreover, the effect of the heating on the cake will depend on the very ingredients it is made of and how these ingredients have been mixed and handled. It is not as if the heat changes the cake (the whole) and this *in turn* changes the properties of the ingredients (the parts). The whole consists of its parts, and intervening with the whole implies influencing its parts. This leaves open the possibility that some parts will be affected more than others; the icing can be burned before the cake is cooked. Here too, different parts may have different thresholds for being affected. Likewise, reading this annoying book affects my amygdala activity, as well as my heart rate and adrenaline levels, but it has no effects on, say, the strength of my toenails (although who knows, maybe prolonged stress and anger will even make my toenails brittle).

Coming back to the two cases of annoyance, we can see that an organisational type of causality can do justice to their differences. For they are different, these two cases, and it does matter for understanding what is going on to understand how it started. The annoyance induced by a book is different from the annoyance induced by a pill – just like the two anxieties are different in the example of Kramer's student. From the mereological perspective of the enactive view, we can still distinguish between perturbations of the system that started from physiological processes (mereologically understood) or from experiential processes (mereologically understood). Even though they both derive their properties from being part of the larger person–world system, there is an asymmetry between them in that experiential processes are more global: they necessarily include certain physiological processes, so that changes in experiential processes always include changes in some physiological processes – whereas physiological processes are more local and not all changes in physiological processes involve or 'add up' to changes in experiential processes. The influence of physiological processes on experiential processes is a *local-to-global* influence (like the amount of sugar changing the taste of the cake), whereas the influence of experiential processes on physiological ones is a *global-to-local* effect (like the effect of the temperature of the oven on the overall state of the cake, including its ingredients).

Kramer is right that the anxiety induced by medication is different from the anxiety induced by a fear of disapproval. They have a different meaning as well as different causal trajectories. But this difference cannot be understood in terms of a simple opposition of meaningless physiological processes on the one hand and meaningful experiential processes on the other hand. This is a mischaracterisation in three ways: there are not just these two hands; experiential and physiological processes are not mutually exclusive and they do not add up to all there is. Besides, they cannot be opposed because both are part of the same larger whole of a living being interacting with its world. Physiological processes are part of experiential processes and physiological processes are what they are because of their being part of an interacting, experiencing being. And, lastly, the distribution of meaningfulness is not so straightforward either. Persons interacting with their worlds form a complex, dynamical system in which physiological, experiential, and environmental processes all play their role and depend on each other, with many complex feedback loops between them. What is meaningful in this system and what isn't?

Physiological processes seem to be more independent and isolatable and as such could be easily imagined to unfold in a meaningless, machine-like fashion. After all, what could be meaningful about the growing of my nails, or the renewal of my blood cells? Some physiological processes indeed operate semi-autonomously. Yet not completely autonomously: in the end, even these semi-autonomous processes in our bodies are dependent on the body as a whole and on this body being alive and thus on this body interacting sensibly enough with its environment. As such they are part of the process of living; a process which installs meaning. How a big a role does something need to play in a meaningful whole to count as meaningful itself? Given that the meaning emerges from the system as a whole, localising and assigning it to its parts may just not be an intelligible thing to do. Besides, physiological events are often part of a larger person-in-her-world story: I am the one deciding to take certain drugs for instance, or to eat or drink certain things that will affect me, including my physiology.

Still, the asymmetry between more local and more global processes does connect to the question of meaningfulness. The more global a process, the closer it is to meaning. So if you ask me what caused my annoyance, why I am annoyed, I will refer to this annoying book and explain why it gets me so worked up. In this case, what is happening in my amygdala in the meanwhile is just a part of the 'how' of me being annoyed, part of the 'machinery' of being in this state. If you ask me for a cause and I start to talk about my amygdala, you will naturally assume there is apparently no such life-world reason, no such 'why' of the state I am in, only a 'how'. When we talk about causality the 'how' and the 'why' aspects sometimes get confounded (Gipps 2018). Especially in the setting of neuroscientific research, the 'how' story can be presented as the answer to the 'why' question as well. But typically we only refer to the 'machinery' of the how, to the unfolding of physiological processes, in answer to a 'why' question if there are no life-world causes to be given. If you ask me why I am annoyed and there is no real reason for me to be annoyed I will tell you so, and suggest that it is probably just a side effect of this pill I have taken for this other reason. In other words, when it comes to meaning, we proceed from the global to the local.

4.6.1 Back to Bieri

Summing up, this enactive view on physiological and experiential processes and their relation can do justice to the kind of differences that we are interested in in psychiatry, such as the difference between taking medication and engaging in psychotherapy, and the difference between psychological and physiological influences in the development of psychiatric disorders. It does not adopt dualism though, as it does not portray what exists as being composed of two, and only two, separate things (or aspects, or tracks, or processes, or levels, or systems) that work on each other. Both physiology and experience need to be understood as parts of larger wholes and this mereological setting prevents any causal interaction between them, if causality be understood in a linear, two-place sense. The enactive view is also not reductive. Since both physiological and experiential processes derive their characteristics from being part of the larger person–world or organism–environment system they can neither be opposed nor reduced to each other. From an enactive perspective, the traditional mind–body problem starts from a misconceived carving up of mind and world. As a result, it is trying to align the wrong things, trying to put incomparable magnitudes into one equation. Both physiology and experience first have to be converted to their common magnitude: that of a person in her world.

If we look again at the mind–body problem as presented in Bieri's (1981) trilemma, we can now see how an enactive view challenges the very conception of the problem. The trilemma is as follows:

1 Mental phenomena are not physical phenomena.
2 Mental phenomena are causally effective in the domain of physical phenomena.
3 The physical domain is causally closed.

From an enactive position, we should start by specifying that we are not interested in any old physical phenomena, but only in a specific subclass of physical phenomena, namely physiological phenomena, or, even better, physiological processes. 'Mental phenomena' is somewhat ambiguous as it could refer to cognition or sense-making in particular, but it probably refers to experiences in general. Proposition (1) then becomes: Are experiences physiological processes? From an enactive perspective this is a strange question, like: is the taste of the cake matter? It is the sort of question that gives rise to dualist bewilderment, like Chalmers' amazement that there should be experiences at all, that on top of the physical phenomena there should be something these physical phenomena feel like (the so-called qualia). The cake is made of matter, but why should it have any taste?

From an enactive perspective, such questions are the result of misunderstanding the nature of both body and mind, of matter and experience. Following the life–mind continuity thesis, experiences are an emergent feature of living beings interacting with their environments: they are the result of the specific self-organisation of living matter, depending on constant exchanges with the environment to sustain itself. Matter in specific configurations gives rise to new processes, with different properties, a different character. Are these new properties matter? Are experiences matter? Well, they do depend on matter, they emerge from this configuration of matter, without matter they would not exist. They are not something 'over and above' matter, they are not something 'extra', something 'on top of' the specific matter of living beings. But to say that experiences are 'nothing but' matter is missing the point too. For that would suggest we can reduce experiences to matter, denying their special nature. A tree consists of wood fibres, but that does not yet make it a sensible thing to ask whether the growth of a tree consists of, or is 'nothing but' its wood fibres.

Experiences are an emergent feature of the configuration of living, interacting beings, and as a feature of the whole they have different characteristics than the parts that gave rise to their occurrence. So in one sense you might say that experiences are physiological processes in that they emerge from physiological processes and are not something *over and above* physiological processes. And in another sense they are not physiological processes if this is meant in the reductionist sense that they are *nothing but* physiological processes, that all their characteristics can be discerned from the study of physiological processes. Digestion, for example, is in a sense the breaking down of starch (and fat and proteins, etc.) by means of acid. But it is also much more than that: putting starch and acid in a petri-dish does not yet amount to digestion taking place. Digestion is an organism's way of staying alive by converting elements of its environment into its own constitution. This conversion is not some magical extra ingredient to the chemical process, something over and above the chemical process: it is rather that digestion is a living being's process, and *it is this wider setting that enables the chemical processes, just as much as these chemical processes are required for the process of living to continue.* The mistaken assumption is that you can get to the core of phenomena by removing things, whereas complex phenomena typically require taking more into account: zooming out instead of zooming in.

Another mistaken assumption is that if experiential processes are different from physiological processes, if they have a different character, this difference or distinctness *implies* that they are something over and above physical processes. But this confuses difference or distinctness with separability. From an enactive view, the global whole can do things that isolated parts cannot: global processes such as experiencing and sense-making are different from local processes, they have different properties, yet they are not distinct in the sense of being *separable* from these local processes. Without the local processes, the global ones would not exist. And vice versa. The phrase 'over and above', however, suggests precisely that the global (i.e. 'the mental') has a separate existence on its own, over and above its parts (i.e. 'the physical').

Proposition (2) is about mental causation: can mental processes causally affect physiological ones? Again, from an enactive perspective the notion of mental causation is misconceived for it presupposes that there is something mental on the one hand and something physiological on the other. The tearing apart and opposing of 'the mental' and 'the physical' (or, in enactive terms, of experiential and physiological processes) also facilitates the idea that they could affect each other in linearly causal ways, as one billiard ball hitting the other. As we saw, an enactive perspective replaces this dualist opposition with a mereological conception of both experiential and physiological processes being part of the larger process of a living being interacting with its environment. Physiological processes can affect experiential processes, as local-to-global influences and experiential processes can affect physiological ones in a global-to-local way. So yes, what I experience, what I do, how I feel, how I think, shapes my physiology. Similarly, being annoyed includes certain processes taking place in my amygdala.

Or, in the longer run, how I move shapes my muscles, my posture, and my metabolism. If I continuously feel stressed, this will affect the connectivity strengths of some neuronal pathways in my brain, and it will affect the tenseness of my muscles, potentially leading to headaches or back pain. But these are not instances of 'mental causation': my experience is not working on my physiology like a mental hammer hitting a physical nail. There are not two separate processes going on, one physiological ('physical') and one experiential ('mental'). There is the one living, interacting being and we can focus on more local or more global processes that are going on in this complex system. From an enactive point of view, there is thus no point in either denying or agreeing with proposition (2); instead, the question itself needs to be rejected and the issue at stake reformulated.

It won't come as a surprise that proposition (3) likewise requires reformulation. The idea that every physical effect has a sufficient physical cause is hard to make sense of from an enactive perspective. For what does 'physical' mean here exactly? What do we buy into with talk of 'physical' causes and effects? If we translate it into a statement about physiological processes it would say that every physiological effect has a sufficient physiological cause. But again, this formulation forces us to think in a confusing, dualist manner, for it assumes that either physiological processes are all there is, or that there are some non-physiological processes. But this very depiction is mistaken.

In some sense, the statement that the physical domain is causally closed is true, namely that there are no mysterious 'other-worldly' substances or processes. But it is not true in a physicalist, reductionist, or atomistic sense. The specific configuration of the matter of living beings gives rise to all sorts of capacities, the sort of capacities that seem mysteriously different from the matter of rocks, like thinking or imagining. And the specific living beings that are persons gives rise to mysterious 'things' like social norms, rituals, or political movements. What could be further removed from the tangible physicality of the matter of a rock? Social norms are intangible and irreducible to matter in that their special nature is lost if one zooms in on what's happening at the level of molecules. Yet they are not a ghostly *addition* to matter either.

The apparent mysteriousness of our experiential capacities and sociocultural 'entities' relies on a narrow conception of what 'the physical' is or encompasses, typically taking dead matter and ever smaller parts like molecules and atoms as the exemplary tokens of the physical. If, however, we adopt a more diversified conception of 'the physical domain', one that allows for the emergence of properties of organisational wholes that are irreducible to the properties of their parts, we can see that we indeed cannot reduce 'mental' capacities to (isolated) physiological processes only, but nor do we need any extra ingredients to explain them. Besides, these physiological processes would not exist if it weren't for these experiential processes. Starting from a dichotomous topology of mind and matter, the term *physical closure* implies that the physical domain is closed off from mental phenomena working on physical phenomena. But from an enactive perspective, the physical matter of living beings depends on their capacity for sense-making – which is an emergent capacity of the specific self-organising structure of matter of living, i.e. interacting, beings. The specific arrangements of physical matter that constitutes a physiological process could not exist without, and derives its characteristics from, this larger constellation of an organism making sense of its environment for survival, and as such the physiological just as well depends on the sense-making.

The enactive perspective thus challenges the very terms in which the debate is framed. The dualism permeating the inner–outer topology leads to the bafflement of how body and mind could possibly relate, how their different natures could meet. If however, one starts from a different view on mind, body, and world such as provided by the enactive life–mind continuity thesis, these problems dissolve – as when an apparent knot turns out to be a slip knot.

4.7   EMERGENCE AND ORGANISATIONAL CAUSALITY

As we saw, the life–mind continuity thesis does not oppose a physical realm on the one hand and an experiential or mental realm on the other, but states that *it is with the emergence of life that mind emerges too.* The qualitative jump from physical aggregates to living organisms is at one and the same time a jump from physical to physiological processes and from non-experiential matter to experiencing being. In contrast to physical aggregates, living beings show that *matter in specific organisations is minded.* Applied to the mind–body problem, enactivism thus argues that 'mind' and 'body' necessarily go together, instead of assuming a fundamental dichotomy between them. Both physiological processes and sense-making derive their characteristics from being part of the system of an organism interacting with its environment. In other words: the capacity for sense-making is an *emergent feature* of a specific self-organising organisation of matter which necessarily includes exchanges of matter between this self-organised unity and its environment.

The enactive position wants to avoid both reductionism and dualism. It wants to acknowledge the special character of our experiences and sense-making without assuming that they are somehow separate or separable from our physiological processes. In order to reconcile the assumption of continuity (sameness, monism) with the possibility of fundamental differences (pluralism), enactivism appeals to *emergence.* Emergence refers to the idea that the whole is more than its parts: that differences in organisational structure can give rise to new processes or new entities. Qualitative changes may emerge from the growing complexity of the organisation of the same basic components. In this way, monism with regard to matter can be reconciled with pluralism with regard to the different processes or features that indeed result from or depend on this matter, but at the same time cannot be reduced to it.

But how should we understand emergence? Emergence can seem like a black box notion: you put in some things on the one end and then something miraculous happens and then you get something different coming out the other end. Given its importance for enactive ontology, we need a clear conception of what emergence is and what it is not. Emergence comes in different kinds and flavours, but the shared assumption is that the whole is more than its parts. The whole can have properties or characteristics that its isolated parts do not have. This can be taken as an *epistemological* issue: we are not able to predict the behaviour of emerged systems out of the laws of matter as determined by physics. This unpredictability could either be an accidental lack of knowledge or rather testify of the irreducible nature of the system and its features. But the latter amounts to *onto-logical* emergence: the idea that an emerged system or entity has features that its parts do not have. Or, in other words, that global processes can have characteristics that are different from the local processes that compose them. This is the kind of emergence that enactivism relies on.

Now there are many different conceptions of emergence. As Bedau and Humphreys (2008) write, 'emergent phenomena are frequently taken to be irreducible, to be unpredictable or unexplainable, to require novel concepts, and to be holistic' (p. 9), and different definitions focus on various of these aspects. There is discussion of what counts as an emergent phenomenon and whether they are rare or common. Examples range from chemical to evolutionary processes, from the shape of piles of sand to the behaviour of swarms, from water turning to ice to experiential processes. There is also discussion of what it is exactly that emerges: properties, entities, features, systems, patterns, or processes? There is discussion too about the status of the emerged process vis-à-vis its constituents: it both depends on them and has a certain independence. And there is discussion of whether emergence is a synchronic or diachronic phenomenon, and on how emergent wholes and constituent parts relate.

Luckily, there is no need to solve all the issues in the discussions on emergence here. For our purpose of developing an integrative account of psychiatric disorders, we are only interested in the emergence of the mind. In particular, we need a concept of emergence that lives up to the non-reductionist and non-dualist agenda of enactivism. Given that the relation between physiological and experiential processes is central to our quest, it is particularly the relation between the emerged processes and its constituents that concerns us. Two main proposals about this relation are the one-way influence of *supervenience*, and the two-way influence of *downward causation*, or circular causality.

4.7.1   *Supervenience*

Many theorists want to combine the intuitions that (1) the emergent properties are new in the sense of qualitatively different, but (2) that they are also 'nothing over and above' their parts, for if they were it seems we have again a dualism going on here. The second intuition is often formulated as *supervenience*: properties or processes supervene on the properties of the underlying or constituting 'subvenient' parts if there can be no difference in the supervenient properties without the underlying or constituting parts also changing (McLaughlin and Bennett 2014). Applied to our problem, the mind and mental processes are taken to supervene on physiological processes, so that whenever mental processes change the physiological processes on which these mental processes supervene change too.

Supervenience is thus a claim about a one-way influence: some set of properties cannot change without the other set of properties changing, but it makes no claim about possible influences the other way around. Supervenience does a good job in capturing the asymmetry that seems to exist between experiential and physiological processes, namely that changes in experiential processes necessarily include changes in physiological ones, whereas not all physiological changes necessarily lead to changes in experiences. Another advantage of supervenience is that it is clearly non-dualist: nothing more than physical (or physiological) processes are required for the emergence of experiences. On the downside: supervenience leaves all relevant questions unanswered. It does not explain anything: it does not give us any clue on *how* the subvenient processes bring forth the supervenient ones. It merely singles out a specific kind of formal relation. A formal relation that is moreover perfectly compatible with both reductionist and epiphenomenalist accounts: so long as the dependence only goes one way, the suggestion is that all the relevant action takes place at the level of the constituting processes. Applied to our subject, this means that our experiences are a causally ineffective by-product of physiological processes, like 'smoke on the fire of the brain' (Humphreys 1997a, p. 2). On an epiphenomenalist account of how supervenient and its constituent processes go together, the supervenient processes may be new, but they are impotent in any relevant sense.

Supervenience is thus not what we are looking for, as we are precisely interested in the emergence of processes or entities that are in some sense new *and irreducible* to their constituent parts.

4.7.2   *Downward Causation and Circular Causality*

A more promising candidate is a conception of emergence in terms of downward causation. The notion of 'downward causation' was introduced by Campbell (1974) to denote the causal influence from higher to lower levels, or from emerged processes to their constituent parts. Taken this way, emergence involves both 'bottom-up' and 'top-down' causation. This position has several advantages: if the emerged process is causally effective in its own right this ensures both its novelty compared to its constituent processes and its irreducibility to them. In fact, causal effectiveness of the emergent process is the most obvious way to cash out both novelty and irreducibility. If an emergent process can have effects that its constituent parts do not have, it is surely new. And this also means that the laws governing the parts fall short of describing these newly emerged effects: they need laws of their own that are not reducible to the laws governing the parts. Besides, the distinction between upward and downward causation still allows there to be an asymmetry between them.

Yet worries remain. Talk of 'the bottom' and 'the top' or 'lower' versus 'higher' levels easily invites a reifying picture of a two-way causality between 'the top' on the one hand and 'the bottom' on the other. The more we see them as different or even independent levels or processes, the easier it becomes to offer a linear reading of the causality that obtains between them. This danger is especially acute when applied to the mind–body problem, which is already so dualistically carved out. Once we conceive of the bottom and the top as two distinct or even independent things, or the lower and the higher level as two independent processes, we get uncomfortably close to traditional dualism: translating bottom-up and top-down causation into mental-to-material and material-to-mental causation respectively.

Several enactivist-minded theorists do talk of downward causation or of *circular* or *reciprocal causality* to denote global-to-local and local-to-global processes (Thompson and Varela 2001; Hanna and Thompson 2003; Fuchs 2011b, 2018).[13] Circular or reciprocal causality is meant to convey the two-way dependence of global and local processes, which is also what we are looking for. Still, these terms are not ideal either since they still invite a conception of a back-and-forth between two separate things that stand in a to-and-from causal relation. And indeed, even enactivists write things like: 'If conscious cognitive acts are emergent phenomena, then accordingly we can hypothesize that they have causal effects on local neuronal activity' (Thompson and Varela 2001, p. 421). Such statements about causal effects suggest that conscious cognitive acts are distinct from local neural activity, for if this neural activity were part of what the cognitive act *is* there could be no causality *between* the cognitive act and the neural activity. Again, this looks uncomfortably like dualism.[14]

---

[13]   Fuchs (2018) further distinguishes between the *vertical* circular causality taking place within an organism and the *horizontal* circular causality between the organism and its environment. Even though the picture of causality that Fuchs sketches is very similar to the one I am advocating here, I prefer neither to speak of circular causality nor of vertical hierarchies, for reasons I explain below.

[14]   In his later work, Thompson (2007) acknowledges the problems with the term *downward causation*. He writes that *downward* should be considered as a 'metaphor for the formal or topological influence of a whole with respect to its parts' and that it is

This shows how easy it is to slip back into divisions that follow the dichotomous moulds that one precisely wanted to overcome. To be on the safe side, we'd better steer clear of terms that allow for a dichotomous reading. Circular or reciprocal causality then seems better suited to describe the workings of thermostats and guided missiles than the emergence of the mind.

Interestingly, while we appealed to emergence as an alternative to both reductionist and dualist explanations of how the physiological and the experiential relate, they seem to creep back through the backdoor. For if emergence is explained in terms of supervenience, we all too easily end up with a reformulation of a reductionist or epiphenomenalist position. In order to avoid this reductionism, emergence in terms of downward causation argues that emergent processes are new and irreducible as is shown by their causal effects on their constituent processes. However, if we assume emerged processes exert causal influence on their parts, we seem to be tied to a dualist position again. The very impasse that emergence was supposed to overcome seems to have only shifted.

4.7.3   Emergence as Fusion and Organisational Causality

Luckily, there are more helpful ways to think about the relation between parts and whole or local and global processes. The way out of the impasse comes from (1) a re-conception of the relation between the emerged whole and its constituent parts in terms of 'fusion' instead of levels; (2) a re-conception of the causal effectiveness of the emerged process in terms of organisational causality rather than interlevel causation; and (3) a reconsideration of what the whole and the parts are that we are trying to relate.

'questionable whether this metaphor is a good one' (p. 426). Thompson refers to Searle's (2000) notion of 'system causation' to replace downward causation, and he concludes, 'from this perspective, the term *downward causation* is symptomatic of a partial recognition of system causation together with an inability to shift completely to a system-causation perspective' (p. 427). Likewise, he points out that when one adopts relational holism, 'the components could not constitute an independent lower level subject to higher-level "downward" influence, as the term *downward causation* cannot help but suggest' (p. 428). Again he concludes that 'given relational holism, downward causation seems a misnomer' (p. 428).

The relation between the emerged process and its constituent parts is often described in terms of 'higher' and 'lower' processes, properties, or levels, with the causality going top-down and bottom-up between them. This inclination is understandable in that the notion of emergence assumes that simpler parts can make up a more complex whole. This incites a picture of the simpler, basic parts being the 'underlying level', at the bottom, and the complex whole being the higher level top of that bottom. That is, we envision a vertical hierarchy of different levels, as a layered pyramid. The danger of this picture is that talk of 'top' and 'bottom' and 'higher' and 'lower' levels could suggest that we have at least two different processes going on within the organism: the processes of the underlying parts and the processes at the emerged top. But this is a mistake. The so-called higher levels *consist* of the so-called lower levels: they do not form a separate entity *over and above* their constituents. And these so-called lower levels too are what they are only as part of this specific configuration. The parts or processes prior to this configuration are thus not the same as the parts or processes after this configuration: their relational structure carves out different 'abilities' and 'inabilities' than they had before, either in isolation or as part of a different constellation.

Talk of 'high' versus 'low' levels easily induces an unwarranted reification of two ways of describing one and the same process: yes, there need to be constituent parts, but once they form a specific organisational structure, they are *part* of that structure. And the structure is the configuration of these parts, not a separate identity opposed to these parts. The parts form the structure, as much as the structure forms the parts. This has been described in various ways: as the *dynamic emergence* (Kronz and Tiehen 2002), *dynamic co-emergence* (Thompson 2007), *relational holism* (Teller 1986) or *fusion* (Humphreys 1997a) of part and whole or local and global. Thompson (2007) for instance describes it as a process of dynamic co-emergence: 'the whole not only arises from the (organisational closure of) the parts, but the parts also arise from the whole' (p. 65).

The clearest description, one that leaves no room for any dualist readings, is Humphreys' (1996, 1997a, 1997b) explanation of emergence in terms of *fusion*. Instead of assuming that the constituent parts can still be discerned and subsequently related to the emerged entity as a whole, he argues that these parts rather *become* the newly emerged entity.[15] Thus: 'when emergence occurs, the lower level property instances go out of existence in producing the higher level emergent instances' (p. 10). We can again take the baking of a cake as an example: although we started out with separate ingredients – flour, eggs, butter, sugar, yeast – we end up with a cake in which these elements can no longer be discerned.

This conception of emergence as fusion fits nicely with the way in which the emergence of organisational structures is described in dynamical systems theory. In dynamical systems theory the emerged pattern is said to 'enslave' its elements (Haken 1983; Tschacher and Haken 2007). That is: the global ordering constraints the local processes. Such constraints are at the same time restricting as well as enabling: in this configuration some behaviours are open to the system, but others are not. The global ordering, the enslavement of the local processes, entails a new behavioural repertoire. In other words: the emerged structure opens up different possibilities, and closes off others, compared to the possibilities that the parts had before, either in isolation or in a different configuration. As Thompson and Varela (2001) write, in a dynamical system 'coherent collective behaviors, called "collective variables", or "order parameters", constrain or

---

[15] Humphreys (1997a) uses a formal notation for his argument. To make his point more easily readable, I have replaced these formal notations by descriptions: 'The key feature of [the emerged entity] ... is that it is a unified whole in the sense that its causal effects cannot be correctly represented in terms of the separate causal effects of ... [the original property instances]. Moreover within the fusion [of the emerged entity] ... the original property instances ... *no longer exist as separate identities* and they do not have all of their i-level causal powers available for use at the (i+1)st level ... Hence, these i-level property instances no longer have an independent existence within the fusion. In the course of fusing they *become* the (i+1)-level property instance, rather than realizing the (i+1)-level property in the way that supervenience theorists allow the subvenient property instances to continue to exist at the same time as the supervenient property instance' (p. 10, italics mine).

prescribe the behavior of the individual components, "enslaving" them, as it were, so that they no longer have the same behavioral alternatives open to them as would be the case if they were not interdependently linked in the system' (p. 421).

Epistemologically it makes sense to discern the encompassing structure and its constitutive elements because the elements may change while leaving the overall structure intact. For example, even though no single cell may remain of me seven years from now, I am in a sense still the same person. There is, however, no need to therefore postulate the *separate* existence of an organisational structure: as long as we keep thinking in terms of dynamical processes rather than static substances we do not need to account for the relative stability of an organism by dividing the explanatory job into one stable thing and one or more changing things. Similarly, while we may want to speak of the elements before and after the emergence of a new structuring pattern for epistemic reasons, we should keep in mind that these are no longer the same. The notion of 'fusion' nicely captures this.

This conception of emergence in terms of fusion has several consequences. Following this view on the relation between parts and whole, the picture of a vertical hierarchy of levels makes little sense – let alone the assumption of there being only two levels, such as 'the physical' and 'the mental'. As Humphreys (1997a) writes:

> At the very least, one would have to consider this [assumption of a hierarchy of levels] an idealization of some kind, and we shall see that the assumption that there is a discrete hierarchy of levels is seriously misleading and probably false. It seems more likely that even if the ordering on the complexity of structures ranging from those of elementary physics to those of astrophysics and neurophysiology is discrete, the interactions between such structures will be so entangled that any separation into levels will be quite arbitrary.

(p. 5)

It would be like explaining the properties of the cake by assuming it consists of the layers of the various ingredients: a layer of flour, a layer of eggs, a layer of butter, a layer of sugar, and on top the layer of the cake itself.

It is more helpful to understand the relations between parts and whole in terms of a *horizontal hierarchy of encompassingness*: to distinguish between more local and more global (i.e. encompassing more local) processes. The local processes can have a certain degree of autonomy (like the renewal of cells) – but their behaviour is still dependent upon the whole they are part of (like the renewal of cells requires the availability of oxygen in the blood which in turn depends on the functioning of the respiratory system, which in turn depends on the functioning of the muscles, and the availability of air, etc. The interconnectedness of these processes, the feedback loops between them, and the different time scales at which they work, all defy an easy stratifying into separate levels or layers.

Emergence as fusion also calls for a reconceptualisation of the causality involved between parts and whole. Top-down and bottom-up causality and even circular causality still allow one to assume the existence of separate levels and, as a consequence, to entertain the possibility of linear causal effects on each other. The regulatory influence of the emerged whole, the enslaving or constraining of its parts, however, cannot be described in terms of linear causality. As we saw in the previous section, this type of causality between more local and more global processes is better understood as *organisational causality* (or implicational causality, or constitutional causality), or, following Aristotle (1989, Book 5, 1013a) as *formal causality*, or following Searle (2000), as *system causation*. What all these terms try to convey is that the relation between local and global processes, between parts and whole, is reciprocally influential, but without the one working on the other as if they were separate.

One of the functions of top-down causality was to ensure that the emerged process was new with respect to its parts. The causal effectiveness of the emerged process proved its novelty. This is indeed a convincing sign. But the remarkable thing is that in the debate on top-down causality this causal effectiveness of the emerged processes has been narrowly understood as the causal effectiveness of the emerged process *on* its constituent processes. The emerged whole is supposed to prove its causal effectiveness by causally working on its parts. Now this would be no problem if the causality in case is understood to be of the organisational or enslavement type. If the causality is understood in a linear way, however, this *is* a problematic idea as this would again introduce dualism in the heart of emergence. Such dualistic tendencies are easily reinforced by the assumption of levels, especially of a top and a bottom level, as it is easy to reify both of them as if they were two different things. We do not need such levels nor a causal force between them to prove the emerged process' novelty though. For that it would be enough to acknowledge that the emerged whole has different (causal) powers of its own as compared to its parts in isolation or in a different configuration.

The conception of emergence as fusion allows us to understand the process of emergence without an appeal to separate levels and without assuming a vertical hierarchy between them. A horizontal perspective better fits with the enactive view. And it also helps to appreciate that what counts as a whole and what counts as parts is a relative matter – dependent upon our specific purposes. That is, the divisions that we are interested in depend upon the kind of questions we are asking. As Searle (2002) remarks: 'there are not two (or five or seven) fundamental ontological categories, rather the act of categorization itself is always interest relative . . . We live in exactly one world and there are as many different ways of dividing it as you like' (p. 59).

In the mind–body debate this question arises too. For what is at stake is not only how parts and whole relate, or how local and global processes relate, but also what *is* the whole that structures its parts, or what *are* the global and the local processes? Which are the parts that we take into consideration? As we saw, the mind–body debate is centred around relating these two: mind and matter, mind and body, mind and brain, mental and neuronal processes. From an enactive perspective we should replace this two-place relation with a three-place one: to explain the mind and the relation between body and mind we should be looking at a different, bigger whole with more parts. We need to include our interactions with our world to understand both physiological and experiential processes. The whole of an enactive approach is thus the person interacting with her world.[16]

4.8   INTERMEDIATE RESULTS

So far, I have described the enactive framework: its historical motivation, some core ideas, and the enactive ontology that can be deduced from this. This ontology is thoroughly relational, which implies that to understand the mind, we need to understand living beings, and to understand living beings we need to understand their fundamental coupling to their environment. An enactive perspective thus involves the adoption of (1) an encompassing system's perspective on organism

---

[16] This is why enactivism is neither a form of identity theory nor a form of aspect dualism – two positions that might at first sight seem similar to enactivism. For these theories both assume that an exhaustive picture can be given by only taking physiological and experiential processes into account. From an enactive perspective, however, they rather both stand in a mereological relation to the more encompassing system of a person interacting with her world. Consequently, physiological and psychological processes are not 'two sides of the same coin' or two aspects of one process – as aspect-dualism would have it – for these are not the only sides or aspects and they are not mutually exclusive either. To stay with the metaphor: if physiological processes would be coins than experiences would be the sociocultural practice of money-use. (It is not an ideal metaphor though as it could easily invite functionalist reading: after all coins could be replaced by paper, credit card, or phone swipe – as opposed to the deep embodiment that enactivism embraces.)

Identity theory advocates a one to one mapping of psychological and physiological or even just neuronal states, relating them to each other, whereas following the enactive perspective that I am proposing here this is simply not possible: my experiences include certain physiological processes but both my experiences and the bodily processes involved depend on being an agent interacting with an environment. Mapping experiences onto neuronal states is like relating the taste of a cake with just the flour used in it: the flour is a necessary component, but so are the yeast and the sugar and the eggs, and so is the mixing of all these ingredients and their heating in the oven.

and environment or person and world as well as of (2) a developmental perspective on the dynamics of the interactional processes as they develop over time. Such a dynamical, complex systems view in turn has implications for how we understand the causality involved, which includes non-linear causal processes, feedback loops, and what we have called organisational causality.

Regarding the question of how physiological processes and experiences are related, the enactive approach argues for the continuity of life and mind. Instead of opposing material and experiential processes, the life–mind continuity thesis argues that they necessarily go together in the process of living. Given the fundamental dependency of living beings on interactions with their environment, they require some (basic) sense-making capacities in order to survive. It is thus the organisational structure of living beings, their self-maintaining structure through interacting with the environment, that gives rise to the process of experiencing. This emergence is best understood in terms of fusion.

From this enactive view the relation between physiological and experiential processes necessarily includes the living beings' relation to their environment. This view is thoroughly non-dualist in that it (1) reconfigures a two-place relation into a three-place one and (2) stresses their mereological co-dependency, and, as a consequence, (3) replaces linear causality between physiological and experiential processes with non-linear, organisational causality within the larger person–world system. At the same time, the enactive view does justice to our intuitions about the differences between physiological and experiential processes and their causal influences by distinguishing between more global and more local processes and effects. Such differences are relevant for our understanding of the different causes and different forms of treatment of psychiatric disorders. Furthermore, as enactivism presents a non-dualist outlook, it therefore does not need reductionism to solve any dualist problems. The fundamental dependency of the body on mind and world, of the mind on body and world, and of our world on body and mind rather implies that none of these dimensions can be reduced to another.

By connecting body, mind, and world it seems that an enactive perspective already integrates three of the four dimensions of psychiatric disorders. But this is not quite the case, for we are not interested in any living beings, but in human beings and their specific difficulties in making sense of themselves, the world, and others. While the enactive life–mind continuity thesis speaks of organisms and their environments, we are interested in persons and their worlds.

At this point we encounter a more general worry about the enactive perspective: can it still do justice to differences with all its emphasis on continuity? How can we combine enactivism's deep continuity of life and mind with the fundamental differences in sense-making capacities across different forms of life? In particular, an enactive approach should be able to account for the special sense-making capacities of human beings, the special, non-metabolic values that guide the lives of human beings, and the special sociocultural communities they are part of. If it cannot do that, it will be of limited use for understanding what is at stake in psychiatric problems. To achieve this we need to bring in the existential dimension.

5   The Existential Dimension and Its Role in Psychiatry

5.1   INTRODUCTION

So far we have looked at the enactive account of the relation between body and mind and saw that following the life–mind continuity thesis we need to understand both physiological and experiential processes as part of a larger system of living beings interacting with their worlds. This relational approach undercuts the dualist confusions that stem from an inner/outer mind and world. Although the enactive account is a promising basis for an integrative framework of psychiatric disorders, it does not yet suffice. And that is because the existential dimension is lacking. The existential dimension is what marks the difference between organisms and persons and between environments and (sociocultural) worlds. In this chapter, I explain what I mean by the existential dimension, explicate how it is at stake in psychiatry, and propose how it could be fitted within an enactive account.

5.2   THE EXISTENTIAL DIMENSION

All organisms stand in relation to their environments, and so do we. However, we are also able to relate to this relation. This ability to take a stance on ourselves and our situation shapes our way of being in the world. We are not only aware, but also *self-aware*, beings. It is because we are able to take such stances that we do not coincide with our biological constitution. Plessner (1928/1981) calls this our 'excentric position', in contrast to the centric position of animals that are fully absorbed by the here and now of their situation and sensations. Heidegger (1927/1978) refers to the same matter when he says that our human existence is characterised by the fact that 'in its very being this being is an issue for it' (p. 32), and that we always relate to our being. Taylor (1985) likewise describes persons as 'self-interpreting animals' – and many more examples could be given. The existential dimension refers to the space of meaning that is opened up by our stance-taking capacities, transforming our way of being in the world.

Stance-taking is not the same as reflection. Reflection is a form of stance-taking: it typically refers to deliberative and explicit instances of stance-taking. Stance-taking is broader than that: it rather refers to *reflexive* relations in general – 'reflexive' in the logical sense of relating to itself. In contrast to the wilful act of reflection, stance-taking is *unavoidable* and usually *implicit* too. It is unavoidable in that once you are able to take a stance, you cannot refrain from doing so. Once you have become conscious of yourself as being visible to others, of the fact that others can see you and have a perspective on you and can evaluate you, there is no going back to oblivion. Or, rather there are ways to temporarily forget about yourself – by being immersed in what you're doing, by using drugs or alcohol – but these moments of living with your eyes closed do not reverse the knowledge of your visibility and judgeability by others. Once you realise that what you say and do says something about you, that you express yourself, this cannot be undone. Think for instance of clothes: we cannot help but express something through what we wear – even if this expression is that I do not care about clothes. My cat's fur is not expressing anything: it can show things about her health, but she is not expressing herself; she is not expressing any choices or values or economic status.

Our excentric position, our ability to take a stance, opens up a huge space of freedom to choose. By not necessarily coinciding with ourselves and our situation we are free to do things differently – to a certain extent at least.[1] This freedom is not free-floating, just as we are not free-floating individuals: like the dove that for its flight

---

[1]   It is feminist theorists especially who have offered a justified critique of the idea that we are all free, self-choosing persons (Mackenzie and Stoljar 2000). This image neglects the fact that we are shaped in many different ways: by our bodies, our gender, our socio-economical position, our ethnicity, our sexual preferences, our religion, our education, and so on, and of course by the prejudices and practices of our specific culture. There is

depends on its body as well as the air, so do we remain specifically bodied beings in specifically configured communities. The freedom that is opened up by our ability to take a stance does not annul the ways in which we are determined by our bodies and worlds: it is rather from this specific anchoring that we can start to reflect on ourselves and our situation. Which in turn opens up the space to start doing things differently, to choose to lay down a different path in walking. And once this possibility is on the table we have to position ourselves. Or rather, we inevitably do position ourselves: even not doing any-thing has become an act, even not choosing is a choice. Sartre (1943/ 1996, p. 553) referred to the unavoidability of stance-taking with his famous assertion that we are 'condemned to be free'.

'Choosing' may sound deliberate, but often our stances are instead implicit in the way we act. Consider again the matter of clothing: on some occasions you may deliberately reflect on what you want to express and how you want to come across; when you are

no neutral starting position, which means that the scope of freedom to act is simply not the same for everybody. How freely you can move in a public space, how free you feel to express yourself, will differ depending on how well you fit in that context. Are you the only black person there, or rather the only white person? Are you familiar with the implicit codes of conduct in this particular setting? In our Western culture, your free-dom to express yourself and to move will generally be greater if you are a white, highly educated, economically prosperous, heterosexual male than if you are black, poorly educated, economically deprived, or homosexual. Our freedom to act and to move is dependent on our specific embodiment and our specific embeddedness and on how these interact. Young's (1980) classical example of 'throwing like a girl' shows how cultural gender biases impact even the very basic scope of our movements: whether we feel comfortable to take up space, stand with our legs wide open, show our strength, sweat, etc. (see also Chapter 6, Section 6.4). And this is only to look at one example and only focusing on the impact of gender, and not yet to touch on the impact of all other factors and their combinations. The enactive, embodied and embedded view fits with taking such differences and determinations seriously. How one is able to move and act and speak is a relational and developmental matter rather than a fixed capacity that all individuals are supposed to have. The freedom that comes from our excentric position is certainly not a free-floating one – yet our capacity for taking a stance does mark a qualitative shift that opens up a new scope of agency and possibilities for change. We cannot help but be determined in one way or another (we cannot help but 'have' bodies and have been born in a certain place and at a certain time), but it is our relating to these determinations and the sociocultural practices in which we enact them that opens the way for emancipation and change. As enactivists like to say, we lay down a path in walking, so if we choose to walk in different directions, different paths will emerge (See also: Ahmed 2006).

having a job interview, or going to a first date, for instance. But usually we just wear what is in our closet, cloths we have bought because we feel they fit us, because they make us feel comfortable, or powerful, or professional, or sexy. What I wear, what I eat, what I drink, how I talk to others, whom I talk to: through all of my actions I express who I am and my stance on things. As Merleau-Ponty (1942/1963) writes: 'Doubtless, clothing and houses serve to protect us from the cold; language helps in collective work ... But the act of dressing becomes the act of adornment or also of modesty and thus reveals a new attitude towards oneself and others. Only men see that they are nude. In the house that he builds for himself, man projects and realizes his preferred values' (p. 174). In other words: the functionality of our behaviour does not exhaust its meaning.

Even our basic biological needs get transformed, and acquire an existentially meaningful dimension. Eating is for instance much more than just filling your stomach with nutrients: what you choose to eat is meaningful, and with whom you eat, and how you eat. We can refrain from eating although we are hungry and there is food available, because of spiritual reasons, or estimations of the social context (it is polite to wait for the host to eat first), or because we want to lose weight. We get out of warm beds in early morning, even though we are still tired (Baumeister 1991). And we do not act on all our sexual desires either. Some people even choose to give their lives for other people, or for their ideals and convictions. The existential dimension, our stance-taking, thus permeates the way we interact with our worlds, and shapes all of our everyday practices.

Another example of how our (implicit) stances permeate our behaviour is gender conventions. As Kelly (2009) explains in one of his lectures on Heidegger 'the distinction between masculinity and femininity is ... a distinction that we are all already taking a stand on in everything that we do. In the way that we sit in a lecture, in the way we ask questions, in the way we interact with our friends, in our writing style, in the way you drink beer at a party. Everything that you do is ... a way of taking a stand on that aspect of being.' Some of our stances on gender may be explicit ('I'm not going to be all humble and apologetic!'), but most will instead be implicit. We express our stances through the way we act. That is, 'express' in the sense that Merleau-Ponty (1945/2002) uses the term: we 'reveal' our stances through our behaviour, but at the same time our stances are constituted by this behaviour. In other words: our actions are enactments of our stance-taking.

Although the existential stance induces what we could call the need for existential meaning – i.e. the need for us to make sense of our lives, to have some notion of how our lives fit in the bigger scheme of things, what living a good life amounts to, etc. – the existential dimension as I use it is much broader than the purview of these big questions. The capacity for stance-taking does imply that we can ask ourselves such questions, the kind of questions that religions and other worldviews provide answers to, and that we can engage with these 'ultimate concerns' (Tillich 1952/2000). But the transformation that results from our stance-taking is both more pervasive and implicit. I use the term *existential* in the broader, Heideggerian sense of how our way of being in the world is shaped by our ability to relate to ourselves and our situation.

5.3   THE EXISTENTIAL DIMENSION IN PSYCHIATRY

In Chapter 1 I proposed that an integrative account of psychiatric disorders should include the existential dimension as it plays a vital role in their development and persistence. So how is the existential dimension at stake in psychiatry? As mentioned in Chapter 1, our stance-taking capacities form the very *precondition* for the development of psychiatric disorders (Fuchs 2011a). Only organisms capable of stance-staking, of being self-conscious, of relating to past and future, of evaluating themselves and others, of making moral judgements, of living a good life are vulnerable to psychiatric disorders. Our excentric position implies not only the expansion of our freedom, but also the possibility of not feeling at home in the world. Because we do not coincide with our present state, because we can take a stance on ourselves and our situation, it becomes possible for us to feel estranged, to feel fundamentally disconnected from our own bodies, from other people, from the world itself. Our excentric position implies an *existential vulnerability*: the possibility of alienation and of anxieties that run deeper than fears.

Our excentric position brings along certain demands. We have to come to terms with our awareness of ourselves and our deeds, of others and how they might judge us, and of the passing of time and the reality of death. We have to find our way in life and are responsible for what we do. And we face the possibility of failing to live a good, meaningful life, the possibility that we are disappointed with ourselves and others and what we have made of what life throws at us. Even if we try our best, it may simply not be possible to reconcile the demands of our sometimes conflicting values. I want to feel free and to belong, to dare and be safe, to trust and not get hurt. I can be torn between loyalty to my family and loyalty to my partner. Or I need my job, but it is corrupting my self-worth. Or I need my job, but my children need me too. The reality we have to deal with is complicated and demanding, and may sometimes be too much to bear, causing us to disconnect, to lose touch, to retreat into a world of our own.

Besides, our stance-taking adds depth not just to the meanings we encounter in the world, but also to our sufferings. The capacity for reflection implies the emergence of guilt and shame, and with more to relate to, we have more to worry about. It is one thing to fear a current threat. It is quite another to be in a constant state of dreadful undertow, of impending disaster. It is one thing to feel out of sorts. It is quite another to feel that all has been lost, that the past is filled with shame- and guilt-provoking deeds, and that the future is just as hopelessly grim and oppressive as the present. With the eccentric position, suffering acquires a different character too. To be sure, stance-taking not only makes things worse: it can be of clear help too in enduring pain and fighting fears. For instance, knowing that *this too shall pass* is a comfort that is not available for non-reflexive beings.

The relevance of the existential dimension for psychiatric disorders has been recognised since the earliest days of psychiatry, for instance in classic phenomenological psychopathology (Janet 1903; Bleuler 1911/1950; Minkowski 1927). Later on, theorists from the existentialist tradition in psychotherapy put the existential dimension at centre stage, arguing that many, or even most, of the problems encountered in psychiatry are the result of existential concerns (Frankl 1963; Yalom 1980; May 1983; van Deurzen-Smith 1988; van Deurzen 2009). For example, in his classic book on existential psychotherapy, Yalom (1980) discerns four main existential concerns that we need to come to terms with: the knowledge of our death and the fear that this evokes, our condition of freedom and the responsibility it implies, our isolation and the difficulties in relating to oneself and others, and finally our quest for meaning. Note that the term *existential* here typically refers to our ultimate concerns specifically. To be sure, these depend on our stance-taking capacities, but stance-taking is broader than only these concerns.

Regardless of whether one accepts these ideas of the existential dimension being a precondition of psychiatric disorders or as being central to them, the existential dimension, broadly understood, is always at play in psychiatric disorders. As mentioned in Chapter 1, the existential dimension can (1) play a primary role, (2) be affected by the disorder, and/or (3) play various modulatory roles in the course of the disorder. Patients' stances towards their experiences and situation play a *primary* role when the psychiatric disorder would not exist as such without this stance. The clearest examples of such a primary role are provided by the anxiety disorders. In anxiety disorders the fear of the fear co-constitutes the very problem. It is one's fear of having a panic attack, one's fear of becoming red and awkward in social situations, one's fear of having a fatal disease that is disabling. For it is such feared risks that make patients avoid the situations in which the dreaded event might occur. This avoidance not only directly impacts patients' lives, but also prevents them from experiencing that reality may not be so dreadful as they fear. Their fears are not corrected by real life and so continue to exert their harmful influence. We can see a similar effect in patients suffering from obsessive-compulsive disorder (OCD): their fearful reaction to the unwanted thoughts and images that pop up sets in motion a negative spiral. Everyone will at some point have aggressive or sexual or blasphemous thoughts, images, or fantasies, but it makes a huge difference whether you are worried about them and fear they reveal something about who you really are, deep down, or whether you see them as *just* a thought or fantasy. Patients with OCD for instance worry that they might 'actually' be paedophiles, or that thoughts like 'I could stab my baby' are indications that they cannot trust themselves. They actively try to suppress such thoughts, but this backfires and increases their occurrence (the pink elephant paradox) (de Haan et al. 2013a). So it's not the thoughts themselves that are the problem, but rather the meaning that patients attach to them and their coping strategies that makes things worse.

Psychiatric disorders can also *affect* patients' stances to themselves and their situation. The disorder has confiscated their existential stance, so to speak. A depression, for instance, not only affects patients' present experiences, but also colours their reflections on their past and future experiences. Patients are convinced of the worthlessness of their past and the impossibility of any improvement of their situation in the future. Their relation to themselves is characterised by feeling insufficient, guilty, and worthless (Fuchs 2002; Ratcliffe 2010). Likewise, in psychotic episodes, patients are completely taken up by their delusions: they are no longer able to reflect on their views and experiences. In the early stages schizophrenic patients are often able to regard their delusional experiences in the 'as if' mode: 'it is as if my girlfriend can read my thoughts', or 'it is as if I control the traffic'. The 'as if' shows they can still take a perspective on their experiences: it feels this way, but I know that it cannot really be the case. In full delusions, this perspective is lost. Such distortions of patients' existential stances are also described as a lack of insight: when patients coincide with their disorder they lack insight into how much the disorder is affecting even their reflections. Not all psychiatric disorders affect patients' existential stance. Patients suffering from OCD, for example, do recognise the oddness of their compulsions, but the impulse to check, or count, or clean is just too strong to resist.

Lastly, patients' stances can play a *modulatory* role in a host of ways. How patients relate to their diagnosis and to their disorder, how the diagnosis and the disorder affect their views on their past and future, how patients relate to (pharmacological) treatment – all of these can have an impact on the (course of) the disorder. Let's take a look at some typical examples.

5.3.1   Relation to Diagnosis and Disorder

Being diagnosed with a psychiatric disorder can have an enormous impact on your sense of self. In fact, even before that it will often already be a huge step to decide to confide in somebody or to seek professional help. One might have experiences that are deeply upsetting and frightening or very difficult to explain. How do you even talk about something that you haven't yet grasped yourself? One might also feel ashamed about one's 'weird' experiences. For what would they think of me if I told them that I sometimes feel like Truman in the movie *The Truman Show*, the unknowing star of a real-life show, surrounded by professional actors? Or that I felt the need to check whether I really locked the door, for the twelfth time? Or what would my partner think if I told him I feel my life is meaningless and oppressive? Another factor that might hamper seeking professional help is that some people feel uncomfortable about talking to a psychologist or psychiatrist as they fear such professionals might somehow 'see through' them, or at least see things about them they are not aware of themselves. And of course there is the unattractive prospect that they might indeed determine you to be 'crazy'.

Once one has sought help and enters the process of being diagnosed a new series of difficulties is opened up. For some the diagnosis may be a relief in that it offers a helpful recognition of what they have been wrestling with, plus the relief of finding that one is not the only one who is experiencing this, that you are not so crazy in that you are not alone. Others may find the label rather alienating, and feel they have been reduced to a being-in-a-box that foregoes their individuality. In either way, the diagnosis forces one to reconsider one's self-narrative. The diagnosis might put events and experiences in the past in a new perspective. Looking back, some of one's troubles may make more sense now; puzzling experiences may fall into place. Or on the contrary, you may feel you need to reconsider old certainties; your understanding of yourself and your past might feel under attack and shaky. Being diagnosed throws a different light on one's future as well. What does it mean to be diagnosed with bipolar disorder? Can I recover from schizophrenia? Do I need to be on medication for the rest of my life? Will I be able to life a normal life, have a job, have a family?

Since psychiatric disorders affect your experiences – your thoughts, feelings, perceptions, and actions – they concern you as a person. As a consequence one has to relate to how one's psychiatric disorder is related to oneself. A broken leg is just that, but a depression is something else. What does it mean to have a psychiatric disorder? What does it say about me? Is my depression an alien force, a meaningless fault of my brain chemicals, much like the randomness of faults in cell-division of some types of cancer? Or does my depression in a sense belong to me? Maybe it fits with the fact that I am not a light-hearted, happy-go-lucky type of person; maybe it is just part of who I am that I am prone to melancholy and depression. Or is my depression a meaningful sign concerning how I live my life, a kind of warning that I should make different choices?

Having a psychiatric disorder opens up the question of what is me and what is my disorder. To what extent does the disorder define who I am? In some psychiatric disorders, or at some stages of psychiatric disorders, one can still take a stance on one's experiences; reflect on these experiences, and put them in perspective. I mentioned patients suffering from OCD or early stages of schizophrenia. But even for these patients their 'healthy' stance is erodible under the pressure of their experiences. If 'knowing that' competes with 'feeling that', the latter is typically more forceful. And for many patients there is no such relativising stance available at all. Or they may have the knowledge that it is only their depression that makes them think their suffering will never end, but as they are nevertheless unable to feel otherwise, it is hard to attach any weight to this knowledge. For bipolar patients the distinction between self and disorder is particularly difficult as well. For when am I too elated? And don't these strong emotions also make me who I am? Do I really want a pharmacological safety net to prevent the depressive episodes if this implies that *all* my emotions will be dulled and that I will probably loose my quick wit? For many patients suffering from anorexia the question of how the anorexia influences their experiences and their stances is a major issue too. Hope and colleagues (2011) conducted in-depth interviews with twenty-nine anorexia patients and the problem of what is one's real self proved to be a major concern. As one participant says: 'Am I being anorexia [sic] because I'm not having a spread [on my sandwich], or is that me being perfectly capable of making my own decision, about what I do and don't like? ... It is difficult to know' (p. 25). Where to draw this line can also be a matter of dispute between patients and their parents: 'I'll say something and my mum will turn around and say, "That's the anorexia", and I'm like "Ugh, what? That's actually me", and she'll go, "No, you know, it's anorexia". So that in that respect, I get scared sometimes because I think, "Oh my God, I don't know who's who!"' (p. 25).

It may thus be difficult to know which experiences one can trust. As Karp (2009) puts it: 'If I experience X, is it because of the illness, the medication, or is it "just me"?' One's trust in the reliability of one's experiences may be profoundly shaken. Especially if you have had psychotic experiences you have to deal with the fact that you have been betrayed by your senses. This can call into question your most basic feeling of trust. For how can you be sure that you are not delusional again? You may be sure now, but you were also sure during your psychosis. And it is not just the trust in one's perceptions and experiences that may be affected, but also one's trust in one's capacity to know the difference between me and my disorder.

How I relate to my disorder, whether I see it as alien or as part of me or something in between, may in turn affect how I feel about having this disorder: whether I am ashamed, or feel guilty, or frightened, or instead accept it. Do I detest myself for my weaknesses or do I rather accept that these specific vulnerabilities are part of who I am? Do I feel there is something deeply wrong with me, or do I feel that all people have their difficulties and vulnerabilities and that these happen to be mine? Do I feel like a freak, or do I feel that my kind of problems are shared by many others around the world? Such stances have an impact on one's situation. Feelings of fear and shame and guilt are making one's condition even lonelier. They make it harder to confide in others, and easier to retract into one's own world. Social isolation is common for many psychiatric patients and it typically makes their problems worse.

As Hacking (1995) points out: 'classifying people works on people' (p. 369). To classify people is to 'change how we can think of ourselves, to change our sense of self-worth, even how we remember our own past' (p. 369). The different behaviour may in turn motivate a change in the classification concept itself, thus generating what Hacking calls a *looping effect*. Whereas Hacking (1986, 1995) is mostly interested in how our conceptions and classifications of human behaviour change over time, I am interested more in the personal looping effect of the existential stance on one's experiences and situation. His work does make clear however, that our self-understanding always takes place in a specific sociocultural context, and that how I understand myself is to some extent mediated by the narratives that are available to me in this context. The relation of patients to their diagnoses is thus not just an individual, private matter: the kinds of narratives that are available or that get promoted by their loved ones, or their therapists, or the public opinion in general are likely to affect this relation.

5.3.2   *Relation to Treatment*

Decisions on treatment have an existential dimension too. One's self-narrative is involved: one could think: 'I am not the kind of person who goes to a therapist', or: 'I never thought I would be one of those people who take anti-depressants.' One's stance on one's disorder may affect one's preferred choice of treatment as well: if you regard your problems as a matter of neuronal chemistry, medication seems the more likely option, whereas psychotherapeutic treatment probably seems preferable when you estimate that your problems are rather of an existential nature.

Amongst the different treatment options, the decision to use psychotropic medication can be particularly difficult. As this medication is meant to change your experiences, it is not surprising that many patients hesitate to take them. There is of course the fear of potentially severe side-effects. But patients may also worry about what it *means* to rely on psychotropic drugs. Will it change one's personality? And if so, will one be able to notice that in time? Are the effects reversible? Should one continue medication for the rest of one's life once one starts taking it? This twenty-four-year-old patient with first onset schizophrenia is struggling with the question of whether she should take medication or not:

> The doctor says I should take medication. But I don't know, I'd rather not take pills. I am afraid they will change me – and that I will not even notice it. As I arrived at the clinic, I was given medication that made me very drowsy. I don't remember a lot of those first days. I am afraid that it will suppress my feelings. Perhaps I rather feel despair than have no feelings at all. Another patient also got really fat because of the medication.
>
> *(unpublished EASE interview, my translation from German)*

Some patients do try medication, but decide to quit because of the side-effects, or because they feel they are less themselves when taking medication. As this male education student puts it: 'I don't feel like the same person on drugs. I feel as though maybe I'm a better person, but it's not who I am' (Karp 2009).

Apart from concerns about the potential effects of medication on one's experiences and personality, other effects of medication may also impact one's life and identity. Many psychotropic drugs should, for example, not be combined with alcohol. For some patients this may be a minor restriction, but for others it can have a big impact: in case drinking figures prominently in one's social life for example. If you primarily meet your friends in the pub for a drink, you may feel uncomfortable to be the only one drinking soft-drinks, and don't look forward to the questions that your friends will surely ask you about it. Not drinking may make it harder to connect to your friends. But avoiding the pub will mean that you miss out on an important part of your social life. Or consider the side effect of becoming fat. Would you rather be fat or anxious? Fat or depressed? It may seem an easy question – until it concerns you. When you don't like yourself much anyway, and are not particularly confident, putting on weight does not help to improve your satisfaction about yourself. And when you're young and susceptible to peer-pressure, the thought of putting on weight can be downright horrifying.

Taking medication thus entails more than merely swallowing a pill at supper – which may explain why psychiatric patients are not always 'compliant' in using the medication their psychiatrists would like them to.

5.3.3   *Relation to Others*

As mentioned, patients' relations to their disorder and to treatment are not formed in a vacuum. What your friends, family, and health care professionals think about the disorder will likely affect you, as will the implicit norms, images, and ideas around psychiatric disorders in popular culture. These views can shape your own – even if only as something to resist. Examples of mentally ill people in movies and other popular media tend to reinforce rather than diminish common prejudices. People with psychiatric disorders are often portrayed as incomprehensible and dangerously disruptive and aggressive. Sometimes they are portrayed as brilliant (as in movies such as *A beautiful mind*, or *Rain man*), but they are still mostly weird. The typical image of psychiatric care is not much better: the movie *One flew over the cuckoo's nest* is a highlight of horror. Of course, there are more positive examples available in popular culture as well, but still the stigma of psychiatric disorders is strong. And as long as there is a negative outlook on your condition in your community, you are encouraged to feel ashamed and keep your experiences and difficulties to yourself. Research has shown that the best way to undo stigma is to familiarise people with psychiatric patients (Walker and Read 2002): if you know someone who suffers from a psychiatric disorder you will know that they are not so scary and, in fact, remarkably like yourself. The nasty catch-22 of stigma, however, is that it precisely causes patients to withhold telling others about their disorder, thus continuing their unfamiliarity. Hopefully at some point it won't be much harder to inform your boss and your colleagues that you suffer from a bipolar disorder than from a somatic disease.

On the positive side: to feel supported and understood and accepted can make a huge difference too. While social isolation can set in motion a negative spiral, social support can do the opposite. Whether online or in real life, exchanging experiences with people suffering from similar problems can be very helpful.[2]

5.3.4   The Possibility of Suicide

A final way in which the existential dimension shows up in psychiatry is that our excentric position enables the possibility of suicide – psychiatry's most common cause of death. We can ask ourselves whether

---

[2]   With the notable exception of so-called pro-ana communities and websites, where patients with anorexia encourage each other and exchange tips on how to lose weight and how to prevent others from finding out about their condition.

we find our lives worth living, and, as an ultimate consequence of our stance-taking capacities, decide that we don't. With over a million suicides a year worldwide, suicide is a common cause of death, especially amongst adolescents and adults under thirty-five (Hawton and van Heeringen 2009). It is estimated that 87 per cent of all suicides are related to psychiatric disorders (Arsenault-Lapierre et al. 2004). The high rates of suicide attest that the question of how to live one's life is not always easy to answer.

For some people the decision to end their lives is a well-deliberated consideration, for instance when they suffer from a chronic, deteriorating disease. Often, however, suicide will rather be a deed out of utter despair, out of a situation that seems to leave no other way out. It is not so much death they wish for, but an end to the wildly overwhelming experience of not being able to cope with this present life anymore. Death can seem the only solution to end one's suffering. It would be a gross distortion to depict these acts as the free choice of an autonomous agent. This twenty-three-year-old female schizophrenic patient recounts her experiences:

> I couldn't control things anymore, I was at mercy. I completely withdrew then; isolated from everything. I mostly stayed at home. I once went jogging with my mother, but I couldn't even do that anymore. It was as if the air to breathe was taken from me, so that I couldn't breathe at all. And all these strange feelings, and all these questions in my head, and I didn't know where it all came from and what I could do against it ... I had again hardly slept. At night, I cut my wrists. At that time, I couldn't find any other solution any more. I did not speak to anyone about it. I just noticed that something is happening with me, that I could no longer control, and I didn't know what it was. I just wanted that these ruminations and this desperation, that it all ended. So then I also wrote letters to my parents, that I just couldn't help it. And I believe, that was the problem, that I wanted to figure things out on my own. I spoke to no one about it, except for my mother. I couldn't handle it all. Only as

the ambulance arrived, and they bandaged me, and I was lying in the ambulance, I realized what I had done. Before I somehow saw it as the solution, that I just would not have those thoughts any longer, and this feeling, and that I would not be so miserable any longer.

(unpublished EASE interview, my translation from German)

To end one's life may seem the only act that one can still control. Accordingly, for some patients it can be a comfort to know that, be things as they may, they still have this last option, this decision that is up to them. This knowledge, having this fall-back option, may be reassuring enough so that one does not need to act on it. Needless to say, for patients' family and friends and for mental health care professionals the possibility of suicide is anything but reassuring.

5.3.5 Summing Up

The existential dimension, our stance-taking capacities and the domain of meaning they open up, plays a significant role in psychiatric problems. The most basic and fundamental reason for this is that psychiatric disorders affect persons in their very personhood (their thoughts, feelings, and actions) and that persons *are* existential, reflexive beings. Persons evaluatively relate to themselves and their situation and this affects the way in which they interact with and make sense of their world. Any disruptions in these interactions and in this sense-making thus imply this reflexive relation as well. How you relate to what happens to you and how you relate to yourself and your experiences matters for how you feel and what you do. The influence of patients' evaluative stances also comes to the fore explicitly when this stance is affected by the disorder, or contributes to the disorder, or modulates patients' choices regarding seeking help and deciding on treatment.

Given these diverse ways in which the existential stance is at stake in the development and persistence of psychiatric disorders, it is no wonder that the existential stance plays an important role in several forms of psychotherapeutic treatment. The existential stance can both be the method of change and the target of treatment. Therapies that use patients' insight into themselves and their situation as a means for change are relying on the transformative power of stance-taking. Insight occurs when one succeeds in stepping back from one's engrained reactions and sees the pattern in these reactions. Reflection reveals how one continues to enact old patterns of relating to others and or to oneself: ways of relating that were once helpful but are now obstructive. The existential stance offers a stepping stone from where one can regard the stream of one's emotions and thoughts instead of being completely immersed in them.

In various therapies patients' stances are targets of treatment too. Cognitive behavioural therapy (CBT) for instance follows a two-track approach: patients are encouraged to change both their behaviour, and their 'cognitions'. These cognitions refer to patients' more or less implicit evaluative attitudes towards themselves and their situation. Practising different ways of interacting is thus combined with challenging and adjusting patients' stances. Mindfulness therapies promote a non-judgemental recognition of the state one is in, silencing one's evaluating, judgemental stance. In acceptance and commitment therapy too, patients' stances towards themselves and their experiences is a target with a similar emphasis on acceptance instead of condemnation. In these and other therapies, the existential stance serves as an important lever for changing someone's stuck way of interacting.

5.4 DIFFICULTIES WITH THE EXISTENTIAL DIMENSION IN PSYCHIATRY

There are some difficulties with the existential dimension in psychiatry though. Or, more precisely, there is one worry and one problem with it. The worry is that by accepting the existential dimension as an intrinsic aspect of psychiatric disorders we run the risk of medicalising existential matters and concerns. After all wrestling with life's big themes shouldn't be counted a disorder, and mental health care professionals should not take on the role of vicars, priests, imams, rabbis, or other existential counsellors. But the first thing to note is that acknowledging the existential dimension of psychiatric disorders does not at all imply that struggling to come to grips with the big questions in life is a disorder. For one, the existential dimension is much broader than such questions, and also: to struggle with them is rather normal. As we will see in Chapter 7, it is only when one's sense-making gets stuck or is biased in a certain direction that we can speak of psychiatric disorders. Religious themes can be included in obsessions or delusions, but then it is the obsessive or delusional character of the preoccupation that constitutes the disorder, not these themes themselves.

The question of how to live a good life can indeed not be answered by medicine. Yet patients' relation to themselves and their situation is implied in their disorder, affected by it and affecting it. It may be precisely in the domain of meaning that is opened up by our existential stance that psychiatric problems emerge. Psychiatric problems are not like allergies, they are not random, meaningless misfits between our bodies and our worlds. It is the world of meaning that may overwhelm us and our existential needs that make us vulnerable.

But if the existential dimension is to be accepted, this brings us another problem. For how can we reconcile the existential dimension with psychiatry as a science? Psychiatry is a medical discipline and science and as such adopts a naturalistic approach. It is unclear how the meaning and values that come with the existential dimension relate to this naturalism. Naturalism is an elusive concept, that can be used in a number of ways, but at least it entails the rejection of the existence of anything supernatural. The idea is that 'all facts are natural facts ... and natural facts are facts about the natural world, facts of the sort in which the natural sciences trade' (Lenman et al. 2017). The problem is how these natural facts relate to our values. Values seem to be of a very different nature than natural facts. If we were to describe all facts about the natural world, would we thereby know anything about whether these are good or bad or valuable or valueless? According to Moore's (1903) famous argument, the question of the goodness of natural facts and properties will always remain an open question, as it will always remain sensibly disputable. If the goodness of a natural property were implied in it, it wouldn't make sense to dispute it; just as it doesn't make sense to dispute whether an unmarried man is a bachelor (Lenman et al. 2017). If Moore is correct, accounting for our values would require something more than naturalism – whatever that may be.

Psychiatric disorders have an existential dimension and psychiatry is committed to naturalism. How are we then to account for the values of the existential dimension within a naturalist approach? It seems we are faced with a dilemma: either psychiatry is scientifically sound but leaves out the existential considerations, or psychiatry does allow for existential considerations but at the cost of its scientific rigour. As we saw in Chapter 2, the first option is taken by the reductionist approach of biological psychiatry. The second option is taken by values-based psychiatry, which argues for distinguishing different realms within psychiatry. In the values-based approach values are presented as complementary to the scientifically wrought, evidence-based psychiatry. But, as I have argued in Chapter 2, both options are unsatisfying. Reductionist models leave out vital aspects, whereas a complementary dualism of facts versus values does not really answer the dilemma but rather circumvents it. Is there a way in which psychiatry can both be scientifically sound and embrace the role of values? Or, in terms of our central integration quest: how are we going to reconcile the existential dimension with the other three dimensions of psychiatric disorders?

In the previous chapter we saw that enactivism offers us an alternative outlook on the problem of reconciling body and mind. The next big challenge is to reconcile the values of the existential dimension with the naturalism of the sciences. We already saw that enactivism is committed to a non-reductionist naturalist approach. But can it account for the existential dimension? The deeper worry is that fitting the existential dimension into a naturalistic framework would require us to give up precisely those characteristics of the existential dimension that are worthwhile and relevant. In other words: isn't it inherently reductionist to try to be integrative here?

6 Enriched Enactivism
Existential Sense-Making, Values, and Sociocultural Worlds

How does this existential dimension and the space of meaning it opens up fit within the enactive picture? The same feature that made the enactive perspective on the body–mind problem so helpful is now the main source of worry: the life–mind continuity thesis. For if we stress the continuity between living and sense-making, we risk equalising or smoothing out fundamental differences between living beings and their sense-making capacities. Are trees that grow towards the light, bacteria that sense sugar, frogs that catch flies, and humans that imagine being rock stars really doing the same thing? Aren't we glossing over some important distinctions between these behaviours by calling them all 'sense-making'?

A common critique of theories of embodied cognition, including enactivism, is that they appear especially suited for explaining 'low-level' types of cognition, but fall short when it comes to explaining full-fledged human cognition such as imagining and reflecting. The idea is that there is a 'cognitive gap' (De Jaegher and Froese 2009) between what insects do and human thinking. The challenge for enactivism, as De Jaegher and Froese put it, is to show how 'an explanatory framework that accounts for basic biological processes can be systematically extended to incorporate the highest reaches of human cognition' (p. 439). Critics of enactivism would say that at least our most abstract capacities do require the kind of dichotomous, representationalist model of the mind that enactivism aims to replace. For the fact that we can think about things that are not present, or highly abstract, or that we can imagine things that we have never even encountered, can be nicely explained by such a model as the manipulations of our stored representations of the world. Clark and Toribio (1994) therefore called these 'representation-hungry problems'. But do these phenomena actually *require* representations and inner models? Or could they also be explained by an enactive account?

And it is not just human *sense-making* that appears to be special. It is also our *values*, our sense of good and bad that surpasses the realm of biological needs and opens up the moral domain. How does enactivism's commitment to naturalism fit with these values? And our *environment* too is special in that we are part of social communities with specific cultural traditions. All of these matter for understanding psychiatric disorders, and all of these are related to the existential dimension. Let us look at these three aspects in turn.

6.2   EXISTENTIAL SENSE-MAKING

The sense-making of organisms varies with their specific bodies, their specific sense-organs and specific needs, and their specific environments they need to make sense of. This makes their sense-making activities hard to compare: the echolocation of bats is so different from the mineral-detection of beeches that the question which of them is 'smarter' does not seem quite apt. We could maybe distinguish between degrees of complexity of sense-making; it seems likely for instance that social animals would require more complex types of sense-making than non-social animals or plants. But then again, one could also argue that these types of sense-making are just *different*, rather than hierarchically scaleable. With the existential stance, however, a new form of sense-making emerges that *is* different as it is different in structure rather than kind. This existential sense-making is a *reflexive* form of sense-making: a sense-making that can turn to itself. An extra loop is added, so to speak. But this loop, this capacity to relate to and take a stance on oneself and others, on one's world and one's interactions with it, changes everything. So existential sense-making does not form an add-on to non-existential or basic sense-making as the icing of a cake: rather the whole system is transformed.

For the sake of clarity I will call this the person–world system instead of the organism–environment system (although, as I mentioned before, it is an empirical matter whether human persons are the only existential beings).

Basic sense-making is direct sense-making, immersed in the present environment. It involves discerning the relevant aspects of the here and now; recognising food, mates, danger, etc., and acting on them. Basic sense-making refers to the direct interaction of organisms with their environments. When sense-making is reflexive, however, the immediacy of this basic sense-making is interrupted. And not just when we actively take a metaphorical step back and deliberately reflect on things, but even when we *are* immersed in what we are presently doing our sense-making is still different. As noted in Chapter 3, we can distinguish three forms of sense-making: (1) basic sense-making; (2) explicit existential sense-making or reflection; and (3) 'existentialised' sense-making as the general sense-making of persons as transformed by (2). Explicit existential sense-making (2) refers to those instances of sense-making when we reflect on something, when we pause and consider our stances, when we deliberately relate to what happens to us and to our own actions. We can ask ourselves, for example, why we are prone to react in certain ways: what makes me lose my temper, why do I so often feel hurt or angry or scared? We can reflect on how we have behaved towards others, evaluating our actions and reactions. We can ask ourselves whether this is really the place we want to be, whether we would not rather work in a different job, live in a different place of the world, whether our present environment fits us. Or when it comes to psychiatric disorders, we can consider how we feel about the diagnosis we have been given, or what our stance on taking psychotropic medication is.

But even if we do not explicitly reflect, our existential stance still permeates our sense-making: transforming also our unreflective, spontaneous, and direct sense-making. For our perception of the world is shaped by our stance-taking capacities and the sociocultural practices and language skills that co-constitute each other. It is a *world* we walk around in, dense with meanings in a way mere environments are not. As I walk through the city, I don't just see people, I see business men and women, students, hipsters, rich people, poor people, I see well-dressed people and awfully dressed people, I see cool people and wannabes, and all of that without even thinking about it. I can find a landscape to be beautiful or ominous or melancholic. It matters whether I hear noise as the result of hard-working people cleaning up garbage, or whether I hear drunken neighbours yelling at each other: the decibels may be the same but my experience is not. Likewise, different tastes and types of food are meaningful to me in ways that have nothing to do with their nutritional value. Food can be comforting, it can remind us of past times, it signals our moral values (e.g. whether or not you eat meat or any animal products, whether or not you eat organic products), it can have a certain socioeconomical status, I can feel ashamed about eating certain foods or instead feel pleased with myself. All these experiences, all the meanings they embody, are dependent upon our existential stance.

Becoming practiced in stance-taking is like doing a bird watching or a wine tasting course: afterwards you do not just see 'a bird' but you see a blue tit, or a goldfinch if you're lucky. Similarly, after your wine tasting course you may be able to perceive hints of fruits or nuts or other things in your wine, which possibility had previously seemed a bit far-fetched. And once you've learned them, you cannot unlearn them. The same goes for the influence of the existential stance: once you are able to reflexively relate to things, you have entered a world of meaning from which you cannot escape. Not only are you surrounded by meaning, but you also emanate it yourself. You cannot escape expressing something by what you wear, what you eat, what you drink, and whom you have sex with. Whether we like it or not, our choices are tied to our personal identities. All our sense-making has become existentialised.

One way of becoming aware of the abundance of such existential meanings and our immediate discrimination of them is when you visit a foreign culture. Suddenly you are not able to read all those signs so easily, or are simply confronted with different expressions of gender, of economical status, of sub-cultures. If I, a Dutch person, would visit Japan for instance, I am sure I would miss many of the meanings of what is going on around me, especially when it comes to social interactions. My sense-making skills have been sensitised in a different sociocultural world.

A fundamental difference between the worlds of existential beings and the environments of non-existential beings is morality. We will get to role of existential values later, but for now it is important to acknowledge that existentialised sense-making is morally sensitive sense-making. As a person, an existential being, you can be thoughtless, you can be cruel, you can be mean – in contrast to babies or to animals who just follow their instincts. As a person, you can be called out regarding your responsibility. Perhaps you had not realised that you were being thoughtless; even so, you can be blamed for that: you *should* have realised that, for example, your irresponsible behaviour puts others into danger. This moral dimension makes us move through the world differently. We can be called out on and we can call out others. We see much of our world in moral tones: we witness admirable deeds, kind deeds, foul deeds, hypocrite deeds. And even if we decide not to let ourselves be directed by the norms of our sociocultural communities this still implies a relation to these norms, and the replacement of these norms by others. With the capacity for stance-taking our worlds are different and our sense-making is different.

6.2.1   Gradual Differences yet a Qualitative Shift

The existential stance presents a qualitative shift in sense-making. Yet becoming an existential being is a gradual process. The capacity for stance-taking does not emerge full-fledged overnight; it is not even one skill, but rather a family of skills, and each of these requires practice.[1] From a very early age, infants practice perspective-taking

---

[1]   As mentioned in Chapter 3, I do not want to claim that only human beings are capable of stance-taking; I only want to point out that once living beings are capable of stance-

mostly in and through their interactions with others; for instance through games such as peek-a-boo and, later on, hide-and-seek they find out when do you see me and when don't you see me and when can I see you and when can't I see you. In triadic interactions between the infant and two caregivers too they develop an awareness of the perspective that others may have on them and their interactions: as when the infant plays with one of the caregivers and sees the other caregiver watching the two of them (Fuchs 2012). Children are also explicitly encouraged to put themselves in the position of others, hence: 'how would *you* feel if she did that to *your* toy?' or 'do you think the cat likes it if you do that?' Or they are taught to reflect on their own behaviour, as in: 'now you go to your room and think about what you have just done'. Not all such lessons are explicit though: children learn a lot about when to feel pride or shame for something they have done simply through the reactions of the people around them. Through all these kinds of interactions, children develop and fine-tune their sensitivity to different perspectives, their capacity to reflect, and to take a stance on themselves and the world around them.[2]

taking, they are markedly different in terms of their concerns, their sense-making, and their relation to their environment compared to living beings that do not have these capacities. It is an empirical question to what extent other animals have such capacities. Besides, stance-taking is not an all or nothing capacity: it is rather a set of abilities that can be more or less developed. Some of these abilities, such as self-recognition (in the so-called mirror test; Gallup 1977), empathy (Preston and De Waal 2002), and altruistic behaviour and social insight (De Waal 1990) have been argued to be present in several other species. Yet these differences in degree can become a difference in kind: at a certain point the way of being in the world of existential, reflexive beings is qualitatively different from that of non-reflexive beings. A mark of full-blown existential beings may be that existential values can override metabolic ones. Furthermore, as stance-taking has to be learned, human beings are not existential beings from the moment they are born: they have to develop and acquire these skills before they are proper existential beings, or persons. Since I am only interested in human beings and their problems of sense-making, I use *persons* as short-hand for existential beings.

[2]   How exactly we develop these capacities is an interesting and relevant matter that I won't address here. I merely want to suggest that it is in and through interactions with others that infants and children practice their perspective-taking, culminating in full self-consciousness, reflective abilities, empathy, and morality (Hobson 2002; Reddy 2008; De Jaegher et al. 2010; de Haan et al. 2011; Di Paolo and De Jaegher 2012; Fuchs 2012). And of course, the use of language plays an important mediating role here (Di Paolo et al. 2018).

There is no clear cut-off point when someone has become an existential being. We do, however, have a sense of when it is appropriate to hold someone accountable for their behaviour and for which part of their behaviour. You can't blame an infant for making noise during a funeral, but you can be cross at an eight-year-old for not behaving. We have different expectations of three-year-olds than of eight-year-olds or fifteen-year-olds with regard to their reflexive capacities to, say, take into account other people's feelings. Similarly, there are cases of severe illnesses, such as when people suffer from dementia or psychotic delusions, when we do not blame them for their behaviour, because 'they do not know what they are doing', as we put it. Despite the lack of a binary boundary, these gradual, developmental differences in stance-taking skills do at some point imply a structural, qualitative shift of the system. A shift from direct sense-makers to reflexive sense-makers, who live in sociocultural worlds that are saturated with (existential) meaning and values.

6.2.2   Coming Back to the Cognitive Gap

Coming back to the critique of the cognitive gap in enactivism, I do agree that enactivism needs to allow for qualitative differences amidst the continuity of life and mind. In particular, it needs to acknowledge that there is a breach in this continuity in the sense that the capacity to take a stance, to reflect, to reflexively relate to yourself, your world, and your interactions transforms the organism's way of being in the world and transforms basic sense-making into existential and existentialised sense-making. So yes, such sense-making as is done by human persons is indeed special compared to basic sense-making. The capacity to reflexively relate (and the social structures that enable this capacity) give rise to novel kinds of behaviour, such as promising, giving reasons, imagining, and fantasising. In contrast to enactivism's critics though, I see no reason why this qualitative shift in capacities and one's relation to one's environment should also require a shift to a dichotomous, representationalist model of the mind.

The so-called representation-hungry phenomena refer to cases of thinking about things that are not present, such as when we remember or imagine something, or when we think about something abstract like 'justice'. What kind of mind can do that? How should this mind be organised? The idea is that, since in such cases the object of our thought is not present in our immediate surroundings, we need some sort of internal stand in for this object: a mental representation of it. From our previous interactions with the world, we have developed an inner model of it, and now our mental representations of things can be summoned up in our mind, even when the things they represent are themselves absent. Enactivism, on the other hand, stresses that we respond to and engage with our environment rather than manipulate representations of it within our minds. This enactive account of cognition, perception, and action may work well in most cases, but how about these seemingly representation-hungry ones?

This challenge has been addressed in a variety of ways by theorists who endorse an embodied, enactive, and/or ecological approach to cognition (Ramsey 2007; Chemero 2009; De Jaegher and Froese 2009; De Bruin and Kästner 2012; Hutto and Myin 2013, 2017; Kiverstein and Rietveld 2018). I won't go into this debate in any detail here, let alone the even larger debate on representations in general, but I just want to highlight one reply that dismantles a fundamental assumption of this critique of enactivism and its threat to enactive continuity. In their paper 'Representation-Hunger Reconsidered', Degenaar and Myin (2014) point out that advocates of a representational model of 'higher' cognition assume that 'cognitive domains which involve 'the absent' or 'the abstract' necessitate representations *because* they involve the absent and the abstract' (p. 3641). They argue that this is a mistake. The fact that something is absent or abstract does not in itself imply the need for a switch in how this works 'in the mind', so to say. In both cases, there is reason to believe that we are actually 'going through the same motions' (p. 3642) as when we are engaged with concrete, present objects in our environment – at least partially (cf. Thomas 2018). To appreciate the logic of this continuity they offer the example of a sideboard in the kitchen that you are used to walking around. At some point the sideboard is removed. In the beginning, however, you still move as though the sideboard was still there: you are going through the same motions even though they are no longer necessary. According to the advocates of a representationalist switch, the mere removal of the sideboard would imply a shift in what's happening 'in your mind' in this situation: the whole procedure has to be different. Yet this seems unlikely, especially since you are doing the same thing as you have been doing for years when the sideboard was still present. Or suppose the sideboard was removed without you knowing it and you walk through the kitchen at night and you don't even notice it has gone. Again, it seems highly unlikely that something has altered: your behaviour is after all the same and so the capacities you use for this behaviour will surely be the same too. Degenaar and Myin thus point out that the 'presence or absence of the environmental stimulus does not have to bring about a fundamental change in the nature of the behaviour, or the capacity displayed in it, and therefore seems not sufficient to render it representational' (p. 3643).

Now an absent sideboard is obviously a different matter than is considered by the standard examples like imagining, remembering, or abstract thinking. But here too, they argue, there is no reason to assume a radical shift rather than a continuity of capacities used. From an enactive perspective we can understand imagining or remembering as the partial *re-enactment* of 'the perceptual acts that would be carried out if one were actually perceiving' (Thomas 2018, section 4.5.1) that which is imagined or remembered.[3] It has for instance been shown that if we hold a certain image in mind, we 'spontaneously and unconsciously make saccadic eye movements that (at least partially) enact the stimulus-specific pattern of such movements that they would make if actually looking at the equivalent visual stimulus' (section 4.5.1). Moreover, if these movements are disrupted, the mental imagery is disrupted too. This has been suggested to

---

[3]   See Thomas (2018) for an overview of the empirical evidence for this view.

explain the effectiveness of EMDR (eye movement desensitisation and reprocessing) therapy for the treatment of post-traumatic stress disorder (Thomas 2018). In EMDR therapy patients are invited to make certain eye movements while recounting their traumatic experiences. In this way, these memories become less poignant and unsettling.

Like in the sideboard example, the idea is that when we perceive virtually we go through (some of the) same moves as when we actually perceive. It is not completely the same – perceiving and imagining are after all different experiences – but there is no need to assume that all of a sudden there are radically different processes going on. Or, as Kiverstein and Rietveld (2018) nicely summarise Degenaar and Myin's (2014) argument: 're-enactments of non-representational processes do not become internal representations just by virtue of being re-enactments' (p. 12). Likewise, instead of simply assuming that thinking about abstract properties requires the manipulation of internal representations, this is something that should be argued for. Degenaar and Myin argue that if simple cases do not require a representational explanation there is no reason to assume that complex cases would require them. I would like to add that dealing with and making sense of an ambiguous environment that is typically open for multiple assessments can already be quite complex. Abstractions – putting together situations or objects that physically do not have much in common – can be understood as a variety of complex sense-making.

From an enactive perspective (and in contrast to functionalist accounts such as extended mind theories, see Chapter 3, footnote 1, and Chapter 4, footnote 9), 'representations' provide a dangerous metaphor because they imply the possibility of separating the represented from its presentation; the 'content' from its 'vehicle', or 'information' from its 'carrier'. Central to enactivism, however, is the commitment to the inseparability of form and matter (cf. Oyama 1985/2000). Thinking form and matter together may be complicated and require some practice, but tearing them apart raises a whole series of problems of its own. As with any dichotomy, mental representations also implicate a bridging difficulty which comes out as soon as one tries to specify how they work; how do the content and the vehicle get coupled and de-coupled and 'read'? We might at first sight be compelled by the idea of a kind of mental filing cabinet that allows us to pull a representation of anything absent out of its drawers. But the closer you look, the less attractive it becomes.[4] For where are these internal images stored and how does 'the mind' know how to access them and where to find them, and how does it get decided what does and what doesn't get stored, and who does this deciding? It may also help break the representationalist spell if you try to specify how this would work in the case of sounds rather than visual perception and imagery. Do we also have inner recording of sounds and how would that work? Where does the one sound end and the other begin?

Of course advocates of representationalist models can in turn take a number of routes to address these problems. They can for instance opt for a run-down version of mental representations, or claim that all is happening at a hidden, sub-personal level. In the end, if one really wants to, one can always hold on to a representationalist model in one way or another. The question is only whether 'representation' does not at some point become an empty notion, and if holding on to it has become an unfalsifiable matter of faith instead of a scientific hypothesis. As I said, this is a huge debate and I won't be able to do it justice here. What matters for our aim of developing an integrative account of how the diverse aspects of psychiatric disorders relate is that an enactive approach allows for both *discontinuity* in the structure of sense-making and the different capacities this enables as well as for *continuity* when it comes to understanding how these capacities are organised; in how mind, world, and body relate. Sense-making capacities are an emergent feature of organisms interacting with their environments. Likewise, existential sense-making capacities too develop from our

4   See also Heil (1981).

interactions with our complex social environments, including our specific language skills and other sociocultural practices that foster them. Our reflective capacities, remarkable and game-changing though they are, remain very much embodied and embedded capacities. We do not need a different model of the mind to explain them. In this sense there is still continuity, for these novel capacities do not require anything to be added to the enactive account: no inner models or representations. What we are witnessing in human beings, in persons, is not so much a cognitive gap, but rather an existential transformation: the emergence of a different *structure of behaviour* (Merleau-Ponty 1942/1963), or *form of life* (Wittgenstein 1958). We will come back to this idea at the end of this chapter.

6.3   VALUES

The existential dimension brings along values. And as this dimension is part of psychiatric disorders, values are also at play in psychiatric disorders. But how can we do justice to values within the naturalist frame of science within which mental health care operates? The worry is that if we do incorporate values into a naturalist frame, we might have to give up precisely their special character as somehow transcending our biological concerns. Could an enactive account incorporate values while remaining true to both its commitment to naturalism and to non-reductionism?

Now what is it exactly that needs to be incorporated? With (existential) values, I refer to what motivates certain actions: actions that are not motivated by the drive to stay alive, but that rather have to do with living a good, meaningful, or dignified life. Examples of values are friendship, dignity, honour, justice, solidarity, honesty, and the like. Most of the time such values are at work implicitly: I live a certain life, make certain choices that are natural to me and these choices reveal what matters to me. I usually don't think about these choices: of course I pick up the phone if I see a friend is calling whose mother is ill. Of course I show up at the meeting that I should attend. Of course I will go to my nephew's birthday. These are all things I do not think about twice or even once.[5] Sometimes, though, our values will be at stake explicitly: you can for instance deliberate about a certain course of action if you want to be the kind of person who does that. When your values conflict they can become explicit too: what is more important to me: being a good friend or being just? Being honest or protecting my own or someone else's dignity? What do I consider a good enough excuse not to keep a promise? What if in my view good care and respecting a patient's autonomy contradict? Whether we think about our actions or not, we enact what we value. Our actions reflect certain ways of living that matter to us, and values are shorthand concepts to refer to these. Note however that behaviours and values cannot simply be mapped one to one onto each other: if kindness for instance is an important value to me, this means that I will try to be kind in many, very different, situations. In each of these situations 'being kind' may consist of different behaviours: it may be kind to ask someone how they feel, but in another situation, it may be kind precisely not to ask that question. On the other hand, similar patterns of behaviour can be motivated by different values too. For example, from the fact that someone eats healthy food and does sports regularly, one may infer that her health is valuable to her. But it may also be that it is not her health, but her physical appearance that motivates her behaviour.

In the following, I will discuss three main perspectives on values: an evolutionary-functionalist, an objectivist, and a subjectivist approach. Each has their own advantages and drawbacks. The enactive, relational view on the relation between body, mind, and world allows for a different perspective on values, one that captures the core concerns that motivate the other views, and manages to reconcile them. The key is to understand values as *relational realities*.

---

5 As the philosopher Bernard Williams (1981) pointed out, if a man were to consider whether he should save the life of his wife or that of the stranger when both have fallen off a boat, he would be having 'one thought too many'. Commenting on this example, Frankfurt (2004) writes, 'It seems to me that the strictly correct number of thoughts for this man is zero' (p. 36).

6.3.1 Evolutionary/Functionalist Accounts of Values

A common route to naturalise values is to provide an evolutionary explanation for them: even though our values may *seem* to transcend our biological needs and constitution, from a broader, evolutionary perspective they can be interpreted as being useful after all. In general, values can be explained as the requirements to avoid social death, which will likely have detrimental effects on survival and procreation for individuals of a species that is as social as ours. Our values reflect the (implicit) rules of the social groups we are part of. They are thus closely tied to social norms for good conduct. Of all the examples of values mentioned above – friendship, dignity, honour, justice, solidarity, honesty – we can easily see how they are helpful in building solid social structures, by being dependable, brave, and unselfish members of a social group. Even in cases in which our existential values override our physiological needs and possibly even motivate us to sacrifice our lives, evolutionary approaches can still point to their biological usefulness as a means for attaining social status and safeguarding social structures which is profitable for the individual and/or the species as a whole. Values are thus always functional from this perspective.

This view has several clear advantages. For one, it explains values in a naturalist way. But it can also account for both the universality of some values and for their cultural diversity. That some values seem to be universally held can be explained by the fact that we share some core biological needs and that there are some norms that are central to the healthy functioning of *any* group (e.g. not to harm the other individuals in your group, the formation of social ties, and certain taboos, like incest). But there are also more peripheral norms (e.g. which social ties are acceptable, how families are organised, how social status is achieved), since there are several ways to organise groups, like there are different forms of government. The cultural diversity of values reflects this bandwidth of varieties of social organisation. And maybe some differences between social groups even strengthens their social cohesion within the group. In line with this, an evolutionary-functionalist perspective can explain values' relative stability over time too, while also allowing for some dynamics. After all, the universal values will be the most stable ones, whereas the groups' norms with regard to more peripheral issues may shift over time. Furthermore, an evolutionary perspective can back up the intuition that what we value is not a matter of arbitrary subjective flings: something is at stake – even if it's not necessarily what we believe to be at stake.

This brings us to a tricky point: how about the intuition that there is something intrinsically valuable in what we value, that they are ends in themselves rather than means for achieving something else? We feel that we value friendship for its own sake, not as a means to secure our friends' care or protection in case we might be in need. We feel that it is valuable in itself to be an honourable person; not because it enables you to fulfil a certain social role. An evolutionary perspective is at odds with this intuition: the instrumental character of values is precisely its core commitment. It could, however, *explain* this intuition as itself being *useful*. If we believe that we care about our friends for who they are and that we care about being a good friend to them, we will be more likely to sustain a beneficial relationship with them. If we feel our children are loveable, this increases our motivation to take good care of them.

Even though an evolutionary perspective can thus explain our experiences, it basically does so by explaining them away. This is not quite satisfactory. It does not take our experiences seriously. The one-sidedness of its instrumental take does not capture the depth of our experiences: surely love plays a role in procreation and social behaviour, but that is not the whole story: it does not do justice to the complexities of our experiences. An evolutionary view on values flattens our existence. It is however notoriously difficult to falsify, as with any view that disregards the validity of one's own experiences: you may think what is going on is X, but what is *actually* going on is Y. How can you argue against that? How can you prove that your experiences are not illusions? (Note that there is a fundamental problem with such experience-undermining accounts though: for what do they base their superior insights on? At some point, one needs a ground in one's experiences – for where else do we have to start from?).

Another, more internal problem is the common assumption that the mere existence of a certain property proves that it therefore must be functional, that it has survived the evolutionary struggle and so must have some evolutionary advantages. This assumption is too strong, however: from an evolutionary perspective it only follows that it has not been so severely dysfunctional that it was ruled out. In fact, we don't even have a guarantee that it will not in the future turn out to finish off the species after all.

In the end virtually anything can be naturalistically whitewashed by an appeal to 'evolution', but it is questionable whether this increases our insights into the phenomena at stake. If we accept that the capacity for stance-taking opens up an existential dimension to our lives, this precisely challenges the idea that the drive to survive determines the whole of our existence. What we set out to do, integrating this existential dimension within a naturalist approach, is thus not achieved by an evolutionary take on values. For what we get from an evolutionary perspective are not the existential kind of values that we are after, but rather basic, metabolic values or 'valences' in disguise. (I spell out this difference below, in Section 6.3.4.)

6.3.2 Objectivist Accounts of Values

In contrast to evolutionary-functionalist approaches, objectivist accounts of values stress that what we value is *intrinsically* good. The value of dignity, justice, friendship, and the like does not depend on it being good for something: it is valuable in itself. This means that their value is also independent of our reactions to them: we do not project their worth onto them; we can rather *recognise* their goodness and respond accordingly. An important exponent of an objectivist account of values is Charles Taylor (1985, 2000a, 2000b, 2003). He argues against evolutionary approaches of values as they can only address the basic, life-related values (that he calls 'L-values' and I call 'valences' or 'basic values'), but not our own (existential) values which are of 'an incommensurably higher range' (Taylor 2000b, p. 245). He writes:

> Whatever the worth of this some sort of genetic account, it plainly fails to capture what we mean by virtue. If we track our sense of the incommensurably higher through our responses of admiration and its opposite, we can see that whatever the ultimate links with survival and group flourishing, the admirable is never simply defined in terms of them, and sometimes even runs athwart them ... That admiration and its opposites are such an ineradicable part of the human life form testifies to the centrality of values which are seen as essentially higher, more worthy.
>
> *(p. 246)*

According to Taylor, this problem arises for all naturalist accounts of values. He assumes that naturalism implies a split between facts and values and is therefore necessarily reductionist (Taylor 2000b). Naturalist accounts of values will thus never be able to capture their special nature. This 'incommensurably higher' status of what we value refers to our experience that what we value is not simply more desirable than other desires and choices: they are not even on the same scale. What we value 'stand[s] independent of our own desires, inclinations, or choices' and rather 'represent[s] standards by which these desires and choices are judged' (Taylor 2000a, p. 20).[6]

The main advantage of an objectivist account is that it accounts for the intuition that what we value has intrinsic worth. It can also explain why at least some values seem to be universally

---

[6] Taylor (2000a) writes: 'I have tried to express what all these distinctions have in common by the term "incomparable". In each of these cases, the sense is that there are ends or goods which are worthy or desirable in a way that cannot be measured on the same scale as our ordinary ends, goods, desirabilia. They are not just more desirable, the same sense though to a greater degree, than some of these ordinary goods are. Because of

shared: we all recognise their inherent goodness. It is, however, less well equipped to explain the plurality and cultural diversity of values. For if we value what we do because of its intrinsic goodness, it is not just valuable to me, but to everybody. In Taylor's (2000a) terms: the special status of values command everybody. But how then are we to account for the personal and cultural diversity of values that we also see?[7] Does an objectivist approach imply that some people get it right and others get it wrong? Typically, proponents of objectivism are willing to bite this bullet. It may even be seen as an advantage as it saves us from moral relativism which assumes that disputing about matters of value is as senseless as disputing about matters of taste. Objectivist accounts on the contrary imply that we can argue about what is valuable and that we can be mistaken and that we can develop and improve our recognition of what is valuable. The difficulty of this position however concerns how we could know whether a change in our values is an improvement or actually a deterioration. From which standpoint could we determine that?

When we look at Taylor's account we can see a tension between on the one hand his acknowledgement that it is with us, humans (or: existential beings) that values come into the world, while their goodness is on the other hand independent of our recognition of or our reaction to them. Values are dependent upon us in the sense that they would not exist if there were no people in the world (Taylor 2000b). Yet their goodness is an inherent property of what we value, not something that we project onto it. In this way Taylor indeed manages to safeguard values from both functionalist and subjectivist reductions. But the price to pay is rather high: the more objective, the more independent of our recognition the special status of values is,

---

their special status they command our awe, respect, or admiration. And this is where incomparability connects up with what I have been calling "strong evaluation": the fact that these ends or goods stand independent of our own desires, inclinations, or choices, that they represent standards by which these desires and choices are judged'.

[7]   Cf. Anderson (1996), who concludes that 'Taylor is poorly placed to conceive the distinction between what is good for me and what is good per se in terms of the permissible and the obligatory' (p. 27).

the more this account presupposes a 'view from nowhere' (Nagel 1989) on the true worth of what we value.

This is a problem not just for Taylor, but for any objectivist account of values: if the worth of what we value cannot be derived from their instrumental value, nor from our subjective reaction to them, then all that seems to be left is this view from nowhere: an essentially supernatural standpoint. This is indeed what we find in Taylor. Where evolutionary-functionalist approaches appear to incorporate existential values but actually reduce them to valences or basic values, objectivist accounts do safeguard values' special nature, but precisely by supernaturalising them. Neither of them thus succeeds in integrating values within a non-reductionist naturalist approach. Now it might be that Taylor is right and that the attempt to naturalise values will necessarily lead to their reduction, but let's not give up yet.

6.3.3   Subjectivist Accounts of Values

A third main approach to values is provided by subjectivist accounts. In contrast to objectivist accounts they stress the role we ourselves play in what we value. What we value is not necessarily shared by everyone; it can be a highly personal matter. Subjectivist approaches typically involve some notion of projection: what we value lies not in its supposedly intrinsic worth; we rather impose the worth onto it. In other words: it is all in the eye of the beholder. An example of a sophisticated subjectivist account can be found in the work of Harry Frankfurt (1988, 2002, 2004). He argues that our valuing something or, in his terms, our caring about something, is not a response to its inherent worth. It is rather the other way around: we deem something good because we value it: 'It is not necessarily as a *result* of recognising their value and of being captivated by it that we love things. Rather, what we love necessarily *acquires* value for us *because* we love it' (Frankfurt 2004, pp. 38–9, italics original). His paradigm example is parental love. It is not the inherent worth or characteristics of my children that make them valuable to me, but it is rather my love for them that makes them valuable: because I love them they are precious to me.[8] What we value is thus the result of what we, as a matter of fact, love. The basis for this 'force of love' lies in our biological make-up combined with more individual grounds: 'What we love is shaped by the universal exigencies of human life, together with those other needs and interests that derive more particularly from the features of individual character and experience' (Frankfurt 2004, p. 47).

Even though what we value is a personal matter, this does not make these values any less compelling; it is just that they are absolutely compelling *for me*, rather than for everyone – as objectivist accounts would have it. Like Taylor, Frankfurt also regards what we value to be 'commanding', calling them the 'commands of love' (Frankfurt 2004, p. 29). Their commanding character is in fact essential for Frankfurt's account: it is because we find we cannot choose what we care about that our values provide us with the boundaries we need in order to function as persons. In particular we need commanding values in order to be able to make decisions. For if we could choose what we value, we would end up in an infinite regress of giving criteria or reasons for our choices.[9] What we value need not be intrinsically worthwhile: they rather need to be *personal necessities*.

---

8   Frankfurt (2004) writes: 'The particular value that I attribute to my children is not inherent in them but depends upon my love for them. The reason that they are so precious to me is simply because I love them so much' (p. 40). Compare this to Taylor (1985), who gives the example of stating that someone is loveable: according to Taylor, this means that there is something more to this person than just that many people in fact love that person, it is rather an independent characteristic of the person. 'We are not just stating in other terms that we experience a certain feeling in this situation. That is, it could not be a sufficient condition of our ascribing what I am calling an import to a given situation that we experience a certain feeling or desire in it or relative to it' (p. 49).

9   Frankfurt's account is in fact a little bit more complicated: he wants these necessities to be both imposed *and* also self-imposed. The first requirement logically follows from their function: necessities need to be imposed, because otherwise they wouldn't be necessities and they would not put an end to an infinite regress of choosing. However, Frankfurt at the same time wants necessities to be self-imposed, because of his theory of autonomy. On Frankfurt's (2004) definition of autonomy, we need to be *active* rather than passive: 'autonomy is essentially a matter of whether we are active rather than passive in our motives and choices' (p. 20, footnote 5). If the necessities that guide our lives were not self-imposed, they would oppose rather than enhance our autonomy and we would no longer be agents. Frankfurt tries to resolve the problem through the notion of identification. Our active part, and thereby our autonomy, comes from the move of *identifying* with that which we cannot help but care about anyway. 'A person is active

Subjectivist accounts like Frankfurt's have the advantage that they can very well explain the diversity in what people as a matter of fact-value, while also being able to account for more universally shared values by simply pointing to our shared human nature and concerns. Subjectivist accounts ground the source of values in the subject. They need not be functionalist, but they are typically compatible with evolutionary-functionalist explanations of this source. As we can see in Frankfurt: on the one hand, he stresses that values need to be ends in themselves in order to fulfil their grounding role in our volitional architecture. On the other hand, values *are* instrumental in the sense that they serve this function. Values could moreover play this role perfectly well while actually being biological instincts – something that Frankfurt for instance has no problem accepting (cf. Frankfurt 2004, pp. 27–9). All that matters is that we experience them as necessities. Frankfurt is even willing to accept that what we value may be completely arbitrary or even morally despicable: as long as it 'binds the will' it is better than caring

when it is by his own will that he does what he does, even when his will is not itself within the scope of his voluntary control' (Frankfurt 1988, p. 88).

However, problems remain. A person who wants X and who moreover wants to want X is autonomous. Autonomy lies in the second-order volitions. But to what extent is this identifying really a volitional or active deed? In fact, if what we care about really is a *necessity*, it seems contradictory to suppose that we bring it about through our own free choice. Moreover, if identifying were an active choice, than this would again invoke the infinite regress problem. For why would we identify with one thing rather than another? It makes more sense to regard the identifying as part of the package, part of the being 'overcome' (p. 89) by something that one cannot help but want. In other words, in order to be liberated from endless choosing, there has to be a necessity that is precisely *not* chosen by me, but that I rather find myself confronted with and have to endorse. The identification cannot be self-imposed and self-initiated, for that would undermine the necessary character of what we value.

One way out would be a Spinozian move: only that will is free that is in accordance with the necessities of nature. But it is doubtful whether this type of freedom satisfies Frankfurt's requirements for *active* autonomy. Another option would be to give up on the claim that autonomy requires the agent to be active. From an enactive perspective, with its focus on the fundamental coupling of person and world, the dichotomy between 'active' and 'passive' is dubious anyway. Following the enactive ontology as outlined in Chapter 3, it makes more sense to adopt a relational concept of personal autonomy (Mackenzie and Stoljar 2000).

about nothing (Frankfurt 2002). What subjectivist accounts give up upfront is the intuition that what we value has intrinsic worth. Like evolutionary-functionalist accounts they might offer explanations for why we may experience values to be intrinsic, but in the end these are illusions.

Summing Up: A Mission Impossible?

These three different ways of explaining values ground values in what we value (objectivist accounts), in ourselves (subjectivist accounts), or in individual or species' survival (evolutionary-functionalist accounts). While objectivist accounts seem incompatible with naturalism, subjectivist and evolutionary-functionalist accounts of values are incompatible with values' special, non-instrumental status. It seems as if we need to give up either a naturalist framework or one of our central intuitions about values. But is there really no way to reconcile them? Does naturalism automatically imply a functionalist perspective on values? And does acknowledging the intrinsic worth in what we value necessarily require supernaturalising them? Let's now turn to enactivism for a different perspective: one that re-thinks the presuppositions about both values and naturalism that underlie this dilemma. It is, in particular, enactivism's relational ontology that can here be of help. Applied to values, it enables us to reconsider them as *relational realities* or facts.

6.4 AN ENACTIVE APPROACH: THE RELATIONAL REALITY OF VALUES

6.4.1 Valences and Values

As we saw in Chapter 3, the enactive life–mind continuity thesis implies that a very basic form of values is always already at stake in the process of living. For all organisms their environment is meaningful to them. Since living beings are per definition needy creatures, they evaluatively relate to their environments according to those needs. That is: as a corollary of their specific bodily make-up and their current needs, some parts of the environment stand out as attractive – because they are food or shelter – while other parts stand out as dangerous and to be avoided. They thus have a certain value for the organism. We can speak of 'good' and 'bad' in a functional sense here: the possibilities offered by the environment are better or worse in light of the organism's survival. We can call these 'basic' or 'metabolic values', or, to avoid confusion, *valences*.

The valences of specific affordances in the environment arise out of the evaluative interaction between an organism and its environment at a specific time: an object X has a specific valence for organism o in situation s. In other words: the organisms' sense-making reveal the valences their present environments hold for them. We could crudely depict this structure as shown in Figure 6.1.

Since the needs of an organism change over time, so do the valences of the environment. Moreover, the environment itself also changes, which means that there will be different opportunities for action, with different valences. Besides, the current capacities and needs of the organism are themselves shaped by its previous interactions with its environment, so its current interaction pattern will testify of their history of coupling. The organism's landscape of valences is thus dynamic.

While valences emerge from an organism's dependence on its environment, values emerge for those beings that can moreover reflexively relate to themselves and their interactions. With this capacity for reflexive stance-taking, an existential dimension and

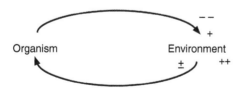

FIGURE 6.1 Valences as a function of an organism–environment system.

a new scope of meaning opens up. Just like all living beings, we evaluatively relate to our environment, but we also evaluatively relate to this relation and to ourselves. If *valences* result from being a living being, depending on an environment, we can say that (existential) *values* emerge for those organisms that can relate to this relation. Because of our stance-taking capacities, it is no longer the here and now that determines all our concerns – nor is the functional our only motivation. We can worry about what we may have done wrong in the past and look forward to the enjoyable things we have planned in the future. We can feel pride and shame and awe. We want to be a good friend, feel appreciated, feel that we are effective agents and that we can live in accordance with what matters to us. We do not only want to stay alive, but also live a good life. A dignified, meaningful life that we can be proud of, or satisfied with, or at least not feel ashamed about. Apart from the will to survive, we also have the 'will to meaning' as Frankl (1946/2009, 1963) calls it.

Both the scope of our concerns and our way of being concerned is altered by our reflexive relating. We need to make sense of more things and by different standards. While organisms make sense of their current environments, noticing what is relevant to them in light of their survival, we need to make sense of a complex social world, of ourselves and others, of past and present, estimating relevances in light of the kind of person we want to be and the kind of life we want to lead. So while for all organisms their environments are meaningful, for us, stance-taking beings or persons, our worlds are imbued with existential meaning. The sense-making of organisms reveals a valenced environment, while our existential sense-making reveals a world of values. Whereas the valences of specific affordances for specific organisms reflect their relevance for survival, the *values* of specific courses of action reflect their relevance for leading a good life for that person.[10]

[10]   Within these two broad categories of basic values or valences on the one hand and existential values on the other hand, further distinctions could of course be made.

Values thus arise out of the evaluative relation of a person to herself, her world, and her interaction with this world. By analogy with the schematic picture of valences, we could depict values as in Figure 6.2.

The capacity for stance-taking transforms our basic sense-making into existential and existentialised sense-making, at the same time transforming our valenced environments into existentially meaningful, value-imbued worlds. And just as existential sense-making is not simply added on top basic sense-making, so too values are not added on top of valences: we rather encounter a different world as the kind of actions we engage in and the kind of things that matter to us amount to a different form of life. Again, this crude, static picture cannot capture the dynamics of how persons are shaped by their bodies and their sociocultural communities and the effects of these communities on our bodies and the effects of persons on their communities and how all of this changes both our worlds and our sense-making of them – including what we value.

6.4.2 Valences and Values as Relational Realities

Valences result from the organism's long-term and current needs paired with its environment. Values result from the person's stance on herself and her interactions with her environment. Valences

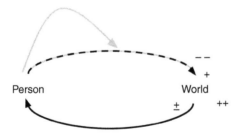

FIGURE 6.2 Values as a function of a person–world system.

With regard to the existential values, Frankl (1963) for instance distinguishes between experiential values (including love, sensual, and aesthetic experiences), creative values (including dedication to work and making art), and attitudinal values (which refer to the stance one takes on what happens to one).

depend on the coupling between organism and environment; values depend on the coupling between person and world. What then, is their ontological status? And, in particular, do they refer to something objective, to some intrinsic quality – or not?

First of all, neither 'valences' nor 'values' refer to some sort of entities; instead they refer to the meaning for organisms or people of specific aspects of the environment or world and specific behaviours or courses of action. A juicy green leaf has the valence of food for the giraffe; being honourable is a value for some persons. That is to say that this value guides their behaviour, often implicitly. As outsiders, we can however look at the choices they make, their courses of action and see that there is a pattern there that reflects this value. Even if one might not be aware of it oneself, such patterns may reveal that one for instance cares about being an honourable person – more than, say, being rich or successful. Our choices testify of what matters to us and what matters to us is what we call values. But how about their objectivity?

Starting with valences, the valence of a specific part of an environment for a specific organism is a function of their coupling. For example, for a fox a mouse is food but bark is not. This valence does not lie in the objects in themselves: for other organisms it may be the other way around. The valence of an object would not be there if the organism weren't there, but now that it is, the valence is a fact. The status of a mouse as food for a fox is the result of the coupling of this specific organism (a fox) with this specific body and this specific metabolism and these specific sense-organs and these specific skills with this specific aspect of the environment (a mouse), with its specific properties and characteristics (its body which is nutritional to a fox, but not to a cow). Does this make valences objective? It all depends on how one defines 'objective'. On the one hand, valences are relative to both sides of the coupling. Valences are not intrinsic in anything. On the other hand, they are not arbitrary. Given this organism and given these surroundings, at this specific point in time, this valence ensues from that. The fox does not *project* the valence of the mouse as food onto it; the mouse *is* food for the fox. Even when valences change – through changes in metabolic processes for instance, such as when calves switch from milk to grass – these changes are not random either. Moreover, valences are not a matter of interpretation: different observers will come to the same conclusion that mice are food to foxes and that grass is food to cows. So in that sense we might still regard them as objective, despite their lack of intrinsicality. As Thompson (2005) writes: 'That sucrose is a nutrient is not intrinsic to the sucrose molecule, but is a *relational feature*, linked to the bacterium's metabolism' (p. 418, italics mine). Avoiding the concept of objectivity all together, we could say that valences are *relational realities*.[11]

Values have a similar structure. For values too emerge from a coupling, in this case between a person (a reflective, existential being) and her world. Values would not exist if there were no existential beings: they are not inherent in what we value – but they are not subjective projections either. Values result from and are thus relative to the configuration of a specific person, with her specific history of interactions, her specific bodily experiences, her specific sociocultural upbringing and the specific sociocultural community of which she is part. But *given* this particular person with this particular history in this particular world, some things simply *are* valuable to her. What she values is not a matter of her choice: from this coupling certain values follow.

[11] Scheler (1976) has advocated a comparable notion (with regard to humans). He introduces the notion of 'existence-relativity' (*Seinsrelativität* or *Daseinsrelativität*) to escape the false Kantian dichotomy between on the one hand the thing in itself, independent of consciousness, and on the other hand the mere object-appearance in consciousness. Scheler points out that our perception, experience, and knowledge of the world is always connected to our specific way of relating to it – and that it is only within this 'sphere' that we can speak of truth and falsity. He gives the example of watching a sunset: if someone would say 'Look, the sun goes down' in an everyday setting, it would be absurd to answer that the sun does not go up and down and that this statement is thus false, because it was not meant as a statement about astronomy. I prefer the notion of 'relational reality' because it stresses both the relational character and its reality – whereas *Seinsrelativität* only stresses the dependence of phenomena on the organism or person. In other words: relational reality is a symmetrical notion, whereas *Seinsrelativität* stresses only one side of the dependence.

Some of the things we value will be highly idiosyncratic, as with some of the things that are meaningful to us, while others are more generally shared. Because of my specific history it follows that fresh ginger tea reminds me of the time I lived in Germany, and that it evokes a whole array of memories. Similarly, it is due to my specific history that I strongly value a holistic approach to psychiatric disorders – whereas I don't have a strong stance on whether we should prefer intuitionistic logic to classical logic: I simply don't care so much about that. But who knows, there might be a point in my life that defending intuitionistic logic will become important to me. Other values are less specific and rather shared by a larger community, or even seem to be universal. This layeredness makes sense: there are after all universal sides to our existence, as well as more culturally determined and idiosyncratic ones. Some of the characteristics of our situation of being persons in the world apply to all of us: we share a similar bodily make-up with similar vulnerabilities and capacities, we are all social beings, we are all capable of reflection, we are all embedded in a sociocultural community.[12] The more universal values are connected to these characteristics, such as the value of a sense of belonging, the value of doing no harm, the value of care for one's kith and/or kin, the value of joy and beauty, the value of protecting the vulnerable. In these respects we are similar to people from all over the world, as well as to people from ancient times.

At the same time, our bodies are not exactly the same: we are female, or male, or neither, our skin colours differ, as well as our heights, our weights, our capacities, our health, whether we are regarded by our communities as beautiful or ugly, our age, etc. Our sociocultural communities too differ in many respects, such as how these various bodily characteristics are valued, which gender roles are promoted, which sexual preferences are accepted, which templates for

---

[12]   In this respect, an enactive account fits with Frankfurt (2004), who also points out that 'people care about many of the same things because the natures of human beings, and the basic conditions of human life, are grounded in biological, psychological, and environmental facts that are not subject to very much variation and change' (p. 27).

how to live your life are present, what the hallmarks of success and failure are, what an ideal family looks like, the kinds of food and music and cultural life that are available, etc. And then there are the unique trajectories of individual persons who are shaped by the practices around them, by their specific bodies and communities and their life-time experiences – while they are also able to relate to and take a stance on these practices and experiences.

Some of our idiosyncratic or cultural values can be seen as particular ways of realising more universal values. The appreciation of music for instance seems to be universal, while the precise kind of music that is considered to be beautiful is a more cultural or personal experience. Idiosyncratic and cultural values will be more liable to change over time than universal ones. A good way to illustrate this variety of dynamics is Wittgenstein's (1975) metaphor of the riverbed and the river: some values change relatively fast (i.e. are more idiosyncratic) and other values change very slowly (i.e. are more deeply anchored in our shared sociobiological constitution), like the riverbed moving place over centuries.

Like valence, values too are relational realities: we can neither locate their source in the person nor in the world. Values are neither projected by us onto neutral situations (as subjectivist accounts claim), nor are they completely *inherent* in the thing or situation as such (as objectivist accounts maintain). In other words: values cannot be reduced or traced back to either one of the relata: it is their coupling that is required. Values are relative to the coupling of persons and their worlds, but like with valences, they are not arbitrary. Their emergence depends on the properties of what we value and on the properties of ourselves.

Colours as an Example of Relational Facts

To get a better grasp of the ontological status of what I have termed relational realities and to see that they are not so extra-vagant or mysterious as they might seem, we can take a look at some other, common examples. Take the perception of colour for instance. We see colours: the lemon is yellow, my curtain is orange, the sky is blue: these are just matters of fact. Still, the colours that we see depend not only on the properties of the object, but also on our perceptual endowment and capacities. We have rods and three types of cone-cells – allowing us to perceive the range of colours that we do. Some birds, however, have four types of cone-cells, and the mantis shrimp is famous for having even twelve different receptor types. We do not really know what the world looks like to them. That is, in virtue of their different perceptual abilities, they pick up on other things than we do. So colours too emerge from the coupling of a specific organism with a specific environment: they result from the coupling of the reflection of waves of light on an object plus the specific characteristics of the organism's perceptual abilities. This dependence on both the properties of the environment and the properties of the organism does not mean that we just make up colours; their being relational does not make them any less real. No colours would exist if there would be no organisms with some kind of eyes, but now that such organisms do exist, colours are a matter of fact.

The same goes for our other sensual experiences, such as taste, hearing, and touch. Here too, the taste or sound or touch comes from the coupling of the objective properties of object on the one hand, and the sensory capacities of the organism on the other hand. And these capacities are again shaped by the organism's previous history of interactions. This means that there are not only differences between species (a dog experiences the same park differently than I do – if only because of his superior smell), but also within one species: a different learning history will lead to different capacities. Dogs can for instance be trained to smell cancer and other diseases, humans can train their detection of bird sounds. Our perceptual expertise carves out what we perceive of our surroundings – as has been pointed out by the likes of theoretical biologists such as von Uexküll (1909), phenomenologists such as Merleau-Ponty (1945/2002), ecological psychologists such as Gibson (1979) and enactive and sensorimotor theorists such as Noë (2004). From an enactive perspective our perceptual capacities afford direct interaction with (a part of) the world. Given the limits of these capacities we can say we experience a certain bandwidth of reality. We cannot perceive all that there is to be perceived, we simply lack the capacities for that: we can hear only a range of frequencies, we cannot see in the dark, we cannot sense subtle vibrations, we cannot use echo location, nor do we see the pee of mice as birds of prey do. But that our perception does not offer complete coverage does not make what we perceive any less real. Whereas a naive realism doesn't do justice to the role of our perceptual capacities and how they co-determine what we see, internalist models on the other hand are too pessimistic in denouncing the possibility of direct engagement with the world.

Evaluation of Values as Relational Realities
This enactive, relational take on values manages to capture the main intuitions on values that were captured by the other three accounts. Like evolutionary-functionalist and subjective accounts, it can account for both universal values and the diversity of values across cultures and individuals, and explain their dynamics. That is because on the enactive account too, values remain embodied and embedded. Objectivist accounts can explain universal values, but are limited when it comes to explaining the cultural and personal diversity of values. An enactive account can also do justice to the main concerns of objectivist accounts: values are ends in themselves; they cannot be reduced to evolutionary-functionalist explanations. We do not chose our values: we rather find ourselves compelled by them. Values are neither arbitrary, nor subjective projections, in that sense the enactive account is on the side of the objectivists rather than the subjectivists. Contrary to objectivist accounts, however, an enactive account does not maintain that values are intrinsic in the things we value. From an enactive, relational point of view, we cannot speak of the intrinsic worth of something in the sense of its worth being *independent of us*. 'Intrinsicality' is just not a helpful

notion within a relational ontology. Values emerge from the coupling between persons and their worlds, so values are only inherent to a specific *relationship* rather than to one of its sides. If we look again at the example of parents' love for their children, we saw that Frankfurt argues that we care about them because we love them, whereas Taylor rather maintains that in general when we find someone to be loveable this is not just a matter of our experiencing certain feelings towards them; we recognise some independent characteristics of this person that makes them loveable. From an enactive perspective, both positions are misguided. The meaning and value of children to their parents is neither dependent upon the children's characteristics, nor on their parents' love for them: their meaning is rather a function of their relationship. It is not because I love my child that she is valuable to me; she is my child and that simple fact implies her relevance to me. Even if I wouldn't love her, or even if I would find her a despicable person, or even if I wouldn't know her, she would still be meaningful to me, I would still have to relate to her in some way, simply because she is my child.[13]

From an enactive perspective we can see that we do not need what we value to have intrinsic worth in order to safeguard it from the reductionism of either a subjectivist or a functionalist account. For when we understand values as relational facts this just as well recognises values' non-arbitrary, non-subjective, and non-functionalist character. Claims about values' intrinsic goodness like those by Taylor and other objectivists are unnecessarily strong: to avoid reducing values then we do not need to declare what we value to be valuable independent from us, nor do we need to grant them some sort of supernatural status. Understanding values as relational realities helps us solve Taylor's dilemma of wanting to retain that valuable goods are valuable, irrespective of our de facto recognition of that fact, while also acknowledging that values depend on our human existence, that without us, there would be no (existential) values.

---

[13]   This is not just a matter of biological parenthood: apart from shared DNA, a shared history or a history of caregiving can just as well make persons meaningful to each other.

Taylor and other proponents of objectivism could however object that the enactive view still leaves us with the threat of moral relativism. Taylor for instance distances himself from what he calls a 'sophisticated naturalism' which 'understand[s] our valuations as among the perceptions of the world and our social existence which are inseparable from our living through and participating in our form of life' (Taylor 2000a, p. 67). This seems close to an enactivist perspective. Taylor rejects this position on the grounds that 'whatever truths were to be found here would nevertheless in a crucial sense be *relative* to the given form of life' (p. 67, italics mine). He writes: 'Precisely because it conceives the 'objectivity' of our valuations entirely in terms of their embedding in our different ways of life, it allows in principle no purchase from which the goods enshrined in a given way of life can be shown as wrong or inadequate' (p. 67). That is: as soon as we regard values as relative to a given form of life rather than as objective characteristics independent of us, we have no firm foundation from which we can dispute and challenge the values of a particular form of life and we are left with the relativism that Taylor wants to avoid. Hence his need for a view from nowhere, or a 'supernatural' status for values: values' objective status implies that there is a human-independent fact of the matter when it comes to debates on values, including moral issues.

An enactive ontology of values as relational realities does not offer such an absolute foundation. But that does not imply the kind of relativism that Taylor fears, the kind of moral relativism that regards values as non-debatable, like matters of taste. Such relativism may follow from subjectivist accounts for whom value is a matter of subjective projection. On an enactive account, however, values are neither subjective projections, nor do they emerge from thin air. For values depend on our embodied and embedded nature, part of which is the universally shared condition of being persons in the world. And our capacity for stance-taking precisely implies that we are capable of critical reflection, of arguing, of learning from each other, from

history, and from other cultural practices. We *can* debate, we *can* try
to convince each other why some practices are morally superior to
others, and we *can* develop our insights. We can become convinced of
the obsoleteness of denying women the same rights as men; we can
learn from people from other backgrounds who point out the implicit
racism of some parts of our cultural folklore. We can see progress if
we look back at the colonialism and sexism of previous times –
although there is obviously still much moral sensitising work to
do. An enactive, relational account of values allows for the possibility of development and progress: we can improve our stance-taking
skills, our empathy, and our moral sensitivity precisely by interacting with others. Yet there is no 'objective measure', no 'superhuman'
or 'supernatural yardstick' to compare our values against.

We are used to assuming that we need a fundament for
development and progress. A strong foundation seems to be the
only possible basis of a building of any kind: we feel we need
a secure ground of departure to start from. But this is just
another example of what Wittgenstein (1958) called 'a picture
[that] held us captive'. Dynamical systems, however, present us
with a different, non-foundational and non-linear template for
thinking about development. For example: what is 'the foundation' of life? That is a somewhat misleading question – as if there
would be one primary thing or ingredient to its development –
whereas it rather takes a certain chemical soup, a specific environment in terms of temperature and air pressure, and a certain
way in which these interact for life to emerge. Ecosystems in
general provide examples of development without proper
foundations.

On an enactive account, there is no such thing as a view from
nowhere. This means it gives up absolute certainty of the kind
Taylor and other objectivists are after. It even questions its very
attainability. For even if there were such a view from nowhere,
who would be able to take it? If you and I disagree about some
value, how would we know which one of us (if anyone) got hold of

the truth? To assume values' human-independent status is an empty reassurance that provides no real hold. It may on the contrary encourage people to assume their moral superiority on the ground that they have seen the light that others haven't – which is hardly an improvement compared to intersubjective debates in which we try to convince each other from the same level, so to speak.

All in all, an enactive view on values as relational realities helps us avoid the problems tied to objectivist, evolutionary-functionalist, and subjectivist perspectives while at the same time capturing their main concerns.

6.4.3 Enactive Values and Naturalism

We ended the previous chapter with the question of how to fit the existential dimension and values within the naturalist framework of psychiatry. Does an enactive account of values stay within the bounds of naturalism? It all depends on where we want to draw those bounds; on how we want to define naturalism and the terms it engages. We used the definition of naturalism as the idea that 'all facts are natural facts ... and natural facts are facts about the natural world, facts of the sort in which the natural sciences trade' (Lenman et al. 2017). Following this language of 'facts', the current debate on naturalism and values focuses on the status of 'moral facts'. This way of putting the question invites two main positions: (1) moral facts are non-natural and (2) moral facts are natural. Those who adopt the first position regard moral facts as belonging to a somehow different realm. Moral facts thus cannot be reduced to 'natural facts'. This would align with Taylor's view. It leaves us with the dualistic problem of how non-natural values could exert influence on or make a causal difference in the natural world. The second position can in turn be divided into (1) irrealist moral naturalists and (2) realist moral naturalists (Lutz and Lenman 2018). According to the irrealists our moral discourse is a social and linguistic practice, but our utterances do not refer to moral facts with a substantial independent existence. So they exist, but as a social construct. According to the realists, moral facts do exist as part of the natural realm: 'there are objective moral facts and properties and these facts and properties are natural facts and properties' (Lenman et al. 2017). These moral facts are real, mind-independent facts.

Now what is striking, from an enactive point of view, is how this debate reflects the same inner mind–outer world topology that we encountered in the mind–body debate, in which 'mind' refers to an inner, mental realm, while 'world' (including our bodies) refers to an outer, physical realm. Following the lines of this topology, naturalism gets equated with this world–minus–mind side of the division, and accordingly, real is defined as 'mind–independent'. As we saw, enactivism advocates a different understanding of the relation between mind and world. The idea of the world as a physical realm does not distinguish between the physical and the physiological, the non-living and the living. In the process of living, however, physiological and sense-making processes necessarily go together, and they are moreover inherently related to interaction with the organism's environment. So we have a three-place relation in which mind (sense-making), body (physiological processes), and environment (other living organisms and non-living matter) co-determine each other and form an intricate, highly interdependent system. The mind emerges from and thus depends on the organisational properties of an organism that depends on interactions with its environment to stay alive. But this environment is not a static 'independent' factor or stage either: environments crucially consist of other organisms, who also adept to each other and to some extent shape the non-living matter of their surroundings too. To define reality in terms of any kind of independence does not make sense from this point of view.

Applied to values, this relational take means that they are neither subjective projections nor subject-independent 'facts-of-the-world'. So does that mean that they do or do not transcend the natural realm? In a sense, our values 'transcend' our biological concerns in the sense that they go beyond our mere need for survival. Our capacity for stance-taking opens up a fundamentally different way of relating, of being in a value-laden world rather than a valenced environment. Our actions are motivated by a broader range of concerns. The aim to lead a good life may even take precedence over basic biological needs: people can be willing to sacrifice those needs in order to maintain what they value. In the most extreme form, people may even sacrifice their lives, may die for what they value.

'Transcendence' is however not quite the right word, for we never really transcend the biological realm. We remain embodied and embedded beings. We can take a stance on ourselves, our situations and others, and this means we do not coincide with our present state: we are in an 'excentric' position, as Plessner (1928/1981) called it. Our capacity to take a stance fundamentally alters our relation to ourselves, our situation and others. Yet our stance-taking is itself an embodied and embedded capacity that is both developmentally dependent upon and continuously shaped by our interactions with others within our worlds. That is: taking a stance on something is still rooted in and motivated by our interactions as bodily and embedded persons. Taking a stance on something is thus not the same as transcending it. That is why 'transcendence', with its connotation of disconnection, is not an appropriate term. Values do not float in mid-air or belong to some kind of non-natural realm. Stance-taking implies a *reconfiguration* rather than transcendence of 'the natural'.

Values emerge from there being stance-taking, existential beings, a capacity that itself emerges from a specific bodily being in specific social relationships. Out of a specific configuration, something new and different emerges. As I argued in Chapter 4, we should not make the mistake of trying to secure the reality of what has newly emerged by trying to define it in isolation from its constituents. That is, the qualitative differences of the whole do not imply a *disconnection* from its constituent parts. The parts are rather 'fused' into a new whole. There is no causation from 'the top' to 'the bottom' or vice versa; there is only a change of the whole system. And this change of the organisational structure of the whole *is* or *implies* a change of the constituent parts. When we look at the existential dimension from this perspective, we can see that even though our capacity for stance-taking implies a new structure and a new order, it just as well remains thoroughly embodied and embedded. The existential stance and the values that these bring along precisely emerge from *and thus depend upon* our embodied (social) interactions with the world.

Values have no separate existence, independent of us, yet they are fundamentally different from and are not reducible to either subjective tastes or physiologically driven needs. So where does that leave us with regard to naturalism? It first of all shows that both 'natural' and 'supernatural' are slippery terms. Following the conception that naturalism implies that all facts are 'natural facts', namely 'facts about the natural world' then it all hinges on how one sees this 'natural world'. From an enactive perspective, meaning and valences are part of living and thus part of the natural world – and the same goes for values and existential meaning. They are not in any way added onto the world, nor are they of a mysterious, supernatural nature. According to enactivism the natural world allows for differentiation, for the emergence of non-reducible phenomena. The natural world of enactivism is thus not a physical-world-as-opposed-to-the-mental-realm or a physical-world-as-devoid-of-meaning or a world-of-natural-facts-as-opposed-to-values. In other words: enactivism adopts a non-reductionist conception of the natural world. This also means that the 'natural sciences' that have the authority to deal with the 'natural facts' should not be confined to physics and chemistry, but rather also include sciences that investigate the natural fact of existential meaning, of human culture, and so on. In short then, enactivism's relational ontology, its dynamical systems approach, and its appertaining acknowledgement of emergence, enable a form of naturalism that needs neither to reduce real differences, nor to safeguard these differences by supernaturalising them.

6.5   A DIFFERENT FORM OF LIFE

Our capacity for stance-taking transforms our basic sense-making into existential sense-making and at the same time the environment we live in becomes a world imbued with existential meaning and values.

The development of this capacity is itself dependent upon and supported by the world we live in; by being part of a sociocultural community with specific sociocultural practices. The existential
dimension is not a mere addition to the other dimensions: we are
rather looking at a different configuration in which our experiences,
our world, and even our physiology are different too.

Starting with our experiences, we can see how our ability to
relate, to reflect, to distance ourselves from the here and now opens up
different ways of relating to the world. We make sense of the world in
a different way – which is just to say that we experience differently.
Compared to non-reflexive organisms, we are guided by different concerns and cares and we are capable of different types of behaviour. We
relate to our future and our past. We reflexively relate to others and to
ourselves. We can deliberate, plan ahead, imagine, and fantasise. We
can experience so-called self–other emotions (Reddy 2003) such as
shame and pride. We can feel empathy with others. We can recognise
the value of love, beauty, loyalty, friendship, and belonging. And we
can experience despair, loneliness, estrangement, hatred, and jea-
lousy. And in line with the finding that the capacity for existential
sense-making transforms even our basic sense-making, our basic sensual experiences are affected too: how we touch and how we feel, what
we see, hear, and taste. For example: my cat and I can both eat fish, we
can both experience its taste, but for me there may be other issues at
stake: ethical issues (for instance, concerning the threatened status of
this specific species), planning issues (I don't want my house to smell
of fish if my sister who is disgusted by fish is coming to visit), senti-
mental issues (this fish reminds me of dinners with my grandmother),
etc. The taste can be enriched by loving memories or spoiled by
feelings of guilt.

That we stand in a different relationship to other people is both
reflected in and enabled by the sociocultural communities we live in.
The sociocultural dimension goes hand-in-hand with the existential
dimension: if it weren't for our culturally embedded social interactions, we probably would not have developed the capacity to take

a stance. Stretching over many generations, we are shaped by the sociocultural practices we participate in, while at the same time we are shaping these practices, sustaining and modulating them. We are not just part of a specific culture or practice, but our stance-taking capacity enables us to evaluatively relate to them. Our material environments are implied too. Like many organisms, we shape our material environments, but with the passing on of knowledge that is made possible by our sociocultural communities and practices, including our use of language, we have managed to do this to an extraordinary extent. The worlds we live in are packed with human-made artefacts, offering us specifically tailored affordances. Even most of our 'natural' environment has been culturally influenced: the trees we see were probably planted there for specific purposes (e.g. forestry, regulating the city's air temperature, to impress the estate's visitors) and might be imported from other parts of the world. The animals we see may also have been imported, and otherwise they are the ones who have managed to survive human influences like agriculture and its pesticides. But even those elements of the environment that are truly untouched by human interference still offer us a different kind of affordance compared to non-reflexive organisms, for they too are imbued with values and existential meanings. We can find landscapes beautiful or be worried about threats to it, we can feel like painting it, or feel lost in it. Our environments then are sociocultural worlds, imbued with values, rich in meanings.

Lastly, in this new configuration, our physiological processes too are affected. This may seem a bit counter-intuitive, for how could it matter to its physiological processes whether or not an organism is capable of stance-taking? From an enactive perspective, it is not such an odd idea though. Following the life–mind continuity thesis and the relational ontology that it implies, we saw in Chapter 3 that physiological processes are neither independent from sense-making nor from interactions with the environment. And since we embark on a different kind of sense-making and engage in different type of interactions with the world when we develop our existential stance, this will likely have an impact on our physiological processes too.

How we live shapes our physiology. And how we live is in turn shaped by our existential stance and the sociocultural group we are part of. It matters for instance how we eat (affecting our digestive system, our metabolism, some of our hormones, our muscle building, our weight, etc.), how we move (affecting our metabolism, our muscle building, some of our hormones, our bone density, our weight, etc.), and how we feel (affecting our muscle tone, some of our hormones, how we eat and move, thereby affecting all of the above). We also intervene in our bodies by means of all sorts of drugs (medical and non-medical), surgeries, pacemakers, cochlear implants, acupuncture, metal back-plates, plastic hips, deep brain stimulation, and so on. All of these behaviours are influenced by a jumble of cultural norms and practices and more or less reflective personal considerations and choices.

The capacity to take a stance fundamentally changes our relation to our bodies. For us reflective beings, our body is not just felt and experienced 'from the inside' so to say, but we are also aware that our bodies are looked at by others. Sartre (1943/1996) famously describes a man who peeks through the keyhole of a hotel room, where he suspects his wife betrays him. Another man appears in the hallway and the spying man is suddenly aware of how he must look to this outsider. Our shame is mediated by the gaze of others – real or imagined (Zahavi 2010). Our body is at the same time 'felt body' (*Leib*), biological object (*Körper*), and body-for others (Slatman 2014). The outsiders' perspective we can take on our bodies in turn modulates the way in which we experience our bodies and the way in which we behave. We try to shape our bodies into our preferred shape and look through diets, tattoos, sports, piercings, plastic surgery, epilation, etc.

But the effects of our sociocultural norms go even deeper. Often without realising it, we adjust how we move and behave according to the prevailing norms, for instance norms on gender, race, and sexuality. Scholars from feminist theory and the new materialism movement in particular have pointed out just how deeply such norms affect us in our (bodily) being in the world (Fanon 1952/2008; Young 1980; Fausto-Sterling 2005; Ahmed 2006; Wilson 2015). In her ground-breaking article 'Throwing Like a Girl', Young (1980) criticised Merleau-Ponty's (1945/2002) phenomenology of the body for not addressing how it matters for your being in the world if your body is male or female. For women, Merleau-Ponty's *'I can'* is often rather an *'I cannot'*, she argues: women simply do not have the same freedom of moving in space. Limiting her scope to 'women situated in contemporary advanced industrial, urban, and commercial society' (p. 140), she uses the example of throwing a ball. How can it be that even young girls already perform so much worse than boys when it comes to throwing balls? Rather than assuming some innate shortcomings in the female body, she points to the fact that schoolgirls typically wear a skirt as part of their school uniform and are therefore taught not to spread their legs as this would be indecent. Making a firm throw, however, precisely requires spreading your legs, and taking up space in general. She writes:

> Even in the most simple body orientations of men and women as they sit, stand, and walk, one can observe a typical difference in body style and extension. Women generally are not as open with their bodies as men in their gait and stride. Typically, the masculine stride is longer proportional to a man's body than is the feminine stride to a woman's. The man typically swings his arms in a more open and loose fashion than does a woman and typically has more up and down rhythm in his step. Though we now wear pants more than we used to, and consequently do not have to restrict our sitting postures because of dress, women still tend to sit with their legs relatively close together and their arms across their bodies. When simply standing or leaning, men tend to keep their feet further apart than do woman, and we also tend more

to keep our hands and arms touching or shielding our bodies. A final indicative difference is the way each carries books or parcels; girls and women most often carry books embraced to their chests, while boys and men swing them along their sides.

(p. 142)

In a similar way, Fanon (1952/2008) addressed how public spaces that are dominated by white people do not offer him as a black man the same freedom of movement. Being a black man means that he always needs to reckon with and relate to white people's prejudices about him.

That such adjustments in behaviour impact not just one's life but include one's physiology too, is nicely shown by Fausto-Sterling's (2005) case study on bones. 'Culture shapes bones', she writes (p. 1491). Osteoporosis, loss of bone density, for instance is much more common in women than in men. This is often explained by pointing to the effects of the menopause, but Fausto-Sterling demonstrates that this picture is much too simplistic. For the structure of our bones develops through our lives and is influenced by many factors, such as 'what we eat, how and when we exercise, whether we drink or smoke, what kinds of diseases we get and how they are treated, and how we age' (p. 1510), so that we need to understand particular bone structures in the context of particular individuals with particular life histories. And these particular life histories are of course shaped by socio-cultural norms. Diets for instance negatively affect bone formation, especially during adolescence, and many more teenage girls than teenage boys go on a diet, even when they have a normal weight. Movement is another important influence and here too we see gendered differences in the way in which boys and girls play and the kinds of sports they typically do. Fausto-Sterling concludes that we need to adopt a dynamical systems approach to connect all these influences and the way in which they develop and impact each other.

Many more examples could be given that testify how our stance-taking and the values and sociocultural practices that imply each other affect our physiology – not just superficially, but fundamentally. Two scientific fields that have been and still are of special importance to psychiatry, neuroscience, and genetics, have made comparable shifts from static to developmental understandings of the brain and our DNA respectively. Both fields have increasingly recognised the crucial role of interactions with the environment. Neuroscience has come a long way since the early days of phrenology: we now know that what we do shapes not only the connectivity between different parts of the brain, but also changes its very anatomy. Much like a muscle gets stronger through using it, specific brain areas that are engaged during specific actions grow 'stronger' and larger too. A famous example is of the enlarged hippocampi of London taxi drivers when they are practising for their exam (Maguire et al. 2000), but many more structural changes have been documented in the brains of dancers (Hänggi et al. 2010), musicians (Gaser and Schlaug 2003), golf players (Bezzola et al. 2011), and many more. Similarly, the idea that DNA functions like the unfolding of a blueprint has long since been discarded. Genetics has adopted the idea of epigenetics that our DNA gets thoroughly shaped by our interactions in the world.[14] What we eat matters (Hardy and Tollefsbol 2011), the amount of stress we experience matters (Franklin et al. 2010), etc. And it is not just the individual's DNA that is influenced, but such effects are moreover heritable.

When it comes to psychiatric disorders, both the brain and the genes have been heralded as forming their underlying causes. The static causal primacy of hard-core reductionism however, has difficulties accounting for the developmental role played by our interactions. From a more nuanced, biopsychosocial perspective, comes

---

[14]   Although it is questionable to what extent the importance of these interactions is really acknowledged as the old ways of carving out form and matter, information and carrier, still deeply resonate in the field, as Oyama (1985/2000) shows.

the idea that we can have both genetic and neuronal vulnerabilities or dispositions to certain disorders. Fully embracing a developmental, interactional account means that we should be wary of assumptions of innateness though, for our genetic and neuronal vulnerabilities are themselves the result of the complex interplay of interactions between individual and environment that go back all the way to the womb. Besides, the idea that certain neuronal networks or a certain set of genes 'code' for a specific disorder appears to be too simplistic too. For example, the same genes that have been proposed to disposition someone to being vulnerable to adversities appear to actually make people *less* vulnerable in case they grow up in supportive environments (Belsky et al. 2009).

In short: our physiological processes are shaped by our experiences and our experiences are shaped by our existential stance and our sociocultural practices and our norms and values. With us, physiology and culture form a mishmash of reciprocal determination. It is good to keep in mind that a large part of this determination does not take the shape of linear, domino-type causation, but rather works in the more complex, non-linear, cake-like ways we discussed in Chapter 4. That is, our stance-taking and sociocultural practices do not function as switches that turn some physiological processes on or off, but physiological processes are rather part of the larger system of an existential person interacting with their worlds and as such influenced by them and influencing them in turn.

The existential dimension is thus not something *over and above* or next to the other dimensions; rather we witness a *transformation* of the whole system from an organism–environment to a person–world system. A new 'form of life' (Wittgenstein 1958) or a new 'structure of behaviour' (Merleau-Ponty 1942/1963) emerges. Merleau-Ponty (1942/1963) describes this as the emergence of the 'human order'. He argues that it would be a misunderstanding to think that we are rational animals. For 'mind is not a specific difference which would be *added* to vital or psychological being [e.g. animal life] in order to constitute a man.

Man is not a rational animal. The appearance of reason and mind does not leave intact a sphere of self-enclosed instincts in man' (p. 181, italics mine). Our mind, or what I call our existential stance, changes it all. As a consequence, 'one cannot speak of the body and of life in general, but only of the animal body and animal life, of the human body and of the human life' (p. 181). The existential stance implies a reconfiguration of the entire system, or as Merleau-Ponty writes:

> A normal man is not a body bearing certain autonomous instincts joined to a 'psychological life' defined by certain characteristic processes – pleasure and pain, emotion, association of ideas – and surmounted with a mind which would unfold its proper acts over this infrastructure. The advent of higher orders, to the extent that they are accomplished, eliminate the autonomy of the lower orders and give a new signification to the steps which constitute them. This is why we have spoken of a human order rather than of a mental or rational order.
>
> (p. 180)

From an enactive perspective, I would avoid any talk of 'higher' and 'lower' orders as this suggests a problematic vertical hierarchy (see Chapter 4, Section 4.7). Merleau-Ponty's clear distinction between plants, animals, and humans can likewise be contested. But he does make clear that there is no independently functioning 'infrastructure': that the whole changes and thereby its parts too – much like we saw in our discussion of emergence as fusion (Chapter 4, Section 4.7).

This new form of life thus implies a qualitative shift compared to organism–environment systems. The emergence of the existential dimension can be seen as another major qualitative jump, comparable to the jump from matter to living beings. As the life–mind continuity thesis argues, it is with the emergence of life that mind emerges too. The qualitative jump from physical aggregates to living organisms is at one and the same time a jump from physical to physiological processes and from non-experiential matter to experiencing beings.

Now, the existential dimension constitutes yet another jump: with the emergence of the capacity for stance-taking, we move from organisms in their environments to persons in their world, implying a whole range of changes too. There is a shift from basic to existential sense-making, from valences to values, from environments to socio-cultural worlds – and all the different forms of experiencing, relating and acting that are implied. We can summarise these major jumps in the schema in Figure 6.3.

Now this is of course a crude simplification. It pictures only two major jumps, whereas it is more likely that there will be different sets of capacities, allowing for all sorts of shades and gradual differences in between. In its full-fledged form though, existential beings do present a different form of life.

Yet there is still continuity too. Enactivism's relational ontology still applies: this new form of life is still a life in which mind, life, and world go together: it has the same embodied and embedded structure. Even though our capacity for stance-taking

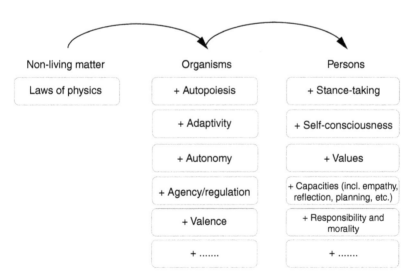

FIGURE 6.3 Qualitative jumps within the life–mind continuity: from lifeless matter to living organisms to existential beings.

implies a new structure or reconfiguration of the system, it nevertheless remains thoroughly embodied and embedded. The existential stance precisely emerges from *and thus depends upon* our embodied, social interactions with the world. The structure is thus still one of interaction, only now between persons and worlds rather than organisms and environments.

A simple example illustrates both the continuity and the differences. Monkeys can be afraid when they see a snake. People can be afraid of becoming afraid in case they would see a snake. The monkey's fear of the snake is the result of a direct perception of a situation, whereas the person's fear of the fear follows from the relation to a potential situation in the future. Both cases consist of an evaluation of a situation. And in both cases, we can only understand the fear as the outcome of an interaction between an animal or person and their environment or world respectively. The structure of their experiences is thus very similar. On the other hand, we also see that the existential stance opens up a new domain of imagining future situations. More generally: even though we can apply our sense-making to ourselves, and to situations in the past or in the future, and even though we can relate to events that are remote from us in time and space, or only take place inside our own heads – this capacity still depends upon the whole system of a person in interaction with her world.

6.6   CONCLUSION: ENACTIVE INTEGRATION OF THE FOUR DIMENSIONS

Where does this leave us with regard to our overall aim of finding an integrative approach to the four main dimensions – experiential, physiological, sociocultural, and existential – of psychiatric disorders? Enriched with the existential dimension, an enactive approach now allows us to relate the four dimensions at stake in psychiatry as different excerpts of one complex person–world system. With the existential dimension the system as a whole is transformed, affecting all other dimensions. The differences between these dimensions are acknowledged, without assigning any of them a special, foundational status: because each dimension depends on and is shaped by the other three, none of them is reducible to any of the others. It is time to take a closer look at some implications of this framework for psychiatry.

7 Enactive Psychiatry
Psychiatric Disorders Are Disorders of Sense-Making

So far, we have been developing an enactive framework to address psychiatry's integration problem. In Chapter 1, we looked at the integration problem and how models of psychiatric disorders could be useful. I argued that a useful framework should integrate all four main dimensions that are at stake in psychiatric disorders (experiential, physiological, sociocultural, and existential); showing how they relate. In Chapter 2, we shortly discussed the advantages and disadvantages of three main groups of models: one-sided and reductionist models, dualist models, and integrative models. The integrative models proved to be most promising, but still fell short when it came to clearly relating the dimensions involved. Also, the existential dimension was missing from these accounts. In Chapters 3 and 4 we investigated what an enactive approach might offer. Since an enactive approach implies a different understanding of how mind, body, and world relate, it has the potential to offer a novel outlook on psychiatry's integration problem. We looked at the enactive life–mind continuity thesis and what it entails for how the experiential, the physiological, and the environmental/sociocultural dimension are related. The notion of emergence proved to be central, so we discussed how to best understand it, as well as its consequences for how to picture the causality involved between dimensions. The existential dimension was still lacking in this enactive account too though. In Chapter 5 we introduced the existential dimension and the roles it plays in psychiatry. In Chapter 6 we discussed how this existential dimension and the values it brings along can be integrated in an enactive framework. In these last two chapters, we will analyse what the adoption of this enriched enactive framework implies for the conception of the nature, causes, and treatment of psychiatric disorders.

7.2 PSYCHIATRIC DISORDERS ARE DISORDERS OF SENSE-MAKING

In the previous chapter we saw that by welcoming the existential dimension in the enactive picture, we arrived at what could be called a new form of life or structure of behaviour in which all four of psychiatry's main dimensions are integrated into one person–world system: bodily, reflexive beings interacting with their socioculturally shaped worlds. But what does this picture about the fundamental coupling of person and world say about psychiatric disorders? It all started out as a way to get a grip on 'the mind', a mind that we can apparently 'lose' or that can be 'disordered' in various ways. We turned to enactivism to find that it had a particular outlook on the mutual dependency of mind and life and on the unavoidable coupling of living, minded beings to their environments. An outlook that is oriented at processes, developing over time, and that embraces a relational ontology in which relational structures can be constitutive of entities. As such, the enactive perspective fits nicely with a dynamical systems approach. This view implies that understanding a specific phenomenon will typically require 'zooming out' in two respects: spatially and temporally. That is, we need to see it in its proper context and to take into account its dynamic character, looking at its developmental trajectory.

Returning to psychiatric disorders, an enactive approach encourages us to do just that: if we want to get a grip on mental disorders, we should see the 'mental' in its proper context. From an enactive perspective, notions like 'mental', 'mind', and 'cognition' are best understood in terms of sense-making: the embodied and embedded activity of organisms or persons who evaluatively orient themselves in their environments or worlds. Psychiatric disorders refer to problems with this sense-making. These problems are obviously very diverse, but what depression, anxiety disorder, schizophrenia, obsessive-compulsive disorder, eating disorder, and other psychiatric disorders have in common is that they refer to cases in which the evaluative interactions of a person with her world go astray. These interactions may include the person's thoughts, feelings, and/or behaviour – towards the world and/or to herself. On a very general level we can say that the way in which the person makes sense of her world is *biased in a specific direction*: the world appears overly threatening, or meaningless, or meaningful, or chaotic. This bias needs to be *structural*: a single instance of inadequate sense-making does not yet amount to a disorder. Psychiatric disorders refer to a more or less stable *pattern* in how someone's sense-making goes astray over time. 'Going astray' means that the person's sense-making is not *appropriate* or insufficiently attuned to her situation. She will find it difficult to *adjust* her sense-making to the situation at hand. This difficulty in adjusting and attuning typically results in overly *rigid patterns of interactions*.

As we saw in Chapter 3, sense-making is first and foremost a bodily and affective affair. For us persons our sense-making includes explicit, reflective sense-making, but even though this capacity affects our basic sense-making it alters neither the bodily and affective nature of our sense-making, nor the fact that most of our sense-making is implicit. Our evaluative 'appraisals' of the situation we are in usually consists of implicit, immediate experiences or senses rather than explicit judgements. For instance, I am immediately aware of the danger of trees or branches falling when I am walking through a squeaky forest in stormy weather. Likewise, I can immediately sense the atmosphere in a group when I enter a room: is everybody chatting cheerfully, or is there rather a tense silence? In both cases I am affected by what concerns me. Sense-making should thus not be understood in an overly reflective way as it includes our perceptions, affects, and bodily feelings as well.

Sense-making refers to how the world is opened up to me, to how I experience the world, and this is what is disordered in the case of psychiatric problems. For depressed patients, for example, the world appears as uninviting and unattractive, even oppressive. The depression affects not only how they feel (hopeless, worthless, heavy), but

also what they perceive (the rejecting, disapproving faces, the phoni-
ness of people's smiles, the litter that has been carelessly thrown onto
the streets, the uselessness of activities), and of course how they act
and interact (avoiding contact with others, staying inside). Their
sense-making is disordered in that it is biased in one direction (perceiving only what is hopeless or meaningless or disconcerting) and in
some cases downright distorted (these smiles may very well be
authentic smiles) and that it is not flexibly attuned to the situation
they are in: they can only feel, experience, and see it that way. Even
activities or interactions that would normally have pleased them do
not manage to affect them anymore. And this is not a matter of having
an off-day: it has to be a longer lasting pattern of biased sense-making
before it amounts to a disorder.

To speak of disorders of sense-making does not mean that there is
only one 'right' or 'proper' way to make sense of a situation. There will
typically be a whole range of viable possibilities. Instances of sense-
making can be wrong or mistaken though: we made an estimation error
of someone's intentions, or could not see an object properly for want of
light, or we projected our own anger on someone else. After all, sense-
making is not a subjective matter: we do not *construe* sense or *project*
sense onto an in itself neutral situation. As we saw in Chapter 3, the
experience of sense rather emerges from the coupling between the
situation and the specifics of our bodies and sense-organs. Like values,
the senses we make of things are relational realities. At least, that is
how it should be. As we will see, when somebody suffers from
a psychiatric disorder, this relational reality is disrupted. Psychiatric
disorders entail more or less one-sided enactments of a specific type of
sense. The sense-making of psychiatric disorders comes close to subjective projection, but that image is generally too simple in its assumption of unidirectionality. For instance, being anxious, I perceive my
surroundings only partly; noticing only what confirms my worries.
The anxious state I am in makes me more susceptible to certain triggers
in my situation than to others – but that does not mean I make them up.
Often there will be reciprocal loops involved: by acting in a certain way,

I elicit a certain type of reaction from others, one that in turn affirms my expectations. It is through my own behaviour that I enlist others to enact certain interaction patterns with me, as when I position myself as submissive and thereby invite the other to behave more dominantly. Here I am not *imagining* the other being dominant towards me: I might even recognise only their dominance and remain unaware of my own submissiveness.

Sense-making is moreover always sense-making in a *context*. Consequently, whether or not someone's sense-making is disordered fundamentally depends upon that context. No behaviour, thought, or feeling is in itself 'disordered': aggression can be called for when under attack, suspicion may be warranted, grief after losing a loved one is but normal, and some situations simply are worrisome or anxiety-provoking. Thus one cannot assess the appropriateness of sense-making without taking its context into account. Besides, our assessment is itself shaped by the norms and values of the sociocultural community of which we are a part. And because norms may shift and social practices are flexible too, the evaluation of what is and what is not appropriate is also not set in stone. Some norms and practices will be more stable or liable to change than others, as was seen with the 'layered' structure of values from universally shared to sociocultural and idiosyncratic ones that we discussed in the previous chapter.

By characterising psychiatric disorders as disorders of sense-making, and sense-making as a fundamentally embodied and embedded activity, an enactive account implies that the proper unit of analysis of psychiatric disorders will be persons in their worlds. Mental or psychiatric disorders are not disorders of the brain, or of the body, but they pertain to *persons*; that is, to bodily and reflexive beings. Persons, moreover, who cannot be understood apart from their sociocultural worlds. From an enactive perspective then, if we want to understand psychiatric disorders, we will have to look at persons in interaction with their worlds.[1] The enactive view on sense-making thus implies an integration

---

[1]   An enactive approach thus takes the whole person–world system as the relevant unit of analysis. Given that the person's relations with her environment are

of the four dimensions of psychiatric disorders with which we started out. Besides, as is already implied by the notion of interaction, we need to look at this complex person–world system *over time* in order to understand its dynamics. How did the person arrive at this pattern in her sense-making?

7.3   WHEN IS SOMETHING A DISORDER OF SENSE-MAKING?

To further flesh out the characterisation of psychiatric disorders as disorders of sense-making it will be helpful to distinguish psychiatric disorders from somatic disorders on the one hand and from normal sense-making on the other hand. In other words: what makes something a *psychiatric* rather than a somatic disorder? And what makes something a *disordered* rather than a normal pattern of sense-making?

7.3.1   Somatic versus Psychiatric Disorders

Given the thorough rejection of mind–body dualism, one might expect that the distinction between 'somatic' and 'mental' disorders is also rejected by an enactive perspective. And in a sense, it is. After all, one cannot cut people into two halves, one somatic, one mental. From an

regarded as co-constitutive, this may prompt the question whether we can still 'locate' psychiatric disorders within individual persons. Or perhaps better put, is it still appropriate to ascribe psychiatric disorders to persons? Why not ascribe them to relationships, families, environments, or to cultures even? On the one hand, these can certainly be toxic in the sense of undermining the person, being highly stressful, gaslighting her, discriminating her, etc. If someone goes on to develop psychiatric problems, they cannot be seen in isolation from her history and interactions with her environment. But that does not yet mean that we can simply apply the concepts of psychiatric disorders to these environments. It is after all still the person who is making sense of the world, and the person who suffers. A 'healthy' sense-making would recognise toxic environments as such. The difficulty is of course that one's sense-making is actually shaped through one's previous interactions, so that recognising detrimental circumstances may be hindered precisely because of these circumstances. In that case, what is disordered is still the *person's* sense-making though, even if we now have a developmental explanation for it. In terms of treatment, someone's sense-making can be changed in various ways, and some of these involve changing their relationships or environments in general, thereby enabling a different kind of interaction. Family dynamics can for instance be the target of treatment, as in systems therapy, or it may be part of treatment that social work helps with a concrete change of environment in terms of housing or jobs.

enactive perspective, to understand psychiatric disorders implies looking at the entire, complex and dynamic, person–world system. The same can be said of 'somatic' disorders. But even though body and mind cannot be separated, this does not yet mean that we cannot distinguish between somatic and psychiatric disorders as different *kinds* of disorders affecting one and the same undivided person. Avoiding dichotomies does not require us to deny all differences.

Psychiatric disorders are disorders of sense-making, while in somatic disorders this sense-making is only secondarily involved – if it is involved at all. Psychiatric disorders pertain to one's thoughts, feelings, and actions; to one's way of being in the world. They affect people in their very personhood, including their relations to the world, to other people, and to themselves. For patients suffering from somatic diseases, their worlds may change too, as well as their relations to the people around them and to themselves and their bodies. These can even be quite dramatic changes, especially in case of chronic diseases and neurological disorders. Some neurological disorders such as Parkinson's disease, Korsakoff's syndrome, and Alzheimer's disease can clearly affect patients' sense-making and even their personalities. Yet these remain secondary effects of the disease. In psychiatric disorders, however, these relations are directly concerned. For psychiatric patients their world changes in character: to the extent that their sense-making is out of tune they can even be said to live in a world of their own (van den Berg 1972).

It is tempting to describe this difference as one of causes versus reasons: in the case of somatic disorders, potential sense-making problems have (somatic) causes, whereas psychiatric disorders have reasons. From an enactive perspective, this is a problematic distinction though, for it implies an opposition between matter and meaning while the enactive life–mind continuity thesis rather implies that matter and meaning necessarily go together in living beings. The distinction between somatic and psychiatric disorders is not that the first has nothing to do with meaning (our physiological processes are after all shaped by our existential form of life, as we saw in the previous chapter), but rather that there is a difference in *the way in which* meaning is involved or the *kind* of meaning that is involved. In psychiatric disorders, there is a different motivation at play. While somatic diseases threaten the precariousness of living being's self-organisation, i.e. the integrity of being a living being, psychiatric disorders result from threats to being an existential self, a person in the world. Here our *integrity as persons* is at stake. Often we protect ourselves – our experience of being an integrated, more or less coherent, able and worthwhile human being – by certain ways of acting, feeling, or thinking. We avoid certain situations or thoughts that make us anxious or uncomfortable about ourselves, we come up with rationalisations for the discrepancies between the values we want to embody and our actual behaviours, we guard ourselves against critique by not taking our criticasters seriously in the first place, etc. Usually such self-protective patterns of behaviour are pretty harmless and may function quite well, but they too can get out of hand. Some reaction type that was once helpful can become detrimental over time and/or in a different environment. It may for instance have been a good strategy to be very careful and alert for danger in a certain time and place, but in safer circumstances the inability to trust may stand in the way of you making appropriate sense of your situation and the people around you. Psychiatric disorders are *enacted*: they dissolve if one succeeds in changing one's way of interacting with the world, opening up one's stuck pattern of sense-making.[2] The paths we have lain

---

2   In the case of psychotic problems, the enaction of fundamental or basic aspects of personhood, such as the boundary between self and others and self and world, is at stake (Gipps, forthcoming-b). Laing (1960/1990) speaks of the 'ontological insecurity' of schizophrenic patients, and I think this notion captures quite well the motivational structure of trying to safeguard yourself as a person by resorting to such drastic means as transitivism, thought disorder, or delusions. Contact with reality is too threatening to the self to be endured. By contrast, neurotic (i.e. non-psychotic) problems concern the safeguarding of one's ideal self by avoiding certain feelings or situations or insights. We could say that here contact with one's self in all its anxiousness, smallness, vulnerability, and dependence is avoided.

down in walking are the problem. The secondary problems of sense-making due to somatic disorders such as Alzheimer's or Parkinson's disease, however, do not typically disappear by interacting with the world in a different way.

Psychiatric disorders should thus be distinguished from somatic disorders, including neurological disorders. Neurological disorders such as Parkinson's disease are brain diseases in the sense that most of their diverse symptoms – such as tremors, slowness and depressed feelings – can be linked to a neurological problem, in the case of Parkinson's disease: the diminished dopamine production in the substantia nigra. This is evidenced by the fact that these complaints are usually diminished by medication that raises dopamine production. No such disturbance in the brain has been found for psychiatric disorders, despite all the research that has been done to try to find such 'underlying mechanisms'. And if we were to find such a neuronal mechanism, this would mean that we had been wrong to think that here we had a psychiatric disorder. This may sound drastic, but there is an intuitive appeal to this idea. Think for instance of a delirium following a physiological trigger (e.g. fever, anaesthesia, or alcohol), or madness following untreated syphilis, or disturbances of sense-making caused by a brain tumour: such cases of disordered sense-making intuitively seem different from problems of sense-making at play in schizophrenia or personality disorders.[3] They also usually require a different type of treatment. Someone who is depressed because of thyroid gland problems, for example, should have these attended to, rather than taking antidepressants or engaging in psychotherapy. This is also reflected in the psychiatric practice of first excluding potential somatic causes of the symptoms at hand. If inexplicable personality changes start to occur,

---

[3]   The *DSM-5* (American Psychiatric Association 2013), on the contrary, does consider these neurologically induced disorders to be psychiatric disorders. They are listed in the category of 'neurocognitive disorders'. Clearly physiologically induced depressions too are considered psychiatric disorders, to be diagnosed as 'depressive disorder due to another medical condition'.

one first wants to exclude the option that these changes may be due to a brain tumour – since that would naturally require a different kind of treatment than those on offer in mental health care.

The brain is obviously implicated in psychiatric disorders as well (amongst other physiological processes) and interventions directed at neuronal features such as neurotransmitters can help diminish psychiatric problems too. The difference between neurological and psychiatric disorders is that in psychiatric disorders the brain is indeed implicated, but in a mereological way; as part of problems taking place at a more global level of the person–world system. It is the global problem of sense-making that affects the more local brain processes in an organisationally causal, cake-like way. In neurological disorders it is the other way around: a local disturbance at the level of brain processes can have global effects on sense-making amongst other things. Here too though we should avoid reductionism about the role of the brain, for in the case of neurological disorders too the brain is not an isolated organ and what happens in the brain is affected by what we do and have done and experienced. That is, what is happening in our brain typically cannot be properly understood without taking our history of interactions with the world into account, interactions which in turn are shaped by our existential concerns and sociocultural practices. Cancer may be an exception to this, and there may be other exceptions too, but in general we also need a developmental, systems approach to diseases of the brain.

But how about the so-called neurodevelopmental disorders, such as autism spectrum disorders and tic disorders? These are difficult cases. If a distinct neurological deficit were to be found, we should not regard them as psychiatric disorders, according to the distinction here proposed. But autism spectrum disorders also confront us with the further question of whether they should actually be seen as disorders. Now this diagnosis (as part of the *DSM-5*) currently includes a range of very different forms of problems, from the former diagnosis of Asperger's to PDD-NOS (Pervasive Developmental Disorder Not

Otherwise Specified). At least for some of these cases one could ask whether they should be considered cases of disordered, or rather of *different*, sense-making (see footnote 6).

Note that the conceptual distinction between somatic and psychiatric disorders will not always be clear-cut in practice. Someone may suffer from both a somatic and a psychiatric disorder and psychiatric disorders may lead to somatic disorders and vice versa. OCD patients may for instance wreck their backs and the skin of their hands because of their hours of bending over the sink to wash their hands. The constant experience of tension due to anxiety disorders can affect one's muscles and tendons and lead to headaches and other problems. Conversely, the social isolation that may follow from being impaired by a chronic illness can in turn lead to depression. Furthermore, the distinction between primary and secondary problems of sense-making does not mean that these secondary problems could not also be attended to by various mental health care professionals. These problems naturally deserve attention and treatment too – the type of treatment required depending on the nature of the problems at hand.

7.3.2   *Normal versus Pathological Sense-Making*

The second even more important and difficult demarcation matter concerns how to distinguish pathological from normal sense-making. This is a charged question – and rightly so because demarcating 'normal' from 'abnormal' is a risky undertaking. There is the danger of pathologising ordinary weirdness, of behaviours of people that somehow stand out from the crowd. Relatedly there is the risk of pathologising those who do not comply with certain oppressive social norms, or those who in some way are socially deviant or resist certain societal expectations or rules. And there is the danger of pathologising what are merely sociocultural differences (e.g. talking with the spirits of one's diseased ancestors should not be confused with hearing voices as a schizophrenic symptom). It is also important to recognise that those who are in the position of deciding whether someone is or is not suffering from a psychiatric disorder are in a position of power. Who gets to decide what is and isn't normal? Being labelled with a psychiatric disorder can have serious effects on people's lives in terms of their self-understanding, social status, possibilities of getting insurances, job assessments, as well as juridical consequences. In many countries psychiatrists are granted the power to admit people to psychiatric wards against their will. Typically according to strict policies, but still. Who gets to develop these policies? one could further ask.

There is an inescapable normativity to drawing a line between the 'normal' and the 'abnormal': after all, statistical rarity alone won't be able to tell us whether a phenomenon is pathological or not. Being exceptionally tall or exceptionally smart or exceptionally large-nosed makes you part of a minority, but it does not amount to a pathology. The history of ascribing 'madness', including the history of the field of psychiatry itself, also inspires caution. Behaviours we do not understand, or that frighten us, or behaviours that were regarded as sinful, or contrary to our norms, have all been labelled as indications of madness, a madness that needed to be repressed or removed from society. A recent shameful example is that homosexuality was included as a psychiatric disorder in the *DSM* until as late as 1973.

With so many pitfalls to avoid, one might wonder why we should even speak of 'disorders' at all, rather than keep simply to differences between people? Why not just say that there are differences in the way in which people make sense of the world, without declaring some patterns of sense-making pathological? Because normalising can fail to do justice to the experiences of those who suffer from psychiatric disorders: their suffering, their feeling out of place, their feeling of something being wrong. By allowing certain ways of interacting with the world, oneself, and/or others to be pathological, we acknowledge that these are conditions in which one's being a person in the world is at stake, in which one's personhood is affected or even damaged. It *is* difficult to be a person in the world, and we all at some point and to some extent struggle with it, so in that sense it is normal – as is reflected by the fact that many people suffer from psychiatric problems at some point in their lives. But to efface these problems as varieties of normality does not do justice to the impairments they present and the suffering that they cause. This of course does not mean that people suffering from psychiatric disorders are in any sense (morally or ontologically) inferior (Gipps, forthcoming-a). It is precisely part of our human condition to be vulnerable in this existential way.

In what follows I will argue that there are four general characteristics of pathological sense-making that have to do with (1) the appropriateness of sense-making, (2) the flexibility of sense-making in relation to the world, (3) the flexibility of the existential stance, and (4) the experience of suffering.

The Appropriateness of Sense-Making

Sense-making is the evaluative interaction of persons with their world, others, and themselves. As sense-making is always of something, the first question is whether this sense is intelligible in light of the person's situation. Do her experiences fit with her situation? Is her reaction or evaluation appropriate to and meaningful in light of her circumstances? Is it appropriate to experience oneself as fat, given one's actual body? Is it appropriate to fear social exclusion, given one's social environment? Is it appropriate to feel offended, given the remarks made? Is it appropriate to be suspicious, given one's situation?[4] As mentioned before, no experience, reaction, or sense-making is in and of itself pathological: their appropriateness after all depends on their context.

For example: to grieve about losing a loved one is fitting and meaningful. When you lose someone you love, grieving is a meaningful directedness to your situation. You are engaged with, involved with your situation of loss. Your suffering makes sense. This

---

[4]   Note that there is a difference between being *appropriate* and being *understandable*: knowing someone's history can help us understand where their reaction is coming from, and we can make sense of their reaction in that way, but that does not yet make their reaction appropriate to the situation.

is not to prescribe one way of grieving as appropriate and others as inappropriate – it does not even mean that grief is what you should experience at all. Again it all depends on the situation: when you lose someone who is close to you, but you had an ambivalent relation with, for instance one of your parents, it can make perfect sense to feel just as ambivalent about their death, maybe even partly relieved or freed. The appropriateness of someone's sense-making can only be determined by taking into account the wider context of someone's current situation as well as her history. In contrast to grief, a depression is not a meaningful connection to the world, but rather *stands between* the person and her world, and makes it impossible for her to relate meaningfully to it. While grief is a way of relating to one's situation, a depression hinders one's relation to the world. Because the sense-making of the situation gets 'stuck' (see the next criterion), it is no longer attuned to the situation and the suffering is no longer a form of meaningful engagement.

A lack of meaning is not the only form of impaired sense-making: the world may also appear as overly meaningful, as we see in the case of delusions when random objects and events become meaningful signs. The contact with reality, the attunedness of the sense-making, is more severely disrupted in case of delusions than in (non-delusional) depression, but in both cases the person suffering from these disorders is in some way out of touch with reality. The same goes for patients with anxiety disorders, sensing more threats than are realistically present, and for those OCD patients who unwarrantedly worry that they may have done harm to others without noticing it.

It may well be that psychiatric disorders are characterised by sense-making that is inappropriate or insufficiently attuned to the situation at hand – but the next question is of course how we estimate or judge this appropriateness. We saw earlier that enactivism's relational view of the fundamental coupling between person and world, and of sense-making as the relational outcome of this coupling, imply that there is no view from nowhere. Any sense-making is necessarily embodied and embedded or situated sense-making: one's bodily constitution, sense-organs, and concerns unavoidably shape one's relation to and perspective on the world. And for us existential beings, our concerns are co-shaped by the sociocultural communities of which we are part. This means that there is not only no neutral point of view from which to establish what is and is not appropriate, but also that the norms of appropriateness will, to some extent, vary over time and place.

All we can rely on is our *common sense*, i.e. the shared sense-making of people within their sociocultural practices. It is against the backdrop of such a body of shared sense-making that we can regard someone's sense-making as disattuned. Our sense-making is to a large extent shared – it is 'common sense'. As we saw in our discussion of values in Chapter 6, our sense-making has more universal aspects (coming from the fact that we are all bodily and social creatures, with similar needs and vulnerabilities) as well as more sociocultural aspects (that come from being brought up in a specific community with specific norms and practices) and idiosyncratic aspects (that depend on our specific life histories and experiences). The first two are shared or common sense. Some examples of this common sense include: the capacity to notice natural dangers such as fires or grizzly bears; to see when someone is in pain, happy, sad, or angry; to sense the atmosphere when you enter a room with people: whether the atmosphere is exuberant or rather gloomy; to know how to behave in a specific social setting like a library, a party, or a public space. There is an increasingly sociocultural aspect to these examples, but they are all examples of immediate, generally implicit, estimations of a situation – with their own norms of attunement or appropriateness.

Since our sense-making is shaped by our sociocultural embeddedness, psychiatry cannot escape this sociocultural dimension either. This does not make the assessment of appropriateness completely arbitrary though: it's not as if we have to rely on majority votes or etiquette to tell us what is sane and what is not. The relational view of enactivism indeed denies a neutral foundation or perspective, but it just as much denies that we construct meaning or project values onto the world. The relational view implies that our common sense does not come from thin air – although some aspects of it will be more arbitrary and thus liable to change than others. We would today find it inappropriate if a teacher were to smoke in front of class of school children, or if a doctor would smoke while consulting her patients, but fifty years ago it would have been normal. As contexts change, our common sense of what is and isn't appropriate changes too. This means that in contexts that are very different from one's own, some aspects of appropriateness will be harder to judge. To think that you are Jesus Christ will probably be seen as inappropriate everywhere, and so too will it be hard to find a context in which being scared of baby strollers makes sense. But other fears, actions, perceptions, thoughts, and feelings – such as 'hearing voices' or being seen as an outcast – may be more difficult to estimate as a sociocultural outsider. Likewise, it is difficult to compare nineteenth-century melancholia with our current major depression: some aspects of these experiences may be similar, but others are so closely tied to the norms and expectations of their time that they cannot simply be regarded as the same condition. In other words: to the extent that our common sense is dependent upon place and time our norms of psychopathology are dynamical too.

Despite all this, the inappropriateness of someone's sense-making is not enough to draw any conclusions regarding psychopathology. Inappropriate behaviour may for instance also be due to a lack of sociocultural know-how, or it may be a deliberate provocation. Besides, not all weirdness is pathological, and there is nothing wrong with eccentricity. But there are further criteria.

The Flexibility of Sense-Making

A second criterion concerns the flexibility of sense-making, in particular the flexibility of someone's pattern of interacting with the world and others. Does the person get stuck in an inflexible pattern of acting and reacting, even when it does not fit the situation? This characteristic is related to the previous one, since sense-making will often be counted inappropriate because someone makes the same sense out of very different situations: they dominantly see the world as threatening (in anxiety disorders), or as meaningless (in case of depression), or as overly meaningful (in case of psychotic disorders). Normally, one's sense-making is attuned or receptive to one's specific situation. In psychiatric disorders this attunement is diminished. Psychiatric disorders often involve a 'freezing' of a certain sense-making.

The rigidity of a particular bias in sense-making is often increased through the development of vicious circles between the sense-making and the world of the patient, reinforcing a specific interaction pattern. For instance, patients suffering from anxiety disorders tend to avoid all kinds of situations that appear threatening to them or that they imagine to be threatening. Because of their avoidance of such situations, no correcting experiences can be formed, and the anxiety remains. The patients' worlds become smaller, and the threshold for going out of the small safe haven becomes larger. Or take depression. For patients suffering from depression hardly anything is inviting anymore, nothing attracts them. This leads them to undertake fewer and fewer activities, thereby shrinking their life-world. This shrunken life-world in turn provides fewer options for action and thus fewer possibilities for positive change.

Self-fulfilling prophecies are another example of a vicious circle that rigidifies a certain pattern of interaction. The person who thinks nobody will find her interesting will (unconsciously) make herself invisible. By radiating her own feeling of being an uninteresting person, she increases the likelihood that people indeed overlook her, which is yet another proof that her self-image is right. Or think of schizophrenic patients who feel a certain general mistrust, a 'delusional mood'. When, looking for signs revealing others' true intentions, they distrustfully stare at them, they find that indeed people look at them weirdly, or stare back at them. This in turn strengthens their belief that these people are up to something, or encourages them to keep an eye on them. In general, how I act towards you will affect how you in turn act towards me. If I find the world to be full of aggressive people, or kind people, or deceitful people, or successful people, that probably says more about me than about those people. The relation between these experiences is me. It may not be something I am aware of: to me it does not feel like I am enacting a type of interaction, it just feels like I happen to be surrounded by people who are keen on humiliating me.

Another solidifying factor for patterns of sense-making comes from social isolation. In many psychiatric disorders, social isolation plays an important modulating role. Sometimes people withdraw from social situations as a direct result of their disorder – such as patients suffering from social anxiety or depressed patients who feel they are a burden to others. In other cases, psychiatric disorders (such as depression and schizophrenia) may involve an experience of estrangement, of being out of tune with the rest of the world. When one feels out of place, social contact may bring this disattunement acutely to the fore, which gives all the more reason to try to avoid such contact. There may also be practical reasons to avoid social situations: OCD patients may fear others' germs, anorexia patients may dread the eating that is often involved in social gatherings. And, last but not least, many patients who suffer from psychiatric disorders are ashamed of their conditions and therefore try to hide either their condition, or, if that becomes impossible, they may hide themselves. But avoiding social situations means that there is less chance that patients may gain positive, supportive experiences that correct their faulty assumptions. Moreover, by withdrawing from social interactions, one also loses the practice of attuning. If you have been in your own world for a while it will take time and effort to re-connect with others again. From an enactive perspective, attuning to others is a *capacity* and social isolation can make this capacity even more rusty – instigating yet another vicious circle.

The Flexibility of Stance-Taking

Apart from the flexibility of the interaction pattern of a person with her world, the flexibility of her stance-taking is also important. Is the person able to relate to herself and her situation? Does she have the ability to take a stance towards what is happening to her and to herself? Is there some inner freedom, or flexibility in this stance-taking? Our existential stance provides the freedom not to coincide with the here and now, to relativise, to take a different perspective on oneself and one's situation. It is through such stance-taking that we may recognise the inappropriateness and inflexibility of our ways of interacting, and this can consequently help us develop and adopt a broader, more attuned way of sense-making. Yet this stance too can itself become rigid or one-sided and thereby less attuned.

As we saw in Chapter 5, the existential stance is often affected by psychiatric disorders. How one evaluates oneself and one's situation may be 'hijacked' by a psychiatric disorder. A depression, for instance, not only affects the primary interactions with the (social) world, but it also affects one's existential stance: one cannot imagine ever being happy again. A depression colonises the existential stance and makes that patients thoroughly coincide with their present, hopeless condition. And even though patients may rationally know that they will probably emerge from this episode, as they have before, it does not feel that way. It is hopeless and it will stay hopeless. The flexibility and attunement of the reflexive relation to oneself and one's situation is impaired. Delusions provide another example of this. Delusions often involve improbable, inapt, or even bizarre convictions: convictions that seem inappropriate. But perhaps even more telling than their content is the rigidity with which these convictions are held. What patients suffering from delusions are incapable of is precisely taking a different perspective and relativising their ideas. It is this absoluteness, this uncompromising holding onto them, that provides an important distinction between merely having unlikely ideas and proper delusions.

Not all psychiatric disorders affect the existential stance, however. Patients suffering from OCD for instance are an exception since they are typically aware of the senselessness of their own compulsive behaviour. They know that what they do does not make sense, but still they feel compelled to perform these behaviours since the pressure and anxiety becomes unbearable if they don't. To them, their disorder is like an alien force, overtaking them. Patients suffering from psychiatric disorders may also be aware of the incongruence of their own sense-making. When one's sense-making is properly attuned, it doesn't draw attention, it goes unnoticed. Patients may however feel that their experiences are not fitting, or lack sense and meaning. The world, and their place in it, has become strange to them. Situations, events, or other people no longer make sense; one cannot sort them out, one does not know how to understand them. Instead of being involved with one's daily projects and concerns one feels there is a rift between oneself and those worldly engagements. One is cut-off from the present situation and the world appears strange and unfamiliar. Such experiences of estrangement can also concern *oneself*. Not only may the world become unfamiliar, but one can also become unfamiliar to oneself. Both experiences can be highly unsettling.

It is not just the stance-taking itself that is at issue; what matters too is the relation between this stance-taking and simply being immersed in the here and now. Given that our capacity for stance-taking implies an excentric position (Plessner 1928/1981), we are characterised by a certain ambiguity: we need to find a balance between deliberation and unreflective action, between being immersed in the present and reflecting on it. In psychiatric disorders, this balance is often disturbed, either by thinking too much ('hyper-reflexivity'[5]) and thereby disrupting the flow of immersed interaction with the world, or by thinking too little (impulsivity) and thereby

---

[5]   To my knowledge, Laing (1960/1990) was the first to use the term *hyper-reflexivity*, in his classical work *The Divided Self*. He argues that schizophrenic patients may experience a gap between their body and mind. They identify with their mind, and feel estranged from their body. Laing describes how 'the unembodied self becomes hyper-conscious' (p. 69); that is, the person observes himself and is continuously aware of himself. *Hyper-reflexivity* thus refers to the exaggerated reflection on and deliberate attention to what one is doing. Every act becomes a conscious, deliberate decision instead of just spontaneous responsiveness. What is normally taken for granted, unthinkingly relied upon, is now brought to awareness. As Fuchs (2011c) points out, making such tacit processes explicit actually *disturbs* their functionality. He writes: 'Self-centeredness and hyper-reflection are ... on the one hand, the result of the illness, but on the other hand, they often additionally contribute to it' (p. 239). For more on

acting too rashly on immediate impulses rather than one's long-term concerns.

In general then, one's stance-taking is disordered when there is reduced flexibility; when there is only a single attitude towards everything that happens, or when the balance between reflection and immersion is disturbed.

Suffering

A final indication of disordered sense-making is that people whose sense-making has become stuck in a rigid pattern and thus disattuned to their actual situation often suffer from this. For many people it is when their suffering becomes too much, and/or when they find they cannot function in the way they want to, that they decide to seek professional help. Suffering or feeling impaired is often a signal that something is going wrong. But it need not be: suffering can just as well be a meaningful and appropriate reaction to a specific life situation. Besides, not all psychiatric patients suffer from their problematic sense-making, as for instance in cases of mania and some delusional psychoses. For these patients, their own behaviour seems meaningful; to them what they do, and how they relate to the world, does make sense. A disordered pattern of sense-making does not have to be experienced by the person in question as disordered, strange, or troublesome – at least not at that moment. In that case, it may be the people close to them that suffer most from their affliction. Despite its personal relevance, suffering thus cannot be the sole or sufficient criterion for the determination of disorders.

Usually psychiatric disorders involve all four aspects – inappropriateness of the experiences or interactions; a lack of flexibility in the way of interacting with the world; a lack of flexibility in one's existential stance-taking; and personal suffering. Not all criteria need to be fulfilled in all disorders though: in different disorders the emphasis is on different aspects and the suffering and problems with the

hyper-reflexivity and psychopathology, see Sass (1992), Sass and Parnas (2003), de Haan and Fuchs (2010), Fuchs (2010b), and de Haan et al. (2015a).

existential stance may even be absent. This may be compared with Wittgenstein's (1958) concept of family resemblances: with some family members I share the shape of my ears, with others my nose or knobbly knees.

Where to Draw the Boundaries?

These four criteria for disordered sense-making, however, do not yet tell us where to draw the lines: when does a pattern of sense-making become so deviant that we should consider it a psychiatric disorder? When is a pattern of sense-making too inappropriate or too inflexible and when is suffering too much? None of the four criteria provides us with a binary outcome: all of them refer instead to gradual phenomena. An enactive approach asks us to focus on processes rather than entities, and invites us to think both in terms of stages and in terms of reinforcing versus undermining influences rather than static states. The importance of evaluating a person's sense-making in their proper context – in terms of their current situation as well as the dynamics of their sense-making over time – makes it hard to draw discrete boundaries around psychiatric disorders. On an enactive account then there simply are no clear, generally valid cut-off points between normality and pathology. Regarding psychiatric disorders as structurally disordered patterns of sense-making implies a continuum rather than discrete states. Both ends of the continuum are clear: we can just as easily recognise normal behaviour as we can recognise a severe major depression or a vigorous psychotic episode. In the middle, it will be more difficult. The fact that the boundaries are vague, however, does not mean that the difference between pathology and normality becomes purely arbitrary: it only means that there will be grey areas. Grey areas are unavoidable. For when is a pattern of sense-making really 'stuck' as compared to merely somewhat biased in a certain direction? When is a kid merely lively or difficult, and when is a diagnosis of ADHD justified? When do we start to consider whether deep mourning after the death of a loved one may be 'turning into' a depression? There are normal differences between people: some are more inclined to being

anxious, to worrying, others more inclined to be orderly or controlling, yet others are more impulsive. Neither normality nor psychopathology has strict boundaries.[6]

The existence of such grey areas may prompt the worry that, in
the absence of clear cut-off points, psychiatry could become over-
inclusive, leading to unnecessary pathologising and treating what
are really varieties of normality. Conversely, it may also prompt concerns about the risk of under-treatment: of not recognising cases of
psychiatric problems and thus not sufficiently helping people who
might need it. The question is whether this lack of clear boundaries
is a fault of the enactive conception or whether this is just the way it
is. As soon as we accept that we need to take into account people's
contexts, we will be confronted with border cases. Following the
enactive view on persons in their worlds as complex dynamical systems implies the need for individual, contextualised assessments –
instead of arbitrarily assigning cut-off points. That the diagnosis of
a psychiatric disorder asks for a careful, contextualised estimation of
a particular person is not a weakness of the enactive approach but
rather a fitting tenet.

Besides, it is good to keep in mind that psychiatry is no different
from other medical specialties in this regard. That is: to the extent that
grey areas may be regarded as a worry, it is not a worry that is specific
of psychiatry. Almost all estimations concerning matters of health
lack universal cut-off points and rather require us to take the person's
context, history, and circumstances into account. When, for example,
do we regard someone's cholesterol level as 'too high'? When is

---

6   Autism spectrum disorders (ASD) are a difficult case. Although autists typically show
rigid and/or limited patterns of interactions and are characterised by disattunement to
social situations in particular, it is still questionable whether they should be seen as
having a psychiatric disorder. Because they are developmental disorders there is no
'before' or 'after' ASD: it is not a temporary condition: for autists there is no other way
of experiencing the world. And do they suffer from their condition? Or do they suffer
from not fitting into our normal ways of life, a way of life that is imposed upon them? In
the right environment, they might be fine. The question who gets to decide what is and
isn't normal acutely comes to the fore in the movement that claims that autistic people
are discriminated against by what they call 'neurotypicals' (see for instance www.neuro
-typical.com). They wonder: why should those neurotypical standards be the norm?

someone's level of haemoglobin too low? Here too, decisions depend on the circumstances (e.g. age, gender, global health, pregnancy) and on agreements: informed estimations of experts of the risks of treating or not treating in specific situations. All medical specialties have their own grey areas, their rules of thumb, and their checklists of reasons to depart from those rules. Do you give an eighty-year-old woman who suffers from cardiac arrhythmia a pacemaker, or do the risks of anaesthesia outweigh the benefits of the operation? Or, even more fundamentally, when exactly do we diagnose 'cardiac arrhythmia'? Just as in psychiatry, there are clear cases on both ends of the healthy to disease continuum, and sometimes difficult considerations in between.[7]

7.4 DISORDERED SENSE-MAKING INVOLVES A DIFFERENT FIELD OF AFFORDANCES

The enactive conception of sense-making as a fundamentally embodied and embedded activity integrates the four dimensions of psychiatric disorders: implicating the body, experiences, the world, and our existential stance. This integrative view on sense-making entails that problems of sense-making are per definition not isolated problems: they involve one's very way of being in the world, one's very existence. In system's terms: they are global not local problems. The way in which one makes sense of the world implicates what world one lives in. It includes one's relation to one's body, one's relation to others, and one's relation to time (i.e. the experience of one's history, present, and future). By deviating from our common sense, patients suffering from psychiatric disorders can even be said to 'live in a world of their own', or to have 'a different existence' as the phenomenological psychiatrist van den Berg (1972) called it. The loneliness of this different existence is the 'nucleus of psychiatry' (p. 105). Since this different existence comes to the fore in very various aspects of life, one could start from any one of them when elucidating someone's specific way of being in the world. Drawing on Binswanger, van den Berg (1972) remarks that it

---

[7]   Note that accepting the idea of a continuum does not preclude the possibility of there being qualitative shifts as well. We will get back to this in Section 7.5.

doesn't matter from which corner you start to lift a carpet; in the end you will lift the whole of it. One way to make this different existence more tangible is by explicating how one's experience of the world amounts to a different *field of affordances*.

Sense-making discloses a world, which is to say: not a neutral collection of objects, but rather a world that is significant to me, offering me various possibilities for action. Affordances refer to the possibilities for action that the environment offers to a specific form of life (Gibson 1979; Chemero 2003; Rietveld and Kiverstein 2014). Affordances are an inherently relational notion: what the world affords me depends on the one hand on what is out there, and on the other hand on me: on my capacities (what are possibilities for action to me?), and my concerns (which of these possibilities are relevant to me?). Depending on my capacities and concerns (which both shaped by my history of interacting with the world), the world opens up as a field of more and less relevant affordances. Sense-making entails perceiving the relevant affordances that the world offers to me. We can distinguish between a *landscape* and a *field* of affordances: the landscape of affordances refers to the possibilities of action that are available to a form of life in general, whereas the field of affordances refers to those possibilities of action that are available to a specific individual in a specific situation (de Haan et al. 2013b). This field is thus an idiosyncratic subset of the general landscape of affordances.

The activity of sense-making discloses the world as a field of relevant affordances. Just as affordances are relational, so too is their relevance. Again, this relevance is neither projected onto these affordances, nor inherent in them: their significance is rather a relational reality. Disordered sense-making discloses an altered field of relevant affordances. The world appears differently to psychiatric patients: their sense-making highlights different aspects of the world and misses others. Their experience has become more of a subjective matter and less part of a relational reality. Such biases may even amount to a deformation of the field of affordances. The depressed patient experiences the world as grey, the paranoid patient experiences the world as threatening, the obsessive-

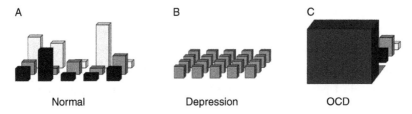

A   B   C

Normal   Depression   OCD

FIGURE 7.1 Different fields of affordances. Adapted from de Haan et al. (2013b).

compulsive patient experiences the world as crawling with bacteria, the anxious patient experiences the world as full of people laughed at her or ridiculing her behind her back. And even if they may be right in one sense (there are bacteria everywhere, sometimes people indeed laugh at you), the relevance or significance encountered in these cases is overestimated. There are bacteria everywhere, but that is typically not relevant: as long as you wash your hands on the appropriate occasions, there is generally nothing to worry about. A substantively different way of making sense of the world implies that the disclosed world, the experienced world, itself is different.

Figure 7.1 gives a schematic depiction of different fields of relevant affordances. Normally, we have a number of short-term and long-term concerns: both immediate needs and more distant goals. These various concerns shape our field of affordances: our concerns determine what appears as salient to us, what attracts our attention and what we react to. For instance, when I am hungry, the chocolate that is lying next to my computer attracts my attention: a nearby affordance of the satisfaction of an immediate need. But more distant goals motivate my actions as well, such as the goal to complete my book. Neither of these motivations needs to be explicit to guide my actions, and many such actions may be performed unthinkingly as well. Besides, we continuously switch between different actions, eating, typing, texting, drinking – often unthinkingly as well. Following Dreyfus (2007), we can say that our affordances have a foreground-background structure.

More can be said about this field of affordances. In particular, we can distinguish its three dimensions (de Haan et al. 2013b): the 'width' refers to the broadness of the scope of affordances that one perceives. This dimension relates to the range of possibilities for action. How many options do I perceive? The 'depth' of the field refers to the temporal aspect: one not only perceives the affordances that are immediately present here and now, but one is also pre-reflectively aware of future plans and possible actions. These are the affordances on the horizon that one is in a sense already responsive to. Besides, one's present field is always shaped by one's history of previous interactions: after eating the chocolate, I'm no longer distracted by being hungry and my goal of finishing my book now makes my computer stand out more forcefully. Lastly, the 'height' of each of the affordances refers to their relevance or salience. Different affordances can however be relevant in different ways. Something can be important because it is dangerous and needs to be avoided (e.g. a softball about to hit your head, a snake on your trail, Facebook when you are trying to work), or because it is highly attractive and pulling us in (e.g. a bar of chocolate when you're hungry, the person you're in love with, Facebook). In the original figure, I used colours to add some differentiation to this dimension of experienced relevance. The height refers to the *intensity* of the relevance, whereas the colours are meant to indicate the *affective* salience of the affordance.[8]

The field of relevant affordances will normally be varied, diverse, and dynamic. It is dynamic in all four aspects: to the extent that both our concerns and the environment change, our field of relevant affordances changes too. Psychiatric disorders involve an alteration, constriction, or deformation of this field. In contrast to the normally extended and differentiated field represented by Figure 7.1A, Figure 7.1B depicts the field of relevant affordances of a depressed patient. Nothing stands out anymore; it is all the same grey, unattractive world that one is surrounded by. And this will go on and on endlessly: nothing sunny can be expected from the future

---

[8] See Dings (2017) for a more elaborate characterisation of the differences in how affordances solicit action.

either. The field of patients suffering from OCD is extremely narrowed down to only the immediate affordance of what *has* to be done *now*. Before any other affordance may announce itself, completing the compulsion has first priority. First, before I can even think of doing something else, I need to thoroughly wash my hands. The field of OCD is very much a field of fear or anxiety: fear too narrows down the focus to just the fearful, and fear also takes primacy over all other perceptions and actions. If, for instance, a fire were to break out, this would immediately draw your complete attention – and all other possibilities for action (drinking your coffee, reading an article, chatting with someone) automatically lose their relevance. Compulsions are like an outbreak of fire in this sense.

'When the psychiatric patient tells what his world looks like, he states, without detours and without mistakes, what he is like', writes van den Berg (1972, p. 46). That is because 'our world is our home, a realization of subjectivity' (p. 40). Our fields of affordances reflect our relations to time, to others (the social affordances we do or do not experience), and to our surroundings in general. More implicitly, they also reflect our relation to ourselves and our bodies, in the way in which possibilities do or do not show up for us. Affordances after all first and foremost concern our bodily responsivity to the world. Besides, our bodies may themselves show up as objects of attention – in contrast to the normal situation in which our bodies remain unnoticed as we are directed at the world.

Many detailed, insightful phenomenological analyses of each of these changed relations have been made for different pathologies; highlighting the experience of the body, the role of intersubjectivity, patients' relation to time, etc. (Broome et al. 2012; Stanghellini et al. 2018). This is not the place to repeat them. What matters here is how to fit such phenomenological accounts of patients' experiences into the bigger picture of psychiatric disorders as phenomena that are also physiologically, socioculturally, and existentially determined.

7.5   SOME CONCEPTUAL CONSEQUENCES

How does this enactive conception of psychiatric disorders as disorders of sense-making relate to other theories of the nature of psychiatric disorders? So many different accounts are on offer that properly discussing all of them would require a book of its own. A helpful way to navigate this conceptual landscape and see where an enactive approach fits in is by using Zachar and Kendler's (2007) conceptual taxonomy. They discerned six main questions about the nature of psychiatric disorders that can be used to compare different approaches. These questions concern the conceptual axes of (1) essentialism-nominalism, (2) objectivism-evaluativism, (3) entities-agents, (4) categories-continua, (5) internalism-externalism, and (6) causalism-descriptivism. I will address each question in turn.

7.5.1   Essentialism-Nominalism

The first question is whether categories of psychiatric disorder are defined by their underlying nature (essentialism), or whether they are rather practical categories identified by humans for particular uses (nominalism) (Zachar and Kendler 2007, p. 558). I want to slightly reformulate this question: the relevant opposition here is between being a *realist* or a *social constructivist* about the existence of psychiatric disorders. Essentialism is a specific form of realism, so you can be a realist about the nature of psychiatric disorders without believing this to entail that they have essences. Nominalism comes in different variants, but is always a negative thesis: it claims certain things (objects, abstractions, universals, etc.) do not exist. A positive reformulation in the context of psychiatric disorders would be social constructivism: the idea that our categories of psychiatric disorders are man-made rather than reflections of reality (which actually fits with how Zachar and Kendler describe nominalist positions). The question then becomes: do psychiatric disorders really exist, independently of our classifications, or are they social constructs, creations of our specific needs that are reflected in our classifications? Do we *discover* psychiatric disorders or do we *invent* them? Biomedical conceptions such as neuroreductionism clearly square with the realist side (in case of neuroreductionism even with its essentialist variant), whereas anti-psychiatry is an example of a social constructivist understanding of psychiatric disorders: what we classify as psychiatric disorders are really just problems in living (Szasz 1961). Psychiatric disorders are the product of our classification schemes which we have harnessed for some (social) purpose.

So where does an enactive approach fit on this axis? It doesn't. From an enactive perspective, the very opposition between realism and social constructivism is questionable. A disordered pattern of sense-making is *both* real *and* socioculturally co-constituted. The opposition between 'real' on the one hand and 'socially constructed' on the other hand is reminiscent of the classical dichotomous mind–world topology we discussed in Chapters 3 and 4: the objective facts are out there in the world and our biggest worry is that we might muddle them with our subjective projections if our representations of this objective world are pure enough. Following this topology we might come to assume that 'biology or physiology = real = universal' whereas 'sociocultural = construct = relative'. From an enactive perspective, however, physiological processes are part of and derive their characteristics from the larger dynamical system of an organism interacting with its environment or a person interacting with her world. Our sociocultural surroundings are thus not a passive background setting but part of the system, affecting our physiological processes as well. As we saw, our physiology is shaped by what we do and what we do is shaped by our sociocultural practices. An opposition between biology and culture is thus untenable.

Similarly, the sociocultural co-constitution of psychiatric disorders does not make them any less real, and even though our classifications, like all of our sense-making, reflect our concerns, this does not yet make them arbitrary. On an inner/outer model of mind and world 'real' means 'independent from us', while enactivism maintains that our perspective on the world is necessarily embodied and embedded and yet instantiates an engagement with reality all the same – even if only with an excerpt of it. Disordered patterns of sense-making are real phenomena and existed before we started categorising them as psychiatric disorders. At the same time, their 'disorderedness' depends on their context and the prevailing sociocultural norms of appropriateness of that time and place. Our classifications of psychiatric disorders thus do not refer to static, universal, never changing 'natural kinds' (another term that an enactive ontology sees as problematic); they will to some extent be dynamic as our common sense is dynamic too. As phenomena then, psychiatric disorders cannot be understood in isolation from our specific, socioculturally co-determined existence – but they are nevertheless real.

7.5.2 Objectivism-Evaluativism

Zachar and Kendler (2007) formulate the second issue as follows: 'Is deciding whether or not something is a psychiatric disorder a simple factual matter (objectivism), or does it inevitably involve a value-laden judgment (evaluativism)?' (p. 558). Objective views on psychiatric disorders typically refer to 'natural functions' and argue that the judgement of a disorder of these natural functions, a dysfunction, is a value-free matter of fact. Eyes that cannot see are dysfunctional, and similarly psychiatric disorders refer to cognitive and emotional dysfunctions. Finding objective measures for psychiatric disorders is one of the key goals of biological psychiatry and its neuroreductionist variants. The idea is that once we have found the underlying (neural) mechanisms of psychiatric disorders, we could in principle diagnose people by looking at their brain scans. On the other side of the axis are those who believe that judgements of health and disease are inherently value-laden; i.e. that the judgement that some condition is 'bad' and the other 'good' necessarily involves values. A middle position is taken by Wakefield's (1992a, 1992b, 1995, 2000) influential conception of psychiatric disorders as harmful dysfunctions. According to him, psychiatric disorders entail both objective dysfunctions of the person's emotional or cognitive functioning and the additional value-laden judgement of their harmfulness: 'a disorder exists when the failure of a person's internal mechanisms to perform their functions as designed by nature impinges harmfully on the person's well-being as defined by social values and meanings' (Wakefield 1992b, p. 373). In the *DSM-5* (American Psychiatric Association 2013) too, we find a hybrid of psychiatric disorders being dysfunctions 'in the psychological, biological, or developmental processes underlying mental functioning' combined with 'significant distress or disability'.[9]

It seems easy to pick the enactive side on this axis, as an enactive view is clearly at odds with the assumption that the determination of dysfunctions of natural functions would be value-free. An enactive approach indeed shares the various critiques that have been formulated against this assumption. It has for instance been pointed out that the notion of 'natural function' presupposes that evolutionary processes are a matter of *design* rather than blind tinkering (Megone 2000; Thornton 2000),[10] and that dysfunctions cannot be value-free

---

[9]   The full definition is as follows: 'A mental disorder is a syndrome characterised by clinically significant disturbance in an individual's cognition, emotion regulation, or behaviour that reflects a dysfunction in the psychological, biological, or developmental processes underlying mental functioning. Mental disorders are usually associated with significant distress or disability in social, occupational, or other important activities. An expectable or culturally approved response to a common stressor or loss, such as the death of a loved one, is not a mental disorder. Socially deviant behaviour (e.g. political, religious, or sexual) and conflicts that are primarily between the individual and society are not mental disorders unless the deviance or conflict results from a dysfunction in the individual, as described above' (American Psychiatric Association 2013).

The definition gives us three characteristics and two disclaimers: mental disorders are (1) syndromes, in which someone's cognition, emotion, or behaviour is disturbed in a 'clinically significant way'. These disturbances are (2) the manifestations of a dysfunction in the 'psychological, biological, or developmental processes underlying mental functioning'. Also, (3) such syndromes are characterised by significant distress or disability in important aspects of an individual's life. The two disclaimers are (1) in case of a common stressor or loss, responses that are 'expectable or culturally approved' do not count as mental disorders, and (2) socially deviant behaviour is not in and of itself sufficient ground for diagnosing a mental disorder.

[10]   Wakefield (2000) for instance refers to the evolutionary basis of functions, claiming that they are 'designed by natural selection'. But 'design' is a metaphor that sits uncomfortably with the 'blind process' of natural selection (Glas 2008). Wakefield (2000) gives the example of the heart as having the natural function to pump our blood: 'the heart exists for the purpose of pumping the blood in the sense that the fact that past hearts

because functions entail purposiveness and these purposes in turn presuppose values (Sadler and Agich 1996; Fulford 1999, 2000; Thornton 2000). The objectivists assume that 'natural' is a means of determining 'normal' in an objective, value-free way. But this shift provides no easy solution, because what is 'natural' and what is not is no less controversial than determining what is and isn't 'normal' (think for instance of the question whether homosexuality is 'natural' or not). Instead of opting for the other side though, an enactive approach again takes issue with the dichotomy itself. For the dichotomous mind–world topology resonates through this opposition as well since it contrasts objective judgement with value-laden judgement and assumes that anything that is value-laden cannot therefore be objective. From an enactive perspective any perceiving, thinking, judging, or other sense-making is 'value-laden' and 'subjective' in that we cannot escape having a specific embodied and embedded perspective. Our sense-making is inevitably shaped by our bodies, our historical and sociocultural context, and our concomitant concerns: a neutral view from nowhere is simply impossible. Yet we have also seen that this enactive relational view does not imply that our sense-making is therefore a matter of mere subjective opinions or projections. From an enactive perspective then, the involvement of values in our judgements about the presence of psychiatric disorders is not only inevitable, but also no automatic threat to their soundness.

7.5.3   Entities-Agents

The third question is: should psychiatric disorders be considered to be 'things' people get, or are they inseparable from an individual's personal subjective make-up (Zachar and Kendler 2007, p. 559)? The contrast is here between entities as generally uniform things and persons as dynamic, intentional agents. Are psychiatric disorders uniform

had this effect causally explains how hearts came to exist and be maintained' (p. 31). But, as Megone (2000) rightly points out: 'it is not the case that hearts pumping blood have simply caused hearts to exist' (pp. 60–1). It is only in hindsight that we can conclude that the heart has this function: there is no sense in which evolution has 'meant' the heart to do that (Glas 2008; Meynen and Ralston 2011).

conditions that befall people, or are they idiosyncratic reactions or expressions of character of individual persons? In line with many somatic disease models, biological psychiatry for instance stresses the common characteristics of psychiatric disorders, while biopsycho-social models are an example of an approach which leaves more room for individual differences.

Characteristic of an enactive perspective is that it favours think-ing in terms of dynamical processes rather than static entities. Following an enactive complex systems perspective, taking into account a person's specific history and context moreover implies that each specific situation is unique. And yet, as a matter of fact, we can recognise certain types of disordered patterns of sense-making. We can recognise a pattern of depression with its guilt and inward directedness, or patterns of delusions with the abundance of suspi-cious meaning, or patterns of anxiety and the pursuit of control. Disordered patterns of sense-making precisely *become* 'types' or 'kinds' of sense-making. Whereas normally our sense-making is flex-ibly attuned to our situation and has a richness and a personal style, disordered sense-making on the contrary entails a restriction, a narrowing down to only one dominant type of sense-making. The process of sense-making gets stuck in a certain form or pattern, instead of the normal process of flexibly attuning to the situation at hand. As these patterns of sense-making are biased in a specific direc-tion – i.e. anxious, depressed, paranoid – they present a limited set of variants. This is not so strange: after all, in our struggles to be a person in the world we share some fundamental concerns, anxieties, and vulnerabilities. Given our shared characteristics as bodily, reflexive, and social beings it is not so surprising that we have to deal with many similar issues, nor surprising that there are common ways in which this can go astray. Our need to belong may for instance conflict with our need to be an autonomous agent. The wish to be liked may conflict with the wish to be authentic. We may long to be among other people, but also be scared of being rejected by them. As Rogers (1961) wrote: 'what is most personal is most general' (p. 26). In psychiatric disorders, the stuck pattern of sense-making makes people more alike than they would otherwise have been: their idiosyncratic styles and personality are to some extent overruled by the rigidity of the pattern they enact. That is, when very different people become depressed, their sense-makings get stuck in similar moulds, making them more alike in that respect. Their confined ways of sense-making do not reflect the full richness of their personality.

This does not mean that we should see psychiatric disorders as entities though: it is not as if people catch a disease that operates the same on each victim, like a cold would: psychiatric disorders are rather enacted. The common structures of disordered patterns of sense-making do not annihilate the importance of taking into account the idiosyncrasies of this particular person with this particular history in this particular situation. Even though different patients suffering from depression show similar patterns of sense-making, their situations remain unique. The trajectories of how they developed their depression will be different, and since they are different persons in different situations the treatment that best suits them may well be different as well.

From an enactive perspective then, the choice between psychiatric disorders having common characteristics and viewing patients as idiosyncratic persons does not make sense as these options are not mutually exclusive. The uniqueness of each patient's situation is not at odds with the universality of the issues that they may struggle with. Likewise the fact of there being differences in patients' individual situations and developmental trajectories is not at odds with there being types of disorders, i.e. common categories of disordered sense-making.

7.5.4   *Categories-Continua*

The fourth question is whether psychiatric disorders are best understood as illnesses with discrete boundaries (categorical) or as the pathological ends of functional dimensions (continuous) (Zachar and Kendler 2007, p. 559). A categorical conception maintains that there are non-arbitrary boundaries between having a psychiatric disorder and being sane. There are qualitative differences between those two conditions and as a consequence we are able to 'carve nature at its joints'. Proponents of a continuous conception in contrast hold that having a psychiatric disorder or being sane is a difference of degree rather than a difference in kind. Dimensional models are an example of such a continuous view, while those models that assume objective judgements can be made about the presence of psychiatric disorders (see the second question) will typically adopt a categorical view.

We already saw that the enactive conception of psychiatric disorders as disorders of sense-making does not provide us with clear boundaries and cut-off points. Disorders of sense-making are typically a matter of degree: one can be a shy or introverted person, but if the shyness turns into downright anxiety, one might develop a social phobia. One's sense-making is more or less strongly biased in one direction, more or less reified in a pattern. For many psychiatric disorders the form of sense-making involved is not itself strange or alien: we may all have experienced feelings of gloominess, despair even, or anxiety, or suspicion. It is rather the consistent inappropriateness of sense-making in light of the situation that makes it disordered, as well as the rigidity, the solidification of just this way of sense-making. This conception in terms of patterns means that there will be clear cases of attuned sense-making and of structurally inapt sense-making as well as grey areas in between. So far, this is in line with a continuous view. The continuous view however implies that there are *only* gradual differences, differences of degree. This is where the continuous and the enactive view part ways, for the enactive adoption of a dynamical complex systems perspective rather implies that there can be both: gradual processes can lead to qualitative differences as well. In complex systems, gradual processes may shift into a qualitatively different state as they reach a certain threshold, leading to a so-called bifurcation of the system (cf. Beer 1995).

With regard to sense-making this means that even though deviations in sense-making can develop gradually, there can still be 'turning points' in which one's sense-making not only differs gradually on a quantitative measure (for instance on a scale of more intense versus flattened emotions), but also differs qualitatively. Psychotic delusions for example differ so radically from normal sense-making that we can regard it as a qualitative difference. In such cases, a suspicious bias may gradually evolve into a delusional mood, which in turn may at some point reach a threshold and shift into a full-blown psychosis. From an enactive viewpoint then the opposition between differences in degree and differences in kind is misguided.

Besides, the assumption that if one accepts continua one also needs to accept arbitrariness is too simple. Within certain grey areas there may indeed be an arbitrariness to the decision to call something a psychiatric disorder or not. In general though what both an enactive and a continuum approach advocate is the acknowledgement of the relevance of someone's specific context when making such decisions. Such a situated approach is apt, not arbitrary.

7.5.5 Internalism-Externalism

Zachar and Kendler's (2007) fifth question is: should psychiatric disorders be defined solely by processes that occur inside the body (internalism), or can events outside the skin also play an important (or exclusive) defining role (externalism)? Proponents of internalism regard processes that happen inside the individual's body or the individual's mind to be of primary importance for explaining the occurrence of psychiatric disorders. External events may play a role, but only a secondary one. By contrast, externalists either see such external events as primary or maintain a more modest interactional view in which external and internal factors both play a role in the development of psychiatric disorders. Neuroreductionism provides a clear example of a body-oriented internalist conception, while cognitivist models are an example of a mind-oriented form of internalism. Some forms of social psychiatry defend a radical externalist position, whereas the biopsychosocial model would be an example of an interactional form of externalism.

It should come as no surprise by now that this dichotomy too is highly problematic from an enactive perspective. Following an enactive relational ontology, it is far from obvious where to draw the boundaries between internal and external processes or events. For how are we to determine what counts as 'internal' and what as 'external' in the complex system of a person interacting with her world? With every breath something external becomes internal and vice versa. We eat, we drink, we breathe: in a very basic sense we are coupled to our environment. But also what we think and how we feel is shaped by our history of interactions with the world and with other people. As soon as one takes the development of a certain state or process into account, the boundaries of internal and external become increasingly fuzzy. Are my coping strategies an internal matter? What if I picked it up from my parents? My hormonal system may be regarded as internal – yet that too is affected by how I behave (how I eat, sleep, and exercise) and how I feel. A traumatic event may be regarded as an external event. But then one may point to certain dispositions or vulnerabilities, to certain characteristics of genes or the brain, that might make someone more or less vulnerable to develop post-traumatic stress disorder. But are these genetic or neural dispositions really 'internal'? They too have developed and been shaped in and through interactions with the world. Within the dynamical, complex system of a person interacting with her world the localisation question becomes rather pointless. Again, we see that this dichotomy depends on the implicit adoption of an inner/outer mind–world topology, in which a certain division of inner and outer is taken for granted.

7.5.6 Causalism-Descriptivism

The sixth and last axis of Zachar and Kendler's (2007) conceptual taxonomy asks if we should categorise psychiatric disorders as a function of their causes (causalism) or of their clinical characteristics (descriptivism). There is at present no agreement on the specific causes of specific psychiatric disorders, nor have single, discrete causes been found. In the absence of such agreement, we now use clinical characteristics to categorise and diagnose psychiatric disorders. Advocates of a causalist approach, however, see the current lack of agreement as a temporary situation, one that is likely to change once we know more about, say, genes, or neurochemistry, or wherever they envision these causes will be found. Any reductionist approach to psychiatric disorders sides with the causalists, with neuroreductionism again being one of its clearest representatives. Those who adhere to descriptivism on the other hand assume that the causality of psychiatric disorders will be too complex, with too many variables and too many individual differences to allow for a causalist approach. For them, sticking to clinical descriptions is not a temporary solution, but rather the optimal manner for categorising psychiatric disorders. Interactionist models, such as the biopsychosocial model, typically favour the descriptivist position.

An enactive approach obviously champions the complexity of psychiatric disorders. Both its integration of the four dimensions as well as its conception of causality in non-linear, organisational ways lead to a complex, dynamical systems view on psychiatric disorders and their causality. Does this then mean that an enactive approach adopts a descriptivist position? Again, from an enactive perspective, the opposition between causes on the one hand and descriptions of clinical symptoms on the other hand is troublesome. The opposition assumes a certain relation between causes and symptoms in which clinical symptoms are regarded as the expressions of underlying causes or causal mechanisms. Symptoms are seen as signs of some underlying pathology or mechanism causing this pathology. This metaphor of *surface* signs and something *underlying* them is deeply problematic on an enactive understanding of psychiatric disorders as disorders of sense-making. In the next chapter, I will get into the issue of causality.

To conclude, we can see how an enactive approach dissolves several conceptual dichotomies since they are corollaries of the implicit adoption of that dichotomous mind–world topology that enactivism challenges. In the next chapter we will look at the implications of the enactive approach for our understanding of the causes and treatment of psychiatric disorders.

8   An Enactive Approach to Causes, Diagnosis, and Treatment of Psychiatric Disorders

8.1   INTRODUCTION

In the previous chapter, I proposed an enactive account of psychiatric disorders that understands them as structurally disturbed patterns of sense-making. We looked at what characterises such disordered patterns: the inaptness of the sense-making in light of its context, the rigidity of both the interactions with the world and the existential stance, and the experience of suffering. We saw that this enactive perspective challenges the main conceptual dichotomies that shape the current debate on the nature of psychiatric disorders. In this chapter, we will flesh out what an enactive approach entails with regard to the causes and treatment of psychiatric disorders.

8.2   CAUSALITY IN PSYCHIATRIC DISORDERS

What causes psychiatric disorders? This is one of the most pressing questions in psychiatry. If we could answer it, we might be able to offer better treatment, or we might even be able to prevent disorders from developing. And, as we saw in the previous chapter, unravelling the causes of psychiatric disorders might also change our diagnostic system: instead of relying on descriptions of clusters of symptoms, we might for instance be able to use 'biomarkers' that reveal whether the cause is present or not. So there is a lot at stake.

Following the enactive approach to psychiatric disorders calls for adopting a complex dynamical systems view on the causality involved in their development and persistence. To recap: the enactive approach understands the mind as sense-making: as a type of interaction that emerges from organisms that depend on their environments, or persons depending on their worlds. Given their fundamental coupling, organisms in their environments and persons in their worlds form complex dynamical systems. This implies that sense-making can only be properly understood by taking this whole system into account: the person's embodiment and embeddedness, their own concerns and capacities as well as the possibilities offered and limits set by their surroundings, plus the way in which these interact and develop. The same goes for disorders of sense-making: here too we need to take into account the whole person–world system, with its physiological, experiential, sociocultural, and existential dimensions. Such a complex dynamical systems approach has several implications regarding causality in psychiatric disorders. But it is obviously not the only way to understand this causality. To clarify what characterises an enactive approach, we can contrast it with a common, opposite view that derives from the traditional inner mind–outer world model that we discussed in Chapters 3 and 4.

8.2.1 The Search for Underlying Mechanisms

Much research in psychiatry is devoted to finding the *underlying* causes or mechanisms of specific disorders.[1] The idea is that the diverse symptoms of specific disorders can be traced back to such underlying faults, for instance in patients' genes or their neuronal architecture. The metaphor of 'underlying' is so ubiquitously used – especially in the neuroscientific research on neural mechanisms – that

---

[1] The terms *mechanism* and *mechanistic* are used in various different ways: while they originally referred to the relatively straightforward causal processes (e.g. 'Mechanisms are entities and activities organized such that they are productive of regular changes from start or set-up to finish or termination conditions'; Machamer et al. 2000) that are characteristic of so-called decomposable systems (i.e. systems in which 'there is a natural projection from component behavior to system behavior, in both the short and the long term'; Bechtel and Richardson 2010), increasingly 'dynamic' versions of mechanisms have been proposed (Bechtel and Abrahamsen 2013), to the extent that the term has become vague (Issad and Malaterre 2015). It is interesting that we apparently do want to hold on to the notion of 'mechanism' – probably because it carries the connotation of giving us a proper explanation rather than a mere re-description of the phenomenon at hand. What matters here is not so much whether and how one precisely uses this term but rather the implications of assuming a vertical model of one thing underlying the other.

it seems innocent, maybe not even that informative. But it *is* informative. Metaphors are never innocent: 'the price of metaphor is eternal vigilance' (Lewontin 2002, citing Norbert Wiener). Talk of 'underlying' imports (implicit) ideas about the nature of causes and symptoms, about what is manifest and latent, about preferred methods, research questions, and even treatment.

Following the idea that we should search for psychiatric disorders' underlying mechanisms, symptoms are taken as signs at the surface: indicators or markers of what is going wrong underneath. Symptoms are thus effects or products of the disorder, but they are not what causes the disorder. This fits with the so-called latent variable model: a statistical model in which the manifest variables (the symptoms) are assumed to depend on one or more latent variables (the underlying causes or mechanisms) (Borsboom 2008; Borsboom et al. 2011; Borsboom and Cramer 2013). As the manifest variables are only affected by changes in the latent variables, there are no causal influences between the manifest variables themselves. With regard to disorders, the idea is that all symptoms derive from one or more underlying cause and that they are independent of the other symptoms. The underlying causes or mechanisms *are* the disorder. An example would be a bacterial infection, say streptococcal pharyngitis, where all symptoms stem from this infection. What is needed is antibiotics: when the bacteria are killed, the symptoms will disappear too (see Figure 8.1).

Dividing disorders into manifest symptoms and latent, underlying causes implies a vertical hierarchy – one that fits well with the sandwich model of the mind (Hurley 1998) that we discussed in Chapter 3. A sandwich model of the mind regards perception as input, behaviour as output, and cognition as the processing of the information from the input and commissioning the adequate behaviour. Behaviour can thus be traced back to its internal source. Likewise, the symptoms of psychiatric disorders can be traced back to faults in the internal mechanisms of patients' cognitive processing. And the idea of internal cognitive mechanisms in turn

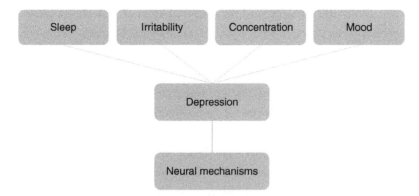

FIGURE 8.1   A latent variable model of depression. After Borsboom (2008).

invites a focus on the brain – for where else would this processing take place? The vertical hierarchy implied by underlying causes invites a physiological reductionism: after all we never hear of research that aims to find the experiences that underlie certain neural phenomena. This again fits with the traditional carving up of the physical versus the mental realm, in which the mental depends on the physical, but not the other way around (see Chapter 4).

In line with this reductionist kinship the conventional methods for finding these underlying mechanisms are localising and decomposing: the aim is to localise the relevant mechanisms and analyse their specific components. Such research often yields very sophisticated and complex (in the colloquial sense of the word) models of the mechanism at stake, models containing many elements and including feedback loops and reciprocal influences. They are far from being simple or crude. Yet they remain part of a vertically hierarchical, reductionist endeavour.

Finally, the assumption that psychiatric disorders have underlying causes or causal structures fosters the idea that treatment should be directed at those causes instead of merely addressing the disorder's symptoms. If one treats these symptoms only, one does not get to the root of the problem.

So far the research into the favoured areas of underlying causes, genes and the brain, has not led to clear answers, but rather attests to the complexity of the processes involved as well as their dependence on interactions with the environment. Research on genes has increasingly turned into epigenetics, i.e. research on genes-in-interaction-with-an-environment. Likewise, neuroscientific research has shifted from focusing on specific brain areas and neurotransmitters to neural networks, connectivity between brain areas, mutual interactions between neurotransmitters, and between neurotransmitters and hormones, and the influence of environmental processes on the brain's structural and functional architecture. What the search for underlying mechanisms has actually revealed are complex networks that span the whole brain-body-world system. Still, the *belief* in finding such underlying mechanisms remains strong, even among those who recognise the modest success of the results so far.[2]

8.2.2 Causality from an Enactive Complex Systems Approach

The enactive complex systems-inspired take on causality is very different. It advocates an integrative relation between psychiatric disorders' four dimensions, where the only hierarchy would be one of horizontal encompassingness (see Chapter 4, Section 4.7). None of the four dimensions 'underlies' any of the other. That is: none of the four dimensions is more fundamental since they refer to different aspects of one and the same system; different excerpts of this system at different levels of zooming in and/or at different time scales. This

---

[2] Kandel (1999a) for instance replies to Rifkin's (1999) critique on the added value of a neurobiological approach to psychotherapy with an insightful statement: 'One has to acknowledge that we are still far from establishing a biological foundation of psychoanalysis. In fact, we do not as yet have a satisfactory biological understanding of any complex mental processes ... Yet ... it is inconceivable to me that biology will not eventually make deep contributions to the understanding of mental processes. There must be a biological basis' (p. 666). It is telling that Kandel does not provide an argument here but rather presents a *testimony of faith* in the biological paradigm. It is simply *inconceivable* to him that biological insights would not transform the central issues in psychotherapy and psychopathology. The fact that we have so far not succeeded in generating these insights is because the research is just 'not yet' far enough developed.

means that there is no a priori causal preference for any of the dimensions involved.

Nothing *underlies* disordered patterns of sense-making either. The pattern itself is all there is to it. Patterns develop through the repetition of certain behaviours. A structure develops out of one's history of interactions, in much the same way that a path is laid down in walking (Machado 1979; Thompson 2007). Applied to sense-making, this means that a certain way of sense-making develops by interacting in a certain way with the world. Depending on how others react, a person will develop a certain style of interacting, with various preferred types of reacting in specific situations. In this continuous cycle of action and reaction, patterns emerge. The development of patterns of sense-making is thus not an internal affair: a person's sense-making is shaped by the people she interacts with and the sociocultural practices that shape these interactions, while she in turn also shapes them. These emergent patterns are not carved in stone: new paths and new ways of interacting develop through new experiences – although the patterns developed early in life may be very persistent.

On this view, the symptoms of psychiatric disorders are not signals of underlying defects; they are rather parts of the problem. What we call 'symptoms' might be better seen as *expressions* of the disorder – expressions in the Merleau-Pontian (1945/2002) sense of the term. He gives the example of sexuality as being an expression of someone's existence: someone's sexual life is not a mere sign of that person's existence, but it is rather itself a fundamental *dimension* of this existence. So an expression expresses something, but at the same time it co-constitutes what it expresses. In a sense it is a sign, but a sign that at the same time 'is what it means' (p. 188). There is more to someone's existence than their sexuality, but their sexual life is part of their existence, and their way of being in the world is also expressed, comes to the fore, in their sexual life. This means that changes in someone's sexuality *are* changes in that person's existence, which can potentially affect other dimensions of their existence as well. In contrast to the latent variable model then, symptoms taken in this way can causally influence each other.

If nothing underlies patterns, does that mean that what you see is what you get? That would be an implausible stance: after all, aspects of psychiatric disorders can be hidden from view, aspects such as neurotransmitter deficiencies or hormonal disbalances, or unrecognised, 'suppressed' anger. Not all aspects of the pattern are immediately or equally visible. But the level of visibility does not imply anything about causal powers: there is no reason to attribute causal powers only to the less readily accessible aspects of the pattern. For example, suppose that I am regularly driven to perform excessive checking rituals. Several physiological processes, like my adrenaline levels and the uptake of certain neurotransmitters, will be part of this disordered pattern of interacting. As we have seen in Chapter 4, an enactive approach rejects the idea that these physiological processes *cause* certain experiences: that would be to confuse mereological relations with causal relations. Such physiological processes are rather *part* of the complex person–world system; *part* of the disturbed pattern of sense-making. Similarly, we might find out that my compulsive behaviour is triggered by situations in which I fear abandonment. I am not aware of this fear and if you were to point it out to me, I might not even immediately recognise it. Does that make my compulsive behaviour a mere indication of my underlying problem of fearing abandonment? Again, an enactive approach would reject this vertical metaphor: my compulsive behaviour is rather a meaningful *part* of the problem. It is not only the fear that is relevant here, but also the way in which I deal with it: I would have a different problem if, for example, I were to deal with this fear by drinking too much alcohol. How I express this fear co-constitutes the problem.

Not only does none of the four dimensions have any a priori causal priority over the others; the very idea of one or more originary causes requires clarification. From a complex systems perspective clear originary causes will in any case be rare given the many mutually influencing processes and feedback loops going on in the person–world system. And even if we do manage to discern an originary cause of someone's psychiatric problems, the effects of this cause will depend on the wider setting of the state of the person in her world at that moment – which of course in turn depends on her previous history. For instance, post-traumatic stress disorder (PTSD) is one of the few disorders in which there is a clear initiating factor, namely the traumatic event(s). But as we saw in Chapter 4, not everybody who has had traumatic experiences will subsequently develop PTSD. One important protective factor for instance seems to be the social embedding of the person in question: the more supportive one's social network, the less likely one is to develop PTSD (Guay et al. 2006). Previous stressful experiences on the other hand may make one more vulnerable. Someone who is already under pressure can take on less. The trauma is then only the originary cause of the PTSD given this person's particular context.

This goes for any influencing factor: its wider context co-determines what comes of this influence: how it is taken up and strengthened or weakened or changed along the way. The aim to find 'the' cause or 'the' pathway to a specific disorder assumes that here we have to do with an originary cause like a falling domino, hitting all the others in a predetermined way. A complex systems approach is more like a metro-network: one delayed metro will not be a big problem, but if it also starts to snow, and some of the tracks become impassable, then a problem may arise. The loss of one's job for example does not automatically lead to a depression. But if someone also has relational problems, and maybe even starts to drink too much because of all these worries, which in turn aggravates the relational problems, the situation may get out of hand. Causes are only causes in specific contexts. It would thus be misleading to trace back all someone's difficulties to just their originary cause, or rather: their initiating trigger. It may have only been the last straw that broke the camel's back.

Besides, a complex systems view also clarifies that the *originating* factors may not be the same as the factors that *maintain* (or even worsen) the present problems. It is not only relevant how patients got to develop their sense-making problems; what also matters is what currently keeps them in this adverse pattern. This distinction is especially relevant for choosing the most adequate targets of treatment. In some cases, such as in case of traumatic events, or poor development of attachment in early life, the original contributing factors may not be alterable any more. But even when it *is* possible to change the instigating factors, that may not be the most effective route to change. In the above example, it may not be a new job that would matter most; improving the patient's relationship may be much more effective. From an enactive complex systems perspective, then, we shouldn't overestimate the role of initiating causes.

Note that the same caution holds the other way around: the effectiveness of a certain treatment or intervention does not allow 'reverse engineering' to conclusions about what caused the problems. It may be tempting to assume that if some intervention manages to solve the problems at hand this must mean that we have apparently addressed their cause – like a reversed version of the falling dominos. But interventions too take place in a certain context, and here too their effect will depend on how they are taken up by the whole person–world system. Think for instance of the example from Chapter 2 of the effects of deep brain stimulation (DBS) on OCD patients. If a severely and chronically ill OCD patient is treated by DBS, we may witness the following effects: she is less anxious, she has less compulsions, she finds a job, and she loses some friends (de Haan et al. 2015b). Are these all separate effects of the stimulation of her nucleus accumbens? Is DBS treatment the latent variable that causes each of these manifest effects? That would be an overly simplistic picture for, as we saw in Chapter 2, the neural stimulation itself takes place in a certain context. With such a special treatment and careful selection trajectory, the expectancy effects will likely be high, plus there are the effects of the weekly meetings with specialised team members, and secondary feedback loops such as the positive effects of being less anxious, of a return to work, etc. Besides, patients often engage in additional psychotherapy and this too seems to play a vital role (Mantione et al. 2014).

Interestingly, there is typically a neuroreductionist bias when it comes to the inclination to 'reversely engineer'. If the price of alcohol goes up this reduces the number of alcoholics (Chaloupka et al. 2002), but we do not assume that the previously lower prices were the cause of people becoming alcoholics. And although exercise can help improve depressive symptoms (Rimer et al. 2012), we do not tend to see depression as the result of a lack of exercise. However, if we find that a certain type of drug working on a specific neurotransmitter is helpful, we may be tempted to conclude that this neurotransmitter was the cause of the problems – although from the outset we have no reason to believe this case is any different from the others.

Finally, the complexity of a person–world system that integrates the physiological, experiential, sociocultural, and existential dimensions of sense-making and its disorders makes it highly unlikely that there would only be one developmental route to each particular psychiatric disorder. With so many processes going on between the person and her world as well as within the person, and with so many feedback loops and (reciprocal) influences between all these processes, it is much more likely that there will be *various developmental trajectories* of disordered patterns of sense-making. Different paths may lead to the same place, and being in a similar state now therefore does not imply that we have arrived there in the same way.

From an enactive perspective, the complex system of a person in interaction with her world can thus become disturbed in many ways, involving factors from any of the four dimensions. There is no reason to regard only some factors (notably physiological processes) and not others as causally influential. Moreover, the relevant quest is not to uncover hidden mechanisms behind or underneath disordered patterns of sense-making, but rather to find out (1) how such patterns develop, and (2) how they persist and solidify. Regarding the first aim, the complexity and dynamics of the system make it likely that a combination of factors are involved and that there are a variety of developmental trajectories leading up to the disordered pattern. Secondly, it is not only the developmental factors that are relevant, but also those factors that maintain the disturbed pattern, as well as the factors that provide a positive influence.

As there is not one recipe for how our sense-making can go astray, we need to develop more personalised models to capture what went wrong and how, and what is keeping one stuck in this state and how. A helpful tool for this are *personalised network models*.

8.3   PERSONALISED NETWORK MODELS

As we saw in Chapter 2, network models consist of elements, so-called nodes, and their relations. Both elements and their relations can refer to anything – the model only provides a template to visualise these elements and their relations. Network models offer an attractive template for an enactive approach to psychiatric disorders in that they present complex processes in a non-reductionist way. They do not assume any predetermined hierarchical ordering of the involved nodes: they provide horizontal rather than vertical models. Likewise, there are no inherent restrictions regarding the relations between nodes: any node can be connected to any other and also reflexively to itself. Moreover, the dynamics of the relations between nodes can be fairly easily visualised by using arrows, which can be thicker or thinner depending on the strength of the connection, or successions of graphs. Network models can thus be used as basic, more manageable simplifications of complex dynamical systems.

The usefulness of a network model depends on (1) *choosing the relevant nodes* as well as (2) an adequate understanding of the *relations between these nodes*. Are they causal, or merely correlational?

Or rather mereological? Network models in themselves do not provide such insights: models after all do not tell you how to apply them; you need a theory for that.[3] In order to be of any practical use, then, network models need to be complemented with a theory of what the important aspects of psychiatric disorders are and how to characterise the relations between them. This is exactly what the enactive framework offers. The four dimensions provide the basic orientation of the network, as four major groupings of relevant factors. Each of these can be further zoomed in on, addressing more specified and fine-grained aspects. Starting from this general network, we can develop personalised network models that are tailored to the individual patient both with respect to which are the relevant nodes to include and how to specify their (mutual) influences. Note that these nodes need not be restricted to factors that contribute to the conservation of the problems at hand. On the contrary, it makes sense to include positive, supportive influences in the model as well.

Figures 8.2–8.4 provide some schematic examples. In Figure 8.2, the person, her (social) world, and her existential stance are schematically depicted, including the four dimensions of psychiatric disorders. Of course these four dimensions are integrated, so putting them in separate boxes provides quite a misleading picture. However, to get a grip on the complexity of the person–world system we need to start from some simplifications. Each of the four dimensions themselves consist of many aspects that are again linked amongst each other. These can also be depicted as network-structures, as in Figure 8.3. Again, each of these nodes can in turn be further specified: which feelings, what sorts of thoughts, what kind of actions are we talking about? If we then focus on one of these aspects, say someone's

---

[3]   As we saw in Chapter 2, the network models for psychiatry that are currently put forward try to solve this problem by relying on the symptoms of disorders as described in the *DSM*. However, this only provides us with a very limited selection of factors that mostly refer to patients' behaviour and experiences. They do not include physiological factors or patients' sociocultural embedding (other than as a generic 'external' factor), nor do they include any positive factors. Lacking a robust theory on the nature of psychiatric disorders, they also cannot give an account of the ontological status of the relations between the symptoms included in the networks.

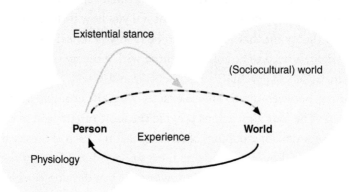

FIGURE 8.2 Schematic of the four dimensions of the person–world system.

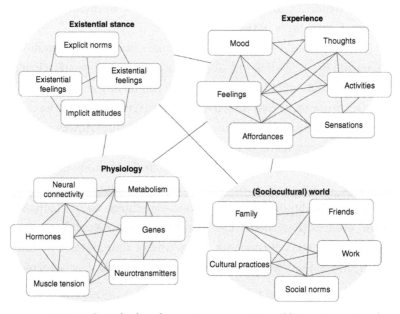

FIGURE 8.3 The four dimensions as groupings of factors in a network.

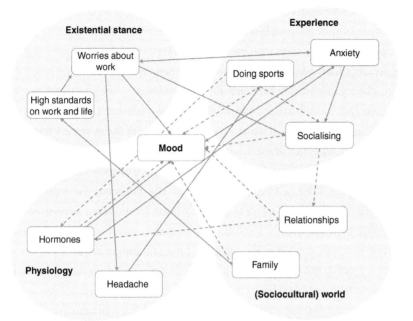

FIGURE 8.4 Mood itself has four dimensions that can be further specified in a network.

depressed mood, we can specify which factors reinforce this mood and which factors instead challenge it – factors such as their social life, their satisfaction with their work, the relationship with their partner, doing sports, their hormonal condition (e.g. premenstrual or not), or ruminating about the future (see Figure 8.4). One's mood thus itself has physiological, sociocultural, and existential dimensions – like any of the examples of the experiential dimension. These heuristic boxes should not trick us into any of the old ontological dichotomies. The level of detail that the network model should provide will depend on the question or issue at stake.

Now these are just static graphics, whereas all of the 'nodes' are in fact *processes* that develop over time. These developments too can be modelled in networks, showing how the relations between the nodes change through time. In this way feedback loops may show up, as well as positive and negative spirals. A network model can also clearly visualise 'tipping points' in which someone shifts from one state to another (in complex systems terms: a shift of the system into an alternative stable state). For instance, there will be several factors that influence whether I might relapse into my former alcohol addiction – such as meeting old friends that I used to drink with, passing the pub that I used to visit, or a conflict at work or with my partner. If one of these things happen, I might manage: the desire to drink is balanced out by other factors that keep me from drinking. However, if two or more of these things happen at the same time, I might crack under the pressure. Generally, we manage to cope with adverse events in our lives, being supported by the things in life that do go well. Yet too much strain or strain from too much different sides and the safety net may no longer hold.

Figures 8.5–8.8 provide a nice example of what such personalised network models look like. They are from Larsen's (2019) research on the factors influencing the intake of cannabis by patients who have been diagnosed with both schizophrenia and substance abuse. He followed twelve patients and conducted six interviews with each of them over the timespan of one year, plotting their personally most relevant – positively and negatively – contributing factors over time. Together these graphs provide an insightful overview of the different developmental trajectories of each participant. Figure 8.5 provides a general depiction of how a network model can be used to map the various factors that influence the use of cannabis by patients diagnosed with schizophrenia. Figures 8.6 and 8.7 are graphs from two different participants, illustrating the individual differences in relevant factors at play. Figure 8.8 shows one participant's transition from smoking lots of cannabis while living a lethargic life (i.e. primarily lying in bed and eating), to having quit smoking, starting an education and reducing her medication.

8.4 IMPLICATIONS FOR TREATMENT

What are the treatment implications of an enactive approach to psychiatric disorders? The enactive framework provides a theoretical grounding

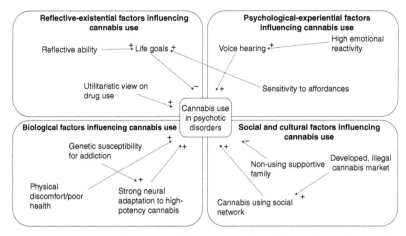

FIGURE 8.5 Illustration of how a network model can be used to map the various factors that influence the use of cannabis by patients diagnosed with schizophrenia, following the four dimensions of the enactive approach as the main groupings of factors. Arrows are marked with a plus if an increase in the originating factor also entails an increase in the target factor. If an increase in the factor entails a decrease in the cannabis use, they are marked with a minus. From Larsen (2019) and Larsen and Johansen (forthcoming).

for a holistic practice of psychiatry. As an integrative model it does not so much advocate a specific, novel form of treatment, but rather helps better understand how various influences cohere, which in turn helps navigate and substantiate treatment decisions. Some general implications on treatment follow from the idea that persons in their world form one dynamical complex system, as well as from the enactive definition of psychiatric disorders as disordered patterns of sense-making.

8.4.1   Complex Systems Offer Many Routes to Change

Taking the dynamical, complex person–world system as the unit of analysis may at first seem too complex to be workable. However, the complexity of the system also implies that there are many routes to change. And because the enactive approach does not prioritise any of the dimensions over the others, it also does not a priori, on purely theoretical grounds, rule out any form of treatment. Instead it

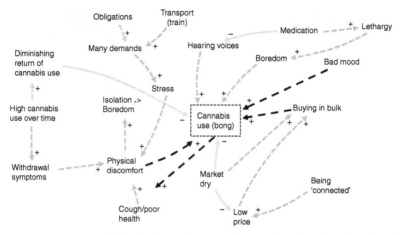

FIGURE 8.6 Graph of a participant in Larsen's (2019) study. Black dotted arrows indicate factors that lead to an increase in cannabis use, grey arrows refer to positive influences and grey dotted arrows refer to indirect influences. A plus signals an increase; a minus signals a decrease.

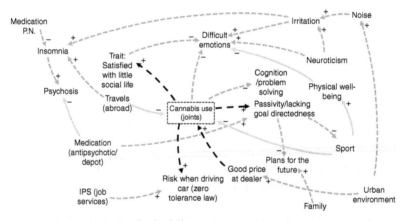

FIGURE 8.7 Graph of a different participant in Larsen's (2019) study. Together, Figures 8.6 and 8.7 illustrate the individual differences between participants' network models.

embraces the full plurality of potential forms of treatment, since a complex system can be stirred in many ways. We just saw that originating causes have a different status in complex systems than in linear approaches to causality. Since causes are only causes in

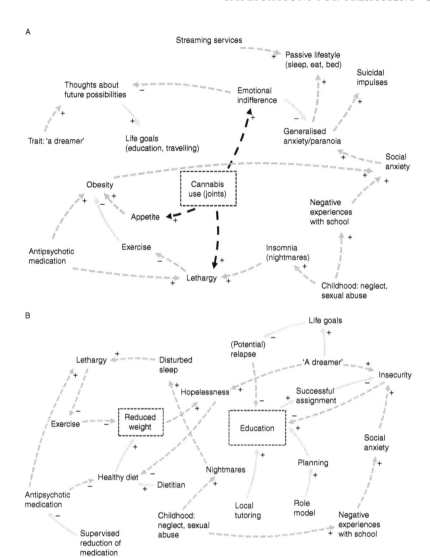

FIGURE 8.8 Graphs of the (a) second and (b) sixth interviews with a twenty-eight-year-old female participant. Together they illustrate the participant's transition from smoking lots of cannabis while living a lethargic life (i.e. primarily lying in bed and eating) to having quit smoking, starting an education and reducing her medication.

a context, the singling out of an initiating cause is not the holy research-grail. Likewise, treatment need not be targeted at such originary factors (if these are even discernible). It may be more effective to intervene on the factors that contribute to the problems' persistence. By shedding the dichotomy of underlying causes and symptoms as their surface signs, treating symptoms is no longer synonymous with 'merely' treating symptoms either. From an enactive perspective a disturbed pattern of sense-making can implicate many diverse factors (from all four dimensions) that are all part of this problematic pattern. Seen in this way, addressing a depressed patient's sleeping problem *is* addressing (part of) the problem. Besides, an integrative complex systems account also makes clear that the strengthening of supportive factors is a valid aim for treatment as well. Given that a cause is only a cause in a certain context, changing that 'context' amounts to changing the problem.

A complex systems perspective also clarifies how removing or dissolving an initial disturbance does not necessarily make someone's problems disappear. The disturbance may have tipped the person into a so-called alternative stable state, and much more may now be required to extricate them. Think for instance of the relation between forest and grazers: a mature forest will remain a forest even though grazers eat young trees. However, a forest destroyed by a fire may not return because all the young trees get eaten by grazers, resulting in a steppe landscape. Return of the forest requires specific measures and time. Similarly, cannabis use may induce a psychotic episode, but quitting smoking does not guarantee full recovery.

Another corollary of the non-linear causality in complex dynamical systems is that it implies that combining various interventions may enhance – or decrease – their effectiveness. The effect may even be disproportional in the sense that the combination of interventions can lead to an increase in effectiveness that is larger than a mere linear addition of the effects of each of the interventions taken on its own. Because of the interconnectedness of the factors involved in sense-making and because of potential feedback loops between them, both positive and negative spirals can occur. Getting a job for instance not only helps to relieve financial worries; it also provides social contacts, self-esteem, and structure to one's week, requiring a normal day-night rhythm. Similarly, medication that helps to lower someone's anxiety levels may allow them to engage in activities that they previously dreaded, which in turn may improve their social network, self-esteem, and well-being. Of course, a combination of treatments does not automatically enhance their effectiveness; undermining effects can occur as well. For example the combination of certain types of medication may be beneficial, but their interactional effects can be detrimental as well.

Furthermore, the complexity of each person in their world, with their own specific developmental trajectories to their disturbed sense-making, and their own specific current maintaining factors, make it highly unlikely that a single type of treatment will work best for all patients who share a diagnosis. Just as drugs do not benefit everyone equally, so too do other forms of treatment vary in their efficacy across individuals. Given that the enactive approach also does not a priori favour a specific type of intervening, one might wonder whether this means that basically 'anything goes': that it does not really matter which type of intervention one chooses. The enactive approach moreover also questions the ideas of both underlying and originating causes; challenging the metaphor of disorders having latent roots with symptoms as their signs, and blurring the distinction between originating and contextual factors. If everything is connected anyway, it may seem as if it does not really matter where one intervenes.

The 'anything-goes-worry' is a lurking risk for all approaches that aim to be integrative, as we also saw with the biopsychosocial model (in Chapter 2). An enactive approach however does not at all imply that anything goes when it comes to treatment. For the mereological relation between the four dimensions as part of one person–world system and the acknowledgement of the (potential) interconnectedness of various factors does not mean that there aren't any differences between them. In complex systems too, it matters where you intervene, as different interventions will have different effects. An enactive model actually helps to clarify both what different interventions are doing and how to understand the effects of interventions in one part of the system (say neuro-physiological processes) on another part of the system (say experiential processes). As we saw in Chapter 4, we can distinguish between more local and more global interventions, and explain their effects as instances of organisational causality. A more locally directed intervention will have a different causal effect on the global system than a more globally directed intervention: they imply different tracks, so to speak, implicating different parts of the person–world system. Think again of the difference between the amount of sugar affecting the rising agent and the taste of the cake as a whole, versus the effects of the oven temperature on the eggs in the dough and on the overall moisture of the cake. Moreover, given that person–world systems differ in many respects, i.e. that persons have their own unique history and context, there will be individual differences in the effects of the same intervention.

Depending on how this particular system is currently structured – i.e. which are the relevant factors involved (nodes) and how are they connected, where are their influences mutual and where are they unidirectional, and where are there feedback loops involved? – different interventions will have different effects. See Figure 8.9a: interventions A and B have different effects on the same system. Besides, as the effect of any specific intervention will depend on the structure of the particular system it works on, the same intervention may well have different effect for different people. See Figure 8.9b: the same interventions A and B have yet again different effects on system two. Since the precise effects of an intervention depend on the person, the prediction of the usefulness of a certain type of treatment will require more information than just the kind of psychiatric disorder from which she suffers. But this does not mean that anything goes: for each individual it is still the case that the one

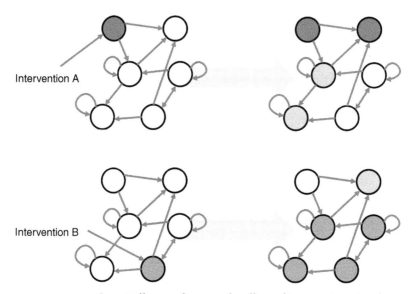

FIGURE 8.9A Differences between the effects of interventions A and B on the same system.

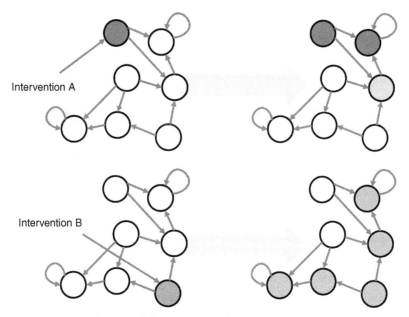

FIGURE 8.9B In a different system, those same A and B interventions will have, yet again, different effects.

intervention has different effects than the other and that some forms of treatment will therefore be preferable over others. Yet what it does mean is that we need more personalised models both to understand what is going on and to predict which treatment will probably be most effective in this particular case.

An enactive approach makes clear that in each individual case an assessment needs to be made of the beneficial interactions and how these might be strengthened, and of the harmful interactions and how they could be changed. Here the personalised network models come into play again. Starting from the four dimensions as four main sets of factors, the network model can be individualised with regard both to the factors to be included and to how they are connected. It makes sense to involve patients in determining the relevant factors to be included in the network and to discuss their likely connections. The relevance of each factor and the extent to which and the way in which they are connected to the other factors is an empirical question. They are moreover likely to change over time: different factors become more or less relevant, different influences between factors become stronger or weaker. In the course of treatment, patients and mental health care professionals can develop a network model to visualise the positive and negative influences on patients' sense-making problems (see again Figure 8.8 for an example). Such an encompassing, personalised overview helps to decide which intervention or combination of interventions is likely to be most effective for this particular patient.

A helpful tool in gathering the relevant information is 'experience sampling' (Csikszentmihalyi and Larson 1987; Myin-Germeys et al. 2009). Experience sampling is a method to collect information from patients, administered by the patients themselves. Typically, patients are asked to record, several times a day, what they are currently doing, what they think, and how they feel. Over time one can, from these data, distil correlations between certain activities and patients' thoughts and feelings. This can lead to the discovery of distinct individual patterns. For example: for one person getting enough sleep may turn out to be very important for his

mood, whereas for another person her mood may be strongly corre-
lated with the amount of physical activity she undertakes. And for
yet another patient, engaging in social activities proves to be particularly uplifting. With the introduction of smartphones, experience
sampling has become less of a hassle for the patient, as the recording
can now be done more easily by using dedicated apps. With help
from the information gathered in this way network models can
elucidate which are the relevant interaction patterns and how they
could be changed.

One may still wonder though if the enactive approach entails
a certain *navigational logic*, a hierarchy of relevance on how to proceed. This is a difficult issue. We already saw that the enactive framework is not a *vertical* hierarchy: none of the four dimensions of
psychiatric disorders is considered to be more basic or fundamental
or 'underlying' than the others. The horizontal person–world system
does allow us to distinguish between more local and more global
processes. Sense-making is the capacity of a person in her world:
a global level capacity. The sense-making problems of psychiatric
disorders are likewise global problems: if a patient's sense-making
difficulties were the result of a local, i.e. physiological, problem like
a brain tumour or a neurological disease, they would be in need of
somatic, not mental health care. The aim of treatment is consequently
on this more global level too, namely to better enable the patient to re-
engage meaningfully with their world.

Should we then privilege global over local interventions?
Psychotherapy over medication? It is not that easy. For the local
depends on and influences the global – and the other way around.
There are indeed differences between local-to-global and global-to-
local influences, but both can be effective. SSRIs can make me less
anxious, and so can psychotherapy, even though the one intervenes
mostly on local and the other on global processes. A change that
starts locally can still have global effects. Besides, we should not
reify either 'local' or 'global': as if we were talking about independent things, the 'local' parts like marbles, the 'global' as the jar that

contains them. The terms *local* and *global* remain imprecise indications anyway. Physiological processes may be more 'local' than experiential processes, but in the end the functioning of the whole complex dynamical system of a person interacting with her world depends on all its parts and as such precisely defies any easy stratification.

From an enactive perspective, there is neither a privileged dimension, nor a single navigational rule. Since all dimensions of the person–world system can only be properly understood in relation to the whole they co-constitute, what follows is a hermeneutical back-and-forth between a focus on the whole *Gestalt* and its dimensions. And even though there are commonalities in different types of disordered patterns (e.g. depressed, anxious, paranoid, controlling biases), it still requires a person-tailored approach to clarify this patients' strengths and weaknesses and decide on treatment options accordingly.

8.4.2   *The Social Sides of Sense-Making*

Even though an enactive approach does not dictate preferred treatment options, it does call attention to the relevance of including patients' bodies, existential stance, and sociocultural embedding in treatment. Sense-making is after all an embodied, embedded, and existential activity. In Chapter 5 we already discussed the various ways in which patients' existential stances towards themselves and their situation, including their disorder, are at play in psychiatric practice and can show up in treatment. The embodied nature of sense-making not only implies the potential effectiveness of treatments directed at our physiological processes (e.g. medication, diets, electrical neurostimulation), but also of various body and movement therapies (Röhricht et al. 2014). Since we interact with the world bodily, our bodies express our personal histories and personhood – from how we move through the world, to how we approach and avoid others, what stresses us and how we relax, and the memories that have become part of our flesh (cf. Koch et al. 2012). Patterns of sense-making are always embodied patterns of sense-making, and so are disordered patterns of sense-making (Fuchs and Schlimme 2009).

The enactive unit of analysis is however not the individual, bodily and existential, person, but the person in her world. In the following, I will highlight some implications of enactivism's relational ontology for the treatment of psychiatric disorders. The embeddedness of our sense-making first of all implies the value of treatments that focus not just on the individual patient but also include the most important people around them, such as systems therapy or relational therapy. Such therapies acknowledge that the sense-making of one person cannot be seen in isolation from the sense-making of those around her. But taking seriously the sociocultural dimension of psychiatric disorders goes further than that: it suggests that irrespective of the form of treatment it will typically make sense to engage family and friends – at least to some extent, and especially in case of severe disorders. Treatment can profit from the perspectives of patients' loved ones and from their support in practising new ways of interacting. An 'open dialogue' (Seikkula et al. 2006; Galbusera and Kyselo 2018) between the patient, caregivers, and family members provides a good example of how this could work, but less ambitious variants can help as well.[4]

Furthermore, the enactive focus on the person-in-her-world helps us see how even though it is the individual person who has sense-making problems, a change of environment may be useful. Which aspects of their surroundings may be reinforcing their problems? And which aspects instead help them to feel more at home? Part of treatment can be to try to find or construct the particular niche in which this person may flourish. This does not mean that patients

---

[4]   Involving patients' families and/or friends in treatment opens up difficult questions regarding autonomy and paternalism. The interests of the patient herself should obviously remain central. What 'personal autonomy' amounts to and how it can best be fostered is far from clear though. Enactivism's relational view could be brought to bear on this issue – but that is beyond the scope of this book. We can at least be sure that an enactive, relational view would reject all too simple independency-based conceptions of personal autonomy.

need to move (although that can sometimes be a good idea): it is rather about the installation of new habits. Just as cardiac patients who should stick to a certain and diet and are encouraged to take the stairs instead of the elevator, to quit smoking and avoid stressful situations, so too psychiatric patients may want to change some of their unhelpful habits. And not just through the sheer use of 'will-power', but by structuring their material and social world in such a way that they support the kind of choices one wants to make. We use all kinds of structures, routines, and habits to help us act in line with our concerns. It is for instance easier to refrain from eating ice-cream if there isn't any in your home. And it is easier to get yourself to exercise regularly if you enrol in a specific programme, or make an appointment with a friend to run together every Tuesday night. Similarly, a dog forces you to go out of the house every day. And if you are recovering from an alcohol addiction it will be helpful to avoid going to bars – and to ask your friends to help you with this. Getting oneself together usually includes shaping one's environment accordingly and these kinds of social and material 'scaffoldings' can help with that (cf. Wood et al. 1976; Anderson and Honneth 2005; Colombetti and Krueger 2015).

Finding or constructing a fitting niche for oneself is important because our surroundings not only influence what we do and how we feel, but also impact our very capacities. From an enactive perspective, our capacities are not simply acquired and completed at a certain age, as if they were a collection of cards that we own; capacities are rather continuously shaped through practising them. We do not *possess* but *enact* them. As a consequence, abilities are not solely an individual's matter: one's abilities also depend on one's specific surroundings and the kinds of interactions they afford. Take our social skills: we can probably all think of examples of social situations in which we felt pretty awkward and other social settings in which we felt completely at ease. In the situations where you felt at ease, you were probably be more likely to join conversations, make jokes, and be open to others, compared to the social situations in which you felt awkward. If someone who didn't know you were to judge your social skills, her assessment would have differed considerably depending on the specific situation in which she witnessed you (cf. De Jaegher and Froese 2009).

Because our capacities and dispositions often have been developed over the course of years, they can have become thoroughly engrained, like deeply worn paths. Yet they are not static: abilities continue to be shaped by present interactions and attitudes. To some extent it will still be possible to practice different interactions, different ways of relating to the world, different ways of evaluating oneself and others. And even if it may prove hard to change one's spontaneous reactions, people can still learn to explicitly 'correct' their initial response, to train themselves to think or look twice before they make sense of the world in their well-worn way. Just like the acquisition of a new skill may take a long time, learning a new way of sense-making may require much practice too.

Such practising of new ways of sense-making is precisely what happens in psychotherapy. From an enactive perspective, psychotherapy can be regarded as the attempt to offer optimal interactions for the patient to learn and practice new ways of sense-making in a durable way. This is in line with the traditional idea of therapy as a 'practice-relationship': within the safe environment of the therapeutic setting, patients can try out a broader range of behaviours, thoughts, and feelings, and thereby practice different ways of relating and sense-making. Disordered patterns of sense-making are *enacted*: you are establishing and maintaining a pattern by continuing to interact in a certain way. This means that when you change your way of interacting, you are thereby changing the pattern.

One's common ways of acting and reacting, the patterns in one's sense-making, will come to the fore in therapy as well. Patients will enact their sense-making within the therapeutic setting. From this enactive perspective, the phenomenon of transference is not a matter of patients projecting their earlier experiences onto the therapist, but rather the enacting of a familiar pattern of interaction, especially one that brings with it an idiosyncratic set of expectations as to how one will be perceived by the other. As van den Berg (1972) writes: 'The patient does not transfer an affect from his father to the psychotherapist; that really is impossible. The neurotic relationship with his father and the neurotic relationship with the psychotherapist have an aspect in common, his contact disturbance in general' (p. 99). 'Resistance' then refers to the difficulty of changing an engrained, incorporated pattern, i.e. to the effort it takes to avoid the well trodden path and start to carve out another path where there isn't one yet.

In therapy, both the aware and unaware sides of patients' sense-making are at stake. The transference, for instance, the re-enactment of familiar patterns of sense-making, is not something the patient is usually aware of: for him this is just the way in which he experiences the world and how he accordingly acts. From an enactive perspective, the notion 'unconscious' does not denote a hidden part of the mind, but rather refers to patterns in one's way of interacting that the person herself is unaware of. Moreover, not only the pattern itself is unconsciously enacted, but alternative possibilities are often not even perceived. It seems so natural to react in a certain way; to avoid conflicts, to keep everybody happy, or rather to defend yourself when you feel attacked, that it seems like this is simply the only way one could possibly react in such circumstances, i.e. that the circumstances just demand this reaction.

Just as there are explicit and implicit processes of sense-making at stake, engaging in therapy will provide both implicit and explicit learning. On the one hand, therapists themselves provide an example of a different way of acting and reacting. Ideally, therapists' non-judgemental, explorative attitude not only sets an example, but also invites a different kind of interaction. On the other hand, therapy enables explicit learning as well. Therapists can for instance offer so-called cognitive challenges which involve spelling out and critically examining the unconscious assumptions of patients. Or they can offer patients 'behavioural challenges' to experiment with other ways of reacting and interacting. Therapies can also be aimed at increasing insight: at helping patients to recognise what they are feeling and to recognise their dominant patterns of sense-making. The collaborative effort of patient and therapist to recognise rigid and inappropriate interaction patterns and to practice with different ways of engaging with the world, oneself, and others, can be understood as a *practice of participatory sense-making*.[5]

8.5 CONCLUSION

Adopting a personalised approach, and considering a plurality of treatment options aimed at different aspects of the problem at hand, is hardly controversial. An enactive approach however clarifies how these aspects are related and how to conceive of their interactions. This was exactly the question we started out with: how can we relate the heterogeneous factors that are at play in psychiatric disorders? In particular, our aim was to find a framework that could integrate the physiological, experiential, sociocultural, and existential dimensions of psychiatric disorders. I turned to enactivism for an alternative view on the nature of the mind as the embodied and embedded activity of sense-making. Instead of adopting a traditional inner mind–outer world topology, the enactive view argues for the continuity of life and mind: in living beings, physiological and experiential sense-making processes necessarily go together because of the organism's fundamental dependency on its interactions with its environment. In order to survive, the organism needs to make sense of its environment, that is: it needs to evaluatively interact with it. From an enactive point of view, we can see the organism in interaction with its environment as one complex, dynamical system.

In this way, an enactive perspective already integrates three out of the four dimensions of psychiatric disorders. We looked at what this view entails with regard to the relations between these dimensions, in

---

[5]   See also Maiese (2016).

particular with regard to causality. I argued that this causality is best understood as organisational causality – in line with a conception of emergence as fusion. One dimension was however still lacking from this enactive framework: the existential dimension, which refers to the fact that persons can take a stance on themselves and their situations. Since this dimension is just as central to understanding the development and persistence of psychiatric disorders as the other three, we elaborated an enriched version of enactivism that integrates the existential dimension. We saw that the existential capacity of stance-taking changes the system as a whole: from an organism–environment into a person–world system. The existential stance transforms our sense-making, implies the emergence of values and of a sociocultural world and at the same time depends on this world for its development. It is this existentialised sense-making of persons in their world that goes astray in psychiatric disorders.

From this enactive perspective we can define psychiatric disorders as structurally disordered patterns of sense-making. Sense-making is disordered if it has become rigid; stuck in a specific pattern rather than flexibly attuned to the situation at hand. The focus on sense-making implies the need to take the whole embodied, existential person in her world as the central unit of analysis for understanding and treating psychiatric disorders – rather than seeing them as problems in individuals' heads. The enactive approach thus integrates psychiatric disorders' diverse dimensions and offers a clear view on how they relate. This in turn helps to understand what is happening in different forms of treatment, to relate findings from different fields of research, and to solve several conceptual issues around the nature of psychiatric disorders. Above all, the enactive approach provides a theoretical framework for a holistic practice of psychiatry, thereby proving that holism does not have to be vague.

References

Adams, F. and K. Aizawa (2008). *The bounds of cognition*. Malden, MA: Blackwell.

Adams, F. and R. Garrison (2013). 'The mark of the cognitive'. *Minds and Machines* **23**(3): 339–52.

Ahmed, S. (2006). *Queer phenomenology: Orientations, objects, others*. Durham, NC: Duke University Press.

Aizawa, K. (2010). 'The coupling-constitution fallacy revisited'. *Cognitive Systems Research* **11**(4): 332–42.

Alexander-Bloch, A. F., P. E. Vértes, R. Stidd, F. Lalonde, L. Clasen, J. Rapoport, J. Giedd et al. (2013). 'The anatomical distance of functional connections predicts brain network topology in health and schizophrenia'. *Cerebral Cortex* **23**(1): 127–38.

American Psychiatric Association (2013). *Diagnostic and statistical manual of mental disorders*, 5th edn. Washington, DC: American Psychiatric Association.

Anderson, J. (1996). 'The personal lives of strong evaluators: Identity, pluralism and ontology in Charles Taylor's value theory'. *Constellations* **3**(1): 17–38.

Anderson, J. and A. Honneth (2005). 'Autonomy, vulnerability, recognition, and justice'. *Autonomy and the challenges to liberalism: New essays*. J. Christman and J. Anderson, eds. Cambridge: Cambridge University Press: 127–49.

Aristotle (1989). *Metaphysics*. Cambridge, MA: Harvard University Press.

Arsenault-Lapierre, G., C. Kim and G. Turecki (2004). 'Psychiatric diagnoses in 3275 suicides: A meta-analysis'. *BMC Psychiatry* **4**(1): 37.

Barandiaran, X. E. and M. D. Egbert (2014). 'Norm-establishing and norm-following in autonomous agency'. *Artificial Life* **20**(1): 5–28.

Barandiaran, X. and A. Moreno (2008). 'Adaptivity: From metabolism to behavior'. *Adaptive Behavior* **16**(5): 325–44.

Barandiaran, X. E., E. Di Paolo and M. Rohde (2009). 'Defining agency: Individuality, normativity, asymmetry, and spatio-temporality in action'. *Adaptive Behavior* **17**(5): 367–86.

Bartz, J. A., J. Zaki, N. Bolger and K. N. Ochsner (2011). 'Social effects of oxytocin in humans: Context and person matter'. *Trends in Cognitive Sciences* **15**(7): 301–9.

Bateson, G. (1972/2000). *Steps to an ecology of mind*. Chicago: University of Chicago Press.

Baumeister, R. F. (1991). *Meanings of life*. New York: Guilford Press.

Bechtel, W. and A. A. Abrahamsen (2013). 'Thinking dynamically about biological mechanisms: Networks of coupled oscillators'. *Foundations of Science* 18(4): 707–23.

Bechtel, W. and R. C. Richardson (2010). *Discovering complexity: Decomposition and localization as strategies in scientific research*. Cambridge, MA: MIT Press.

Beck, A. T. and D. A. Clark (1997). 'An information processing model of anxiety: Automatic and strategic processes'. *Behaviour Research and Therapy* 35(1): 49–58.

Bedau, M. A. and P. Humphreys, eds. (2008). *Emergence: Contemporary readings in philosophy and science*. Cambridge, MA: MIT Press.

Beer, R. D. (1995). 'A dynamical systems perspective on agent-environment interaction'. *Artificial Intelligence* 72: 173–215.

Beer, R. D. (2000). 'Dynamical approaches to cognitive science'. *Trends in Cognitive Sciences* 4: 91–9.

Belsky, J., C. Jonassaint, M. Pluess, M. Stanton, B. Brummett and R. Williams (2009). 'Vulnerability genes or plasticity genes?' *Molecular Psychiatry* 14: 746–54.

Bennett, C. M. (2009). 'The story behind the Atlantic Salmon'. Prefrontal.org.

Bennett, C. M. and M. B. Miller (2010). 'How reliable are the results from functional magnetic resonance imaging?' *Annals of the New York Academy of Sciences* 1191(1): 133–55.

Bernstein, R. J. (1983/2011). *Beyond objectivism and relativism: Science, hermeneutics, and praxis*. Philadelphia: University of Pennsylvania Press.

Bezzola, L., S. Mérillat, C. Gaser and L. Jäncke (2011). 'Training-induced neural plasticity in golf novices'. *Journal of Neuroscience* 31(35): 12444–8.

Bieri, P. (1981). *Analytische philosophie des geistes*. Hain: Königstein.

Bleuler, E. (1911/1950). *Dementia praecox or the group of schizophrenias*. New York: International Universities Press.

Borsboom, D. (2008). 'Psychometric perspectives on diagnostic systems'. *Journal of Clinical Psychology* 64(9): 1089–108.

Borsboom, D. (2017). 'A network theory of mental disorders'. *World Psychiatry* 16 (1): 5–13.

Borsboom, D. and A. Cramer (2013). 'Network analysis: An integrative approach to the structure of psychopathology'. *Annual Review of Clinical Psychology* 9: 91–121.

Borsboom, D., A. O. J. Cramer, V. D. Schmittmann, S. Epskamp and L. J. Waldorp (2011). 'The small world of psychopathology'. *PLoS ONE* **6** (11): e27407.

Broome, M. R., G. S. Owen and A. Stringaris (2012). *The Maudsley reader in phenomenological psychiatry*. Cambridge: Cambridge University Press.

Bruineberg, J. and E. Rietveld (2014). 'Self-organization, free energy minimization, and optimal grip on a field of affordances'. *Frontiers in Human Neuroscience* **8**: 1–14.

Bruineberg, J., J. Kiverstein and E. Rietveld (2018). 'The anticipating brain is not a scientist: The free-energy principle from an ecological-enactive perspective'. *Synthese* **195**(6): 2417–44.

Calvo, P. (2016). The philosophy of plant neurobiology: A manifesto. *Synthese* **193** (5): 1323–43.

Calvo, P. and F. Keijzer (2011). 'Plants: Adaptive behavior, root-brains, and minimal cognition'. *Adaptive Behavior* **19**(3): 155–71.

Campbell, D. T. (1974). 'Downward causation'. *Studies in the philosophy of biology*. F. Ayala and T. Dobzhansky, eds. Berkeley: University of California Press: 179–86.

Chalmers, D. J. (1995). 'Facing up to the problem of consciousness'. *Journal of Consciousness Studies* **2**(3): 200–19.

Chaloupka, F. J., M. Grossman and H. Saffer (2002). 'The effects of price on alcohol consumption and alcohol-related problems'. *Alcohol Research and Health* **26** (1): 22–34.

Chemero, A. (2003). 'An outline of a theory of affordances'. *Ecological Psychology* **15**(2): 181–95.

Chemero, A. (2009). *Radical embodied cognitive science*. Cambridge, MA: MIT Press.

Chiel, H. J. and R. D. Beer (1997). 'The brain has a body: Adaptive behavior emerges from interactions of nervous system, body and environment'. *Trends in Neurosciences* **20**(12): 553–7.

Clark, A. (1999). 'An embodied cognitive science?' *Trends in Cognitive Sciences* **3**: 345–51.

Clark, A. (2001). *Mindware: An introduction to the philosophy of cognitive science*. Oxford: Oxford University Press.

Clark, A. (2008). *Supersizing the mind: Embodiment, action, and cognitive extension*. Oxford: Oxford University Press.

Clark, A. and D. Chalmers (1998). 'The extended mind'. *Analysis* **58**(1): 7–19.

Clark, A. and J. Toribio (1994). 'Doing without representing?' *Synthese* **101**(3): 401–31.

Colombetti, G. (2007). 'Enactive appraisal'. *Phenomenology and the Cognitive Sciences* 6(4): 527–46.

Colombetti, G. (2010). 'Enaction, sense-making and emotion'. *Enaction: Towards a new paradigm for cognitive science*. Cambridge, MA: MIT Press: 145–65.

Colombetti, G. (2013). 'Psychopathology and the enactive mind'. *The Oxford handbook of philosophy and psychiatry*. K. W. M. Fulford, M. Davies, R. G. T. Gipps et al., eds. Oxford: Oxford University Press: 1083–102.

Colombetti, G. and J. Krueger (2015). 'Scaffoldings of the affective mind'. *Philosophical Psychology* 28(8): 1157–76.

Colombetti, G. and E. Thompson (2008). 'The feeling body: Towards an enactive approach to emotion'. *Body in mind, mind in body: Developmental perspectives on embodiment and consciousness*. W. F. Overton, U. Mueller and J. Newman, eds. New York: Erlbaum: 45–68.

Cooper, R. (2017). 'Where's the problem? Considering Laing and Esterson's account of schizophrenia, social models of disability, and extended mental disorder.' *Theoretical medicine and bioethics*, 38(4), 295-305.

Corrigan, P. and A. Watson (2004). 'At issue: Stop the stigma: Call mental illness a brain disease'. *Schizophrenia Bulletin* 30(3): 477.

Csikszentmihalyi, M. and R. Larson (1987). 'Validity and reliability of the experience-sampling method'. *Journal of Nervous and Mental Disease* 175(9): 526–36.

De Bruin, L. C. and L. Kästner (2012). 'Dynamic embodied cognition'. *Phenomenology and the Cognitive Sciences* 11(4): 541–63.

Degenaar, J. and E. Myin (2014). 'Representation – hunger reconsidered'. *Synthese* 191(15): 3639–48.

Degenaar, J. and J. K. O'Regan (2015). 'Sensorimotor theory of consciousness'. *Scholarpedia* 10(5): 4952.

de Haan, S. (2017). 'The existential dimension in psychiatry: An enactive framework'. *Mental Health, Religion and Culture* 20(6): 528–35.

de Haan, S. and T. Fuchs (2010). 'The ghost in the machine: Disembodiment in schizophrenia – two case studies'. *Psychopathology* 43(5): 327–33.

de Haan, S., H. De Jaegher, T. Fuchs and A. Mayer (2011). 'Expanding perspectives: the interactive development of perspective-taking in early childhood'. *The implications of embodiment: Cognition and communication*. W. Tschacher and C. Bergomi, eds. Exeter, UK: Imprint Academic: 129–51.

de Haan, S., E. Rietveld and D. Denys (2013a). 'On the nature of obsessions and compulsions'. *Anxiety disorders*. D. S. Baldwin and B. E. Leonard, eds. Basel: Karger: 1–15.

de Haan, S., E. Rietveld, M. Stokhof and D. Denys (2013b). 'The phenomenology of deep brain stimulation-induced changes in OCD: An enactive affordance-based model'. *Frontiers in Human Neuroscience* 7: 1–14.

de Haan, S., E. Rietveld and D. Denys (2015a). 'Being free by losing control: What obsessive-compulsive disorder can tell us about free will'. *Free will and the brain: Neuroscientific, philosophical, and legal perspectives.* W. Glannon, ed. Cambridge: Cambridge University Press: 83–102.

de Haan, S., E. Rietveld, M. Stokhof and D. Denys (2015b). 'Effects of deep brain stimulation on the lived experience of obsessive-compulsive disorder patients: In-depth interviews with 18 patients'. *PLoS ONE* **10**(8): 1–29.

de Haan, S. (forthcoming). 'An enactive approach to psychiatry.' *Philosophy, Psychiatry and Psychology.*

De Jaegher, H. (2013). 'Embodiment and sense-making in autism'. *Frontiers in Integrative Neuroscience* 7: 1–19.

De Jaegher, H. and E. Di Paolo (2007). 'Participatory sense-making: An enactive approach to social cognition'. *Phenomenology and the Cognitive Sciences* **6**(4): 485–507.

De Jaegher, H. and T. Froese (2009). 'On the role of social interaction in individual agency'. *Adaptive Behavior* **17**(5): 444–60.

De Jaegher, H., E. Di Paolo and S. Gallagher (2010). 'Can social interaction constitute social cognition?' *Trends in Cognitive Sciences* **14**(10): 441–7.

Dew, R. E. (2009). 'Why psychiatry is the hardest specialty'. *American Journal of Psychiatry* **166**(1): 16–17.

De Waal, F. B. (1990). *Peacemaking among primates.* Cambridge, MA: Harvard University Press.

Dings, R. (2017). 'Understanding phenomenological differences in how affordances solicit action: An exploration'. *Phenomenology and the Cognitive Sciences* **17** (4): 681–99.

Di Paolo, E. (2005). 'Autopoiesis, adaptivity, teleology, agency'. *Phenomenology and the Cognitive Sciences* **4**(4): 97–125.

Di Paolo, E. (2009a). 'Extended life'. *Topoi* **28**(1): 9–21.

Di Paolo, E. (2009b). 'Shallow and deep embodiment: Reasons for embracing enactivism'. Online talk available at www.cast.switch.ch/vod/clips/74nrkbwy s/quicktime. mov.

Di Paolo, E. A. and H. De Jaegher (2012). 'The interactive brain hypothesis'. *Frontiers in Human Neuroscience* **6**: 1–16.

Di Paolo, E. and E. Thompson (2014). 'The enactive approach'. *The Routledge handbook of embodied cognition.* L. Shapiro, ed. New York: Routledge: 68–78.

Di Paolo, E., M. Rohde and H. De Jaegher (2011). 'Horizons for the enactive mind: Values, social interaction, and play'. *Enaction: Towards a new paradigm for cognitive science*. J. Stewart, O. Gapenne and E. Di Paolo, eds. Cambridge, MA: MIT Press: 33–89.

Di Paolo, E., T. Buhrmann and X. Barandiaran (2017). *Sensorimotor life: An enactive proposal*. Oxford: Oxford University Press.

Di Paolo, E. A., E. C. Cuffari and H. De Jaegher (2018). *Linguistic bodies: The continuity between life and language*. Cambridge, MA: MIT Press.

Disner, S. G., C. G. Beevers, E. A. P. Haigh and A. T. Beck (2011). 'Neural mechanisms of the cognitive model of depression'. *Nature Reviews Neuroscience* 12: 467–77.

Donne, J. (1624). *Devotions upon emergent occasions*. London: Thomas Iones.

Dougherty, D. D., A. R. Rezai, L. L. Carpenter, R. H. Howland, M. T. Bhati, J. P. O'Reardon, E. N. Eskandar et al. (2015). 'A randomized sham-controlled trial of deep brain stimulation of the ventral capsule/ventral striatum for chronic treatment-resistant depression'. *Biological Psychiatry* 78(4): 240–8.

Drayson, Z. (2009). 'Embodied cognitive science and its implications for psychopathology'. *Philosophy, Psychiatry, and Psychology* 16(4): 329–40.

Dreyfus, H. L. (2007). 'The return of the myth of the mental'. *Inquiry* 50(4): 352–65.

Dreyfus, H. and C. Taylor (2015). *Retrieving realism*. Cambridge, MA: Harvard University Press.

Engel, G. (1977). 'The need for a new medical model: A challenge for biomedicine'. *Science* 196(4286): 129–36.

Engel, G. L. (1980). 'The clinical application of the biopsychosocial model'. *American Journal of Psychiatry* 137(5): 535–44.

Fanon, F. (1952/2008). *Black skin, white masks*. New York: Grove Press.

Fausto-Sterling, A. (2005). 'The bare bones of sex: Part 1—sex and gender'. *Signs: Journal of Women in Culture and Society* 30(2): 1491–527.

Figee, M., M. Vink, F. de Geus, N. Vulink, D. J. Veltman, H. Westenberg and D. Denys (2011). 'Dysfunctional reward circuitry in obsessive-compulsive disorder'. *Biological Psychiatry* 69(9): 867–74.

Fontenelle, L. F., S. Oostermeijer, B. J. Harrison, C. Pantelis and M. Yücel (2011). 'Obsessive-compulsive disorder, impulse control disorders and drug addiction'. *Drugs* 71(7): 827–40.

Frankfurt, H. (1988). *The importance of what we care about: Philosophical essays*. Cambridge: Cambridge University Press.

Frankfurt, H. (2002). 'Reply to Susan Wolf'. *The contours of agency: Essays on themes from Harry Frankfurt*. S. Buss and L. Overton, eds. Cambridge, MA: MIT Press: 245–52.

Frankfurt, H. G. (2004). *The reasons of love*. Princeton, NJ: Princeton University Press.

Frankl, V. (1946/2009). *Ärztliche Seelsorge. Grundlagen der Logotherapie und Existenzanalyse, mit den zehn Thesen über die Person*. Munich, Germany: Deutscher Taschenbuch Verlag.

Frankl, V. E. (1963). *Man's search for meaning: An introduction to logotherapy*. New York: Washington Square Press.

Franklin, T. B., H. Russig, I. C. Weiss, J. Gräff, N. Linder, A. Michalon, S. Vizi et al. (2010). 'Epigenetic transmission of the impact of early stress across generations'. *Biological Psychiatry* 68(5): 408–15.

Froese, T. and E. Di Paolo (2009). 'Sociality and the life–mind continuity thesis'. *Phenomenology and the Cognitive Sciences* 8(4): 439–63.

Froese, T. and E. Di Paolo (2011). 'The enactive approach: Theoretical sketches from cell to society'. *Pragmatics and Cognition* 19(1): 1–36.

Fuchs, T. (2001). 'Melancholia as a desynchronization: Towards a psychopathology of interpersonal time'. *Psychopathology* 34: 179–86.

Fuchs, T. (2002). 'The phenomenology of shame, guilt and the body in body dysmorphic disorder and depression'. *Journal of Phenomenological Psychology* 33(2): 223–43.

Fuchs, T. (2005). 'Corporealized and disembodied minds: A phenomenological view of the body in melancholia and schizophrenia'. *Philosophy, Psychiatry, and Psychology* 12(2): 95–107.

Fuchs, T. (2007). 'Psychotherapy of the lived space: A phenomenological and ecological concept'. *American Journal of Psychotherapy* 61(4): 423–39.

Fuchs, T. (2008). *Das Gehirn – ein Beziehungsorgan. Eine Phänomenologisch-Ökologische Konzeption*. Stuttgart: Kohlhammer.

Fuchs, T. (2009). 'Embodied cognitive neuroscience and its consequences for psychiatry'. *Poiesis and Praxis* 6: 219–33.

Fuchs, T. (2010a). 'Phenomenology and psychopathology'. *Handbook of phenomenology and cognitive science*. S. Gallagher and D. Schmicking, eds. Dordrecht: Springer.

Fuchs, T. (2010b). 'The psychopathology of hyperreflexivity'. *Journal of Speculative Philosophy* 24(3): 239–55.

Fuchs, T. (2011a). 'Are mental illnesses diseases of the brain?' *Critical neuroscience: A handbook of the social and cultural contexts of neuroscience*. S. Choudhury and J. Slaby, eds. London: Wiley-Blackwell: 331–44.

Fuchs, T. (2011b). 'The brain: A mediating organ'. *Journal of Consciousness Studies* 18(7–8): 196–221.

Fuchs, T. (2011c). 'The psychopathology of hyperreflexivity'. *Journal of Speculative Philosophy* **24**(3): 239–55.

Fuchs, T. (2012). 'The phenomenology and development of social perspectives'. *Phenomenology and the Cognitive Sciences* **12**(4): 655–83.

Fuchs, T. (2018). *Ecology of the brain*. Oxford: Oxford University Press.

Fuchs, T. (forthcoming). 'Delusion, reality, and intersubjectivity: A phenomenological and enactive analysis'. *Philosophy, Psychiatry and Psychology*.

Fuchs, T. and H. De Jaegher (2009). 'Enactive intersubjectivity: Participatory sense-making and mutual incorporation'. *Phenomenology and the Cognitive Sciences* **8**(4): 465–86.

Fuchs, T. and J. Schlimme (2009). 'Embodiment and psychopathology: A phenomenological perspective'. *Current Opinion in Psychiatry* **22**(6): 570–5.

Fulda, F. C. (2017). 'Natural agency: The case of bacterial cognition'. *Journal of the American Philosophical Association* **3**(1): 69–90.

Fulford, K. (1999). 'Nine variations and a coda on the theme of an evolutionary definition of dysfunction'. *Journal of Abnormal Psychology* **108**(3): 412–20.

Fulford, K. W. M. (2000). 'Teleology without tears: Naturalism, neo-naturalism, and evaluationism in the analysis of function statements in biology (and a bet on the twenty-first century)'. *Philosophy, Psychiatry, and Psychology* **7**(1): 77–94.

Fulford, K. W. M. (2008a). 'Values-based practice: A new partner to evidence-based practice and a first for psychiatry?' *Mens Sana Monographs* **6**(1): 10–21.

Fulford, K. W. M. (2008b). 'Values-based practice: From the real to the really practical'. *Philosohy, Psychiatry, and Psychology* **15**(2): 183–5.

Fulford, K., M. Broome, G. Stanghellini and T. Thornton (2005). 'Looking with both eyes open: Fact and value in psychiatric diagnosis?' *World Psychiatry* **4**(2): 78–86.

Galbusera, L. and M. Kyselo (2018). 'The difference that makes the difference: a conceptual analysis of the open dialogue approach'. *Psychosis* **10**(1): 47–54.

Gallagher, S. (2004). 'Understanding interpersonal problems in autism: Interaction theory as an alternative to theory of mind'. *Philosophy, Psychiatry, and Psychology* **11**(3): 199–217.

Gallagher, S. (2017). *Enactivist interventions: Rethinking the mind*. Oxford: Oxford University Press.

Gallagher, S. and M. Væver (2004). 'Disorders of embodiment'. *The philosophy of psychiatry: A companion*. J. Radden, ed. Oxford: Oxford University Press: 118–32.

Gallup, G. G. (1977). 'Self recognition in primates: A comparative approach to the bidirectional properties of consciousness'. *American Psychologist* **32**(5): 329–38.

Garofoli, D. (2015). 'A radical embodied approach to lower palaeolithic spear-making'. *Journal of Mind and Behavior* **36**(1–2): 1–26.

Gaser, C. and G. Schlaug (2003). 'Brain structures differ between musicians and non-musicians'. *Journal of Neuroscience* **23**(27): 9240–5.

Gazzaniga, M. (2012). *Who's in charge?: Free will and the science of the brain*, Constable & Robinson.

George, M. S. and G. Aston-Jones (2009). 'Noninvasive techniques for probing neurocircuitry and treating illness: vagus nerve stimulation (VNS), transcranial magnetic stimulation (TMS) and transcranial direct current stimulation (tDCS)'. *Neuropsychopharmacology* **35**: 301–16.

George, M. S., S. H. Lisanby, D. Avery, W. M. McDonald, V. Durkalski, M. Pavlicova, B. Anderson et al. (2010). 'Daily left prefrontal transcranial magnetic stimulation therapy for major depressive disorder: A sham-controlled randomized trialmagnetic stimulation for major depressive disorder'. *Archives of General Psychiatry* **67**(5): 507–16.

Ghaemi, N. S. (2007). 'Feeling and time: The phenomenology of mood disorders, depressive realism, and existential psychotherapy'. *Schizophrenia Bulletin* **33** (1): 122–30.

Ghaemi, S. N. (2009). 'The rise and fall of the biopsychosocial model'. *British Journal of Psychiatry* **195**(1): 3–4.

Gibson, J. J. (1979). *The ecological approach to visual perception*. Boston: Houghton Mifflin.

Gipps, R. G. T. (2018). 'How matters mereological constrain reason-giving'. *Philosophical Perspectives in Clinical Psychology* (blog). Available at: https://clinicalphilosophy.blogspot.com/2018/02/psychological-and-neurological.html.

Gipps, R. G. T. (forthcoming-a). 'Conditions and implications of compromised ego boundaries'. *Philosophy, Psychiatry and Psychology*.

Gipps, R. G. T. (forthcoming-b). 'Disturbance of ego boundary enaction in schizophrenia'. *Philosophy, Psychiatry and Psychology*.

Glas, G. (2008). 'Over het psychiatrisch ziektebegrip'. *Kernproblemen van de psychiatrie*. J. A. Den Boer, G. Glas and A. W. M. Mooij, eds. Amsterdam: Boom: 328–70.

Glas, G. (forthcoming). 'An enactive approach to anxiety and anxiety disorders'. *Philosophy, Psychiatry and Psychology*.

Greenberg, B. D., L. A. Gabriels, D. A. Malone Jr., A. R. Rezai, G. M. Friehs, M. S. Okun, N. A. Shapira et al. (2010). 'Deep brain stimulation of the ventral internal capsule/ventral striatum for obsessive-compulsive disorder: Worldwide experience'. *Molecular Psychiatry* **15**(1): 64–79.

Guay, S., V. Billette and A. Marchand (2006). 'Exploring the links between posttraumatic stress disorder and social support: Processes and potential research avenues'. *Journal of Traumatic Stress* **19**(3): 327–38.

Gupta, M. (2014). *Is evidence-based psychiatry ethical?* Oxford: Oxford University Press.

Hacking, I. (1986). 'Making up people'. *Reconstructing individualism: Autonomy, individuality and the self in Western thought*. T. C. Heller, ed. Stanford, CA: Stanford University Press: 222–36.

Hacking, I. (1995). 'The looping effects of human kinds'. *Causal cognition: A multidisciplinary approach*. D. Sperber, D. Premack and A. J. Premack, eds. New York: Oxford University Press: 351–83.

Haken, H. (1983). 'Synopsis and introduction'. *Synergetics of the brain*. E. Başar, H. Flohr, H. Haken and A. J. Mandell, eds. Berlin: Springer: 3–25

Hänggi, J., S. Koeneke, L. Bezzola and L. Jäncke (2010). 'Structural neuroplasticity in the sensorimotor network of professional female ballet dancers'. *Human Brain Mapping* **31**(8): 1196–206.

Hanna, R. and E. Thompson (2003). 'The mind-body-body problem'. *Theoria et Historia Scientiarum* **7**(1): 24–44.

Hardy, T. M. and T. O. Tollefsbol (2011). 'Epigenetic diet: Impact on the epigenome and cancer'. *Epigenomics* **3**(4): 503–18.

Hawton, K. and K. van Heeringen (2009). 'Suicide'. *The Lancet* **373**(9672): 1372–81.

Heidegger, M. (1927/1978). *Being and time*. Malden, MA: Blackwell.

Heijmans, B. T., E. W. Tobi, A. D. Stein, H. Putter, G. J. Blauw, E. S. Susser, P. E. Slagboom et al. (2008). 'Persistent epigenetic differences associated with prenatal exposure to famine in humans'. *Proceedings of the National Academy of Sciences of the United States of America* **105**(44): 17046–9.

Heil, J. (1981). 'Does cognitive psychology rest on a mistake?' *Mind* **90**(359): 321–42.

Hobson, R. P. (2002). *The cradle of thought*. London: Macmillan.

Hobson, R. P. (2009). 'Wittgenstein and the developmental psychopathology of autism'. *New Ideas in Psychology* **27**(2): 243–57.

Hoffman, G. A. (2016). 'Out of our skulls: How the extended mind thesis can extend psychiatry.' *Philosophical Psychology*, 29(8), 1160-1174.

Hohwy, J. (2016). 'The self-evidencing brain'. *Noûs* **50**(2): 259–85.

Hope, T., J. Tan, A. Stewart and R. Fitzpatrick (2011). 'Anorexia nervosa and the language of authenticity'. *Hastings Center Report* **41**(6): 19–29.

Humphreys, P. (1996). 'Aspects of emergence'. *Philosophical Topics* **24**(1): 53–70.

Humphreys, P. (1997a). 'How properties emerge'. *Philosophy of Science* **64**(1): 1–17.

Humphreys, P. (1997b). 'Emergence, not supervenience'. *Philosophy of Science* **64**: 337–45.

Hurley, S. (1998). *Consciousness in action*. London: Harvard University Press.

Hurley, S. (2008). 'The shared circuits model (SCM): How control, mirroring, and simulation can enable imitation, deliberation, and mindreading'. *Behavioral and Brain Sciences* **31**(01): 1–22.

Hutto, D. D. (2010). 'Radical enactivism and narrative practice: Implications for psychopathology'. *Coherence and disorders of the embodied self*. T. Fuchs, P. Henningsen and H. Sattel, eds. Stuttgart: Schattauer: 43–66.

Hutto, D. D. and E. Myin (2013). *Radicalizing enactivism: Basic minds without content*. Cambridge, MA: MIT Press.

Hutto, D. D. and E. Myin (2017). *Evolving enactivism: Basic minds meet content*. Cambridge, MA: MIT Press.

Insel, T. R. (2013). 'Transforming diagnosis'. www.nimh.nih.gov/about/directors/ thomas-insel/blog/2013/transforming-diagnosis.shtml.

Issad, T. and C. Malaterre (2015). 'Are dynamic mechanistic explanations still mechanistic?' *Explanation in biology: An enquiry into the diversity of explanatory patterns in the life sciences*. Dordrecht: Springer Netherlands: 265–92.

Janet, P. (1903). *Les obsessions et la psychasthénie*. Paris: Alcan.

Jaspers, K. (1913). *Allgemeine Psychopathologie: ein Leitfaden für Studierende, Ärzte und Psychologen*. Berlin: Springer.

Jonas, H. (1966/2001). *The phenomenon of life: Toward a philosophical biology*. Evanston, IL: Northwestern University Press.

Kandel, E. R. (1999a). 'Dr. Kandel replies'. *American Journal of Psychiatry* **156**(4): 665–6.

Kandel, E. R. (1999b). 'Biology and the future of psychoanalysis: A new intellectual framework for psychiatry revisited'. *American Journal of Psychiatry* **156**(4): 505–24.

Kant, I. (1787/1998). *Critique of pure reason*. Cambridge: Cambridge University Press.

Kapur, S., A. G. Phillips and T. R. Insel (2012). 'Why has it taken so long for biological psychiatry to develop clinical tests and what to do about it?' *Molecular Psychiatry* **17**: 1174–9.

Karp, D. A. (2009). *Is it me or my meds? Living with antidepressants*. Cambridge, MA: Harvard University Press.

Kelly, S. (2009). 'Introduction to Heidegger's "Being and time"'. Lecture. E. Rietveld, Boston.

Kelso, J. A. S. (1995). *Dynamic patterns: The self-organization of brain and behaviour*. Cambridge, MA: MIT Press.

Kincaid, H., J. Dupré and A. Wylie, eds. (2007). *Value-free science? Ideals and illusions*. Oxford: Oxford University Press.

Király, I., G. Csibra and G. Gergely (2013). 'Beyond rational imitation: Learning arbitrary means actions from communicative demonstrations'. *Journal of Experimental Child Psychology* **116**(2): 471–86.

Kirchhoff, M. D. (2015a). 'Experiential fantasies, prediction, and enactive minds'. *Journal of Consciousness Studies* **22**(3–4): 68–92.

Kirchhoff, M. D. (2015b). 'Extended cognition & the causal-constitutive fallacy: In search for a diachronic and dynamical conception of constitution'. *Philosophy and Phenomenological Research* **90**(2): 320–60.

Kirchhoff, M. D. (2018). 'Autopoiesis, free energy, and the life–mind continuity thesis'. *Synthese* **195**(6): 2519–40.

Kiverstein, J. D. and E. Rietveld (2018). 'Reconceiving representation-hungry cognition: An ecological-enactive proposal'. *Adaptive Behavior* **26**(4): 1–17.

Klin, A., W. Jones, R. Schultz and F. Volkmar (2003). 'The enactive mind, or from actions to cognition: Lessons from autism'. *Philosophical Transactions of the Royal Society of London, Series B* **358**(1430): 345–60.

Koch, S. C., T. Fuchs, M. Summa and C. Müller, eds. (2012). *Body memory, metaphor and movement: Advances in consciousness research*. Amsterdam: John Benjamins.

Koenigs, M. and J. Grafman (2009). 'Posttraumatic stress disorder: The role of medial prefrontal cortex and amygdala'. *The Neuroscientist* **15**(5): 540–8.

Kopell, B. H., B. Greenberg and A. R. Rezai (2004). 'Deep brain stimulation for psychiatric disorders'. *Journal of Clinical Neurophysiology* **21**(1): 51–67.

Kramer, P. D. (1997). *Listening to Prozac*. New York: Penguin.

Krickel, B. (2017). 'Making sense of interlevel causation in mechanisms from a metaphysical perspective'. *Journal for General Philosophy of Science* **48**(3): 453–68.

Kronz, F. M. and J. T. Tiehen (2002). 'Emergence and quantum mechanics'. *Philosophy of Science* **69**(2): 324–347.

Krueger, J. (2011). 'Enacting musical content'. *Situated aesthetics: Art beyond the skin*. R. Manzotti, ed. Exeter: Imprint Academic: 63–85.

Krueger, J. (2018). 'Schizophrenia and the scaffolded self'. *Topoi*, 1–13.

Krystal, J. H. and M. W. State (2014). 'Psychiatric disorders: Diagnosis to therapy'. *Cell* **157**(1): 201–14.

Kyselo, M. (2016). 'The enactive approach and disorders of the self: The case of schizophrenia'. *Phenomenology and the Cognitive Sciences* **15**(4): 591–616.

Laing, R. D. (1960/1990). *The divided self*. London: Penguin Books.

Larsen, J. L. (2019). 'An examination of factors influencing cannabis use in psychosis: A network perspective'. Unpublished manuscript.

Larsen, J. L. and K. S. Johansen (2019). 'Dobbeltdiagnose – en ubekvem betegnelse i det tværsektorielle arbejde?' *Rusmiddelbrugere i krydsfeltet mellem sektorer og fagligheder*. B. Bjerge and E. Houborg, eds. Aarhus: Aarhus University Press.

Lenman, J., S. Finlay and M. Lutz (2017). 'Moral naturalism'. *The Stanford encyclopedia of philosophy*. E. N. Zalta, ed. https://plato.stanford.edu/archives/sum2017/entries/naturalism-moral/.

Leshner, A. I. (1997). 'Addiction is a brain disease, and it matters'. *Science* **278** (5335): 45–7.

Lewontin, R. C. (2002). 'Foreword'. *The ontogeny of information*. Durham, NC: Duke University Press: xix–xv.

Luigjes, J., B. P. de Kwaasteniet, P. P. de Koning, M. S. Oudijn, P. van den Munckhof, P. R. Schuurman and D. Denys (2013). 'Surgery for psychiatric disorders'. *World Neurosurgery* **80**(3–4): S31.e17–28.

Lutz, M. and J. Lenman (2018). 'Moral naturalism'. *The Stanford encyclopedia of philosophy*. E. N. Zalta, ed. https://plato.stanford.edu/archives/fall2018/entries/naturalism-moral/.

Machado, A. (1979). *Selected poems by Antonio Machado*. Baton Rouge: Louisiana State University Press.

Machamer, P., L. Darden and C. F. Craver (2000). 'Thinking about mechanisms'. *Philosophy of Science* **67**(1): 1–25.

Mackenzie, C. and N. Stoljar, eds. (2000). *Relational autonomy: Feminist perspectives on autonomy, agency, and the social self*. New York: Oxford University Press.

Maguire, E. A., D. G. Gadian, I. S. Johnsrude, C. D. Good, J. Ashburner, R. S. Frackowiak and C. D. Frith (2000). 'Navigation-related structural change in the hippocampi of taxi drivers'. *Proceedings of the National Academy of Sciences of the United States of America* **97**(8): 4398–403.

Maiese, M. (2016). *Embodied selves and divided minds*. Oxford: Oxford University Press.

Maiese, M. (2018). 'An enactivist approach to treating depression: Cultivating online intelligence through dance and music'. *Phenomenology and the Cognitive Sciences*, 1–25.

Malafouris, L. (2013). *How things shape the mind*. Cambridge, MA: MIT Press.

Mantione, M., D. Nieman, M. Figee and D. Denys (2014). 'Cognitive–behavioural therapy augments the effects of deep brain stimulation in obsessive–compulsive disorder'. *Psychological Medicine* **44**(16): 3513–21.

Marneros, A. (2008). 'Psychiatry's 200th birthday'. *British Journal of Psychiatry* **193** (1): 1–3.

Maturana, H. R. (1980). 'Autopoiesis: Reproduction, heredity and evolution'. *Autopoiesis, dissipative structures, and spontaneous social orders.* M. Zeleny, ed. Boulder, CO: Westview Press.

Maturana, H. and F. Varela (1972/1980). *Autopoiesis and cognition: The realization of the living.* Dordrecht: D. Reidel.

Maturana, H. R. and F. J. Varela (1987). *The tree of knowledge: the biological roots of human understanding.* London: Shambhala.

Matyja, J. R. and A. Schiavio (2013). 'Enactive music cognition: Background and research themes'. *Constructivist Foundations* **8**(3): 351–7.

May, R. (1983). *The discovery of being.* New York: W. W. Norton.

Mayberg, H. S., A. M. Lozano, V. Voon, H. E. McNeely, D. Seminowicz, C. Hamani, J. M. Schwalb et al. (2005). 'Deep brain stimulation for treatment-resistant depression'. *Neuron* **45**(5): 651–60.

McGann, M., H. De Jaegher and E. Di Paolo (2013). 'Enaction and psychology'. *Review of General Psychology* **17**(2): 203–9.

McLaughlin, B. and K. Bennett (2014). 'Supervenience'. *The Stanford encyclopedia of philosophy.* E. N. Zalta, ed. https://plato.stanford.edu/archives/win2018/en tries/supervenience/.

Mead, G. H. (1934/1962). *Mind, self and society.* Chicago: University of Chicago Press.

Megone, C. (2000). 'Mental illness, human function, and values'. *Philosophy, Psychiatry and Psychology* **7**(1): 45–65.

Merleau-Ponty, M. (1942/1963). *The structure of behavior.* Boston: Beacon Press.

Merleau-Ponty, M. (1945/2002). *Phenomenology of perception.* London: Routledge.

Metzinger, T. (2003). *Being no one: The self-model theory of subjectivity.* Cambridge, MA: MIT Press.

Meynen, G. and A. Ralston (2011). 'Zeven visies op een psychiatrische stoornis'. *Tijdschrift voor Psychiatrie* **53**(12): 895–903.

Minkowski, E. (1927). *La schizophrénie: psychopathologie des schizoïdes et des schizophrénes.* Paris: Payot.

Minuchin, S., B. L. Rosman and L. Baker (1978/2009). *Psychosomatic families: Anorexia nervosa in context.* Cambridge, MA: Harvard University Press.

Mitchell, P. B. and C. K. Loo (2006). 'Transcranial magnetic stimulation for depression'. *Australian and New Zealand Journal of Psychiatry* **40**(5): 406–13.

Moore, G. E. (1903). *Principia ethica.* Cambridge: Cambridge University Press.

Moreno, A., K. Ruiz-Mirazo and X. Barandiaran (2011). 'The impact of the paradigm of complexity on the foundational frameworks of biology and cognitive science'. *Philosophy of complex systems*. Vol. 10. C. Hooker, ed. Amsterdam: Elsevier: 311–34.

Myin, E. and J. Degenaar (2014). 'Enactive vision'. *The Routledge handbook of embodied cognition*. L. Shapiro, ed. New York: Routledge: 90–8.

Myin-Germeys, I., M. Oorschot, D. Collip, J. Lataster, P. Delespaul and J. van Os (2009). 'Experience sampling research in psychopathology: Opening the black box of daily life'. *Psychological Medicine* 39(09): 1533–47.

Myin, E., J. K. O'Regan and I. Myin-Germeys (2015). 'From a sensorimotor account of perception to an interactive approach to psychopathology'. *Disturbed consciousness: New essays on psychopathology and theories of consciousness*. R. Gennaro. Cambridge, MA: MIT Press: 347–69.

Nagel, T. (1989). *The view from nowhere*. New York: Oxford University Press.

NIMH (2008). *The National Institute of Mental Health strategic plan*. Washington, DC: National Institute of Mental Health.

Noë, A. (2004). *Action in perception*. Cambridge, MA: MIT Press.

Noë, A. (2009). *Out of our heads*. New York: Hill and Wang.

Noël, X., D. Brevers and A. Bechara (2013). 'A neurocognitive approach to understanding the neurobiology of addiction'. *Current Opinion in Neurobiology* 23(4): 632–8.

Nutt, D. J. (2008). 'Relationship of neurotransmitters to the symptoms of major depressive disorder'. *Journal of Clinical Psychiatry* 69: 4–7.

Olff, M., J. L. Frijling, L. D. Kubzansky, B. Bradley, M. A. Ellenbogen, C. Cardoso, J. A. Bartz et al. (2013). 'The role of oxytocin in social bonding, stress regulation and mental health: An update on the moderating effects of context and interindividual differences'. *Psychoneuroendocrinology* 38(9): 1883–94.

O'Neill, A. and T. Frodl (2012). 'Brain structure and function in borderline personality disorder'. *Brain Structure and Function* 217(4): 767–82.

O'Regan, J. K. and A. Noë (2001). 'A sensorimotor account of vision and visual consciousness'. *Behavioral and Brain Sciences* 24(5): 883–917.

Oyama, S. (1985/2000). *The ontogeny of information: Developmental systems and evolution*. Durham, NC: Duke University Press.

Oyama, S., P. E. Griffiths and R. D. Gray (2003). *Cycles of contingency: Developmental systems and evolution*. Cambridge, MA: MIT Press.

Parrish, T. (2006). 'Proper masking to show the true activation'. *American Journal of Neuroradiology* 27(2): 247–9.

Pescosolido, B. A., J. K. Martin, J. S. Long, T. R. Medina, J. C. Phelan and B. G. Link (2010). '"A disease like any other"? A decade of change in public reactions to schizophrenia, depression, and alcohol dependence'. *American Journal of Psychiatry* **167**(11): 1321–30.

Pfeifer, R. and F. Iida (2004). 'Embodied artificial intelligence: Trends and challenges'. *Embodied artificial intelligence*. F. Iida, R. Pfeifer, L. Steels and Y. Kuniyoshi, eds. Berlin: Springer: 1–26.

Plessner, H. (1928/1981). *Die Stufen des Organischen und der Mensch*. Frankfurt am Main: Suhrkamp.

Preston, S. D. and F. B. De Waal (2002). 'Empathy: Its ultimate and proximate bases'. *Behavioral and Brain Sciences* **25**(1): 1–20.

Raja, V. (2018). 'A theory of resonance: Towards an ecological cognitive architecture'. *Minds and Machines* **28**(1): 29–51.

Ramsey, W. M. (2007). *Representation reconsidered*. Cambridge: Cambridge University Press.

Ratcliffe, M. (2008). *Feelings of being: Phenomenology, psychiatry and the sense of reality*. Oxford: Oxford University Press.

Ratcliffe, M. (2009). 'Existential feeling and psychopathology'. *Philosophy, Psychiatry and Psychology* **16**(2): 179–94.

Ratcliffe, M. (2010). 'Depression, guilt and emotional depth'. *Inquiry* **53**(6): 602–26.

Rauch, S. L., P. J. Whalen, L. M. Shin, S. C. McInerney, M. L. Macklin, N. B. Lasko, S. P. Orr et al. (2000). 'Exaggerated amygdala response to masked facial stimuli in posttraumatic stress disorder: A functional MRI study'. *Biological Psychiatry* **47**(9): 769–76.

Reddy, V. (2003). 'On being the object of attention: Implications for self-other consciousness'. *Trends in Cognitive Sciences* **7**(9): 397–402.

Reddy, V. (2008). *How infants know minds*. Cambridge, MA: Harvard University Press.

Reed, E. S. (1996). *Encountering the world: toward an ecological psychology*. Oxford: Oxford University Press.

Rietveld, E. and J. Kiverstein (2014). 'A rich landscape of affordances'. *Ecological Psychology* **26**(4): 325–52.

Rifkin, A. (1999). 'Kandel's challenge to psychoanalysts'. *American Journal of Psychiatry* **156**(4): 663.

Rimer, J., K. Dwan, D. A. Lawlor, C. A. Greig, M. McMurdo, W. Morley and G. E. Mead (2012). 'Exercise for depression'. *Cochrane Database of Systematic Reviews* 7.

Roberts, T., Krueger, J., and Glackin, S. (forthcoming). 'Psychiatry beyond the brain: Externalism, mental health, and autistic spectrum disorder.' *Philosophy, Psychiatry and Psychology*.

Robinson, H. (2017). 'Dualism'. *The Stanford encyclopedia of philosophy.* E. N. Zalta, ed. https://plato.stanford.edu/archives/fall2017/entries/dualism/.

Rogers, C. (1961). *On becoming a person: A therapist's view of psychotherapy.* Boston: Houghton Mifflin.

Röhricht, F., S. Gallagher, U. Geuter and D. D. Hutto (2014). 'Embodied cognition and body psychotherapy: The construction of new therapeutic environments'. *Sensoria: A Journal of Mind, Brain and Culture* **10**(1): 11–20.

Rorty, R. (1979). *Philosophy and The mirror of nature.* Princeton, NJ: Princeton University Press.

Ryle, G. (1949). *The concept of mind.* London: Hutchinson.

Sadler, J. Z. and G. J. Agich (1996). 'Diseases, functions, values, and psychiatric classification'. *Philosophy, Psychiatry and Psychology* **2**(3): 219–31.

Sartre, J. (1943/1996). *Being and nothingness.* Abingdon, UK: Routledge.

Sass, L. A. (1992). *Madness and modernism: Insanity in the light of modern art, literature and thought.* New York: Basic Books.

Sass, L. A. and J. Parnas (2003). 'Schizophrenia, consciousness, and the self'. *Schizophrenia Bulletin* **29**(3): 427–44.

Scheler, M. (1976). *Späte Schriften.* Bern: Francke.

Schiavio, A. and S. Høffding (2015). 'Playing together without communicating? A pre-reflective and enactive account of joint musical performance'. *Musicae Scientiae* **19**(4): 366–88.

Searle, J. R. (2000). 'Consciousness, free action and the brain'. *Journal of Consciousness Studies* **7**(10): 3–22.

Searle, J. R. (2002). 'Why I am not a property dualist'. *Journal of Consciousness Studies* **9**(12): 57–64.

Seikkula, J., J. Aaltonen, B. Alakare, K. Haarakangas, J. Keränen and K. Lehtinen (2006). 'Five-year experience of first-episode nonaffective psychosis in open-dialogue approach: Treatment principles, follow-up outcomes, and two case studies'. *Psychotherapy Research* **16**(2): 214–28.

Sellars, W. (1956). 'Empiricism and the philosophy of mind'. *Minnesota Studies in the Philosophy of Science* **1**(19): 253–329.

Servello, D., M. Porta, M. Sassi, A. Brambilla and M. M. Robertson (2007). 'Deep brain stimulation in 18 patients with severe Gilles de la Tourette syndrome refractory to treatment: The surgery and stimulation'. *Journal of Neurology, Neurosurgery and Psychiatry* **79**(2): 136–42.

Slaby, J., A. Paskaleva and A. Stephan (2013). 'Enactive emotion and impaired agency in depression'. *Journal of Consciousness Studies* **20**(7–8): 33–55.

Slatman, J. (2014). 'Multiple dimensions of embodiment in medical practices'. *Medicine, Health Care and Philosophy* **17**(4): 549–57.

Sorce, J. F., R. N. Emde, J. Campos and M. D. Klinnert (1985). 'Maternal emotional signaling: Its effect on the visual cliff behavior of 1-year-olds'. *Developmental Psychology* **21**: 195–200.

Stanghellini, G., M. Broome, A. Raballo, A. V. Fernandez, P. Fusar-Poli and R. Rosfort (2018). *The Oxford handbook of phenomenological psychopathology*. Oxford: Oxford University Press.

Stein, D. J., K. A. Phillips, D. Bolton, K. W. M. Fulford, J. Z. Sadler and K. S. Kendler (2010). 'What is a mental/psychiatric disorder? From DSM-IV to DSM-V'. *Psychological Medicine* **40**(11): 1759–65.

Stern, D. N. (1985). *The interpersonal world of the infant: A view from psychoanalysis and developmental psychology*. New York: Basic Books.

Sterzer, P., R. A. Adams, P. Fletcher, C. Frith, S. M. Lawrie, L. Muckli, P. Petrovic et al. (2018). 'The predictive coding account of psychosis'. *Biological Psychiatry* **84** (9): 634–43.

Stewart, J. R., O. Gapenne and E. A. Di Paolo, eds. (2010). *Enaction: Toward a new paradigm for cognitive science*. Cambridge, MA: MIT Press.

Stoffregen, T. A. (2003). 'Affordances as properties of the animal-environment system'. *Ecological Psychology* **15**(2): 115–34.

Szasz, T. S. (1961). *The myth of mental illness: Foundations of a theory of personal conduct*. New York: Dell.

Taylor, C. (1985). *Human agency and language*. Cambridge: Cambridge University Press.

Taylor, C. (2000a). *Sources of the self: The making of the modern identity*. Cambridge: Cambridge University Press.

Taylor, C. (2000b). 'McDowell on value and knowledge'. *Philosophical Quarterly* **50**(199): 242–9.

Taylor, C. (2003). 'Ethics and ontology'. *Journal of Philosophy* **100**(6): 305–20.

Teller, P. (1986). 'Relational holism and quantum mechanics'. *British Journal for the Philosophy of Science* **7**(1): 71–81.

Thomas, N. J. T. (2018). 'Mental imagery'. *The Stanford encyclopedia of philosophy*. E. N. Zalta, ed. https://plato.stanford.edu/archives/sum2019/entries/mental-imagery/.

Thompson, E. (2005). 'Sensorimotor subjectivity and the enactive approach to experience'. *Phenomenology and the Cognitive Sciences* **4**(4): 407–27.

Thompson, E. (2007). *Mind in life: Biology, phenomenology, and the sciences of mind*. Cambridge, MA: Harvard University Press.

Thompson, E. and M. Stapleton (2009). 'Making sense of sense-making: Reflections on enactive and extended mind theories'. *Topoi* 28(1): 23–30.

Thompson, E. and F. J. Varela (2001). 'Radical embodiment: Neural dynamics and consciousness'. *Trends in Cognitive Sciences* 5(10): 418–25.

Thornton, T. (2000). 'Mental illness and reductionism: Can functions be naturalized?' *Philosophy, Psychiatry and Psychology* 7(1): 67–76.

Tillich, P. (1952/2000). *The courage to be*. New Haven, CT: Yale University Press.

Torrance, S. (2005). 'In search of the enactive: Introduction to special issue on Enactive Experience'. *Phenomenology and the Cognitive Sciences* 4(4): 357–68.

Tschacher, W. and H. Haken (2007). 'Intentionality in non-equilibrium systems? The functional aspects of self-organized pattern formation'. *New Ideas in Psychology* 25(1): 1–15.

Tsigos, C. and G. P. Chrousos (2002). 'Hypothalamic–pituitary–adrenal axis, neuroendocrine factors and stress'. *Journal of Psychosomatic Research* 53(4): 865–71.

Turvey, M. T. (1992). 'Affordances and prospective control: An outline of the ontology'. *Ecological Psychology* 4(3): 173–87.

van den Berg, J. H. (1972). *A different existence: Principles of phenomenological psychopathology*. Pittsburgh, PA: Duquesne University Press.

van den Herik, J. C. (2017). 'Linguistic know-how and the orders of language'. *Language Sciences* 61: 17–27.

van Deurzen, E. (2009). *Everyday mysteries: A handbook of existential psychotherapy*. London: Routledge.

van Deurzen-Smith, E. (1988). *Existential counselling in practice*. London: Sage.

van Dijk, L., R. Withagen and R. M. Bongers (2015). 'Information without content: A Gibsonian reply to enactivists' worries'. *Cognition* 134: 210–14.

van Orden, G. C., B. F. Pennington and G. O. Stone (2001). 'What do double dissociations prove?' *Cognitive Science* 25(1): 111–72.

van Os, J. and S. Kapur (2009). 'Schizophrenia'. *The Lancet* 374(9690): 635–45.

van Oudenhove, L. and S. Cuypers (2014). 'The relevance of the philosophical "mind–body problem" for the status of psychosomatic medicine: A conceptual analysis of the biopsychosocial model'. *Medicine, Health Care and Philosophy* 17(2): 201–13.

Varela, F. G., H. R. Maturana and R. Uribe (1974/1984). 'Autopoiesis: The organization of living systems, its characterization and a model'. *Cybernetics Forum* 10(2–3): 7–13.

Varela, F. J. (1996). 'Neurophenomenology: A methodological remedy for the hard problem'. *Journal of Consciousness Studies* 3(4): 330–49.

Varela, F. J. (1997). 'Patterns of life: Intertwining identity and cognition'. *Brain and Cognition* **34**(1): 72–87.

Varela, F. J. (1999). 'The specious present: A neurophenomenology of time consciousness'. *Naturalizing phenomenology*. J. Petitot, F. J. Varela, B. Pachoud and J.-M. Roy, eds. Stanford, CA: Stanford University Press: 266–314.

Varela, F. J., E. Thompson and E. Rosch (1991). *The embodied mind: Cognitive science and human experience*. Cambridge, MA: MIT Press.

Villalobos, M. and D. Ward (2014). 'Living systems: Autonomy, autopoiesis and enaction'. *Philosophy and Technology* **28**(2): 225–39.

Villalobos, M. and D. Ward (2016). 'Lived experience and cognitive science: Reappraissing enactivism's Jonasian turn'. *Constructivist Foundations* **11**(2): 802–10.

von Bertalanffy, L. (1950). 'An outline of general system theory'. *British Journal for the Philosophy of Science* **1**(2): 134–65.

von Uexküll, J. (1909). *Umwelt und Innenwelt der Tiere*. Berlin: Springer.

von Uexküll, J. and G. Kriszat (1956). *Streifzüge durch die Umwelten von Tieren und Menschen. Bedeutungslehre*. Reinbek: Rowohlt.

von Uexküll, T. and W. Wesiak (1986). 'Wissenschaftstheorie und Psychosomatische Medizin, ein bio-psycho-soziales Modell'. *Psychosomatische Medizin*. R. Adler, J. M. Herrmann, K. Kohle et al., eds. Munich: Urban und Schwarzenberg.

Wakefield, J. C. (1992a). 'Disorder as harmful dysfunction: A conceptual critique of DSM-III-R's definition of mental disorder'. *Psychological Review* **99**(2): 232–47.

Wakefield, J. C. (1992b). 'The concept of mental disorder: On the boundary between biological facts and social values'. *American Psychologist* **47**(3): 373–88.

Wakefield, J. C. (1995). 'Dysfunction as a value-free concept: A reply to Sadler and Agich'.*Philosophy, Psychiatry and Psychology* **2**(3): 233–46.

Wakefield, J. C. (2000). 'Aristotle as sociobiologist: The "function of a human being" argument, black box essentialism, and the concept of mental disorder'. *Philosophy, Psychiatry and Psychology* **7**(1): 17–44.

Walker, I. and J. Read (2002). 'The differential effectiveness of psychosocial and biogenetic causal explanations in reducing negative attitudes toward "mental illness"'. *Psychiatry: Interpersonal and Biological Processes* **65**(4): 313–25.

Weber, A. and F. J. Varela (2002). 'Life after Kant: Natural purposes and the autopoietic foundations of biological individuality'. *Phenomenology and the Cognitive Sciences* **1**(2): 97–125.

Wegner, D. M. (2003). 'The mind's best trick: How we experience conscious will'. *Trends in Cognitive Sciences* 7(2): 65–9.

Weizsäcker, V. von (1940/1986). *Der Gestaltkreis. Theorie der Einheit von Wahrnehmen und Bewegen*. Stuttgart: Thieme.

Wichmann, T. and M. R. DeLong (2006). 'Deep brain stimulation for neurologic and neuropsychiatric disorders'. *Neuron* 52(1): 197–204.

Williams, B. (1981). 'Persons, character, and morality'. *Moral luck: Philosophical papers 1973–1980*. Cambridge: Cambridge University Press: 1–19.

Wilson, E. A. (2015). *Gut feminism*. Durham, NC: Duke University Press.

Wilson, R. A. (2010). 'Extended vision'. *Perception, action and consciousness: Sensorimotor dynamics and two visual systems*. N. Gangopadhyay, M. Madary and F. Spicer, eds. Oxford: Oxford University Press: 277–90.

Wimsatt, W. C. (1974). 'Complexity and organization'. *Proceedings of the 1972 biennial meeting of the Philosophy of Science Association*. Vol. 20. K. F. Schaffner and R. S. Cohen, eds. New York: Springer: 67–86.

Wimsatt, W. C. (2000). 'Emergence as non-aggregativity and the biases of reductionisms'. *Foundations of Science* 5(3): 269–97.

Wittgenstein, L. (1958). *Philosophical investigations*. Oxford: Blackwell.

Wittgenstein, L. (1975). *On certainty*. Oxford: Blackwell.

Wood, D., J. S. Bruner and G. Ross (1976). 'The role of tutoring in problem solving'. *Journal of Child Psychology and Psychiatry* 17(2): 89–100.

Wyllie, M. (2005). 'Lived time and psychopathology'. *Philosophy, Psychiatry and Psychology* 12(3): 173–85.

Yalom, I. D. (1980). *Existential psychotherapy*. New York: Basic Books.

Young, I. M. (1980). 'Throwing like a girl: A phenomenology of feminine body comportment motility and spatiality'. *Human Studies* 3(1): 137–56.

Zachar, P. and K. S. Kendler (2007). 'Psychiatric disorders: A conceptual taxonomy'. *American Journal of Psychiatry* 164(4): 557–65.

Zahavi, D. (2010). 'Shame and the exposed self'. *Reading Sartre: On phenomenology and existentialism*. J. Webber, ed. London: Routledge: 211–27.

Zahidi, K. and E. Myin (2016). 'Radically enactive numerical cognition'. *Embodiment in evolution and culture*. G. Etzelmüller and C. Tewes, eds. Tübingen: Mohr Siebeck: 57–71.

Ziguras, S. J., S. Klimidis, T. J. R. Lambert and A. C. Jackson (2001). 'Determinants of anti-psychotic medication compliance in a multicultural population'. *Community Mental Health Journal* 37(3): 273–83.

Index

For EU product safety concerns, contact us at Calle de José Abascal, 56–1°, 28003 Madrid, Spain or eugpsr@cambridge.org.

www.ingramcontent.com/pod-product-compliance
Ingram Content Group UK Ltd.
Pitfield, Milton Keynes, MK11 3LW, UK
UKHW020357140625
459647UK00020B/2528